AFRICA

Africa's
Land
Rush

AFRICAN ISSUES

●

AFRICAN ISSUES

Africa's Land Rush

Rural Livelihoods & Agrarian Change

Edited by
Ruth Hall,
Ian Scoones
& Dzodzi Tsikata

JC JAMES CURREY

James Currey
an imprint of
Boydell & Brewer Ltd
PO Box 9, Woodbridge
Suffolk IP12 3DF (GB)
www.jamescurrey.com
and of
Boydell & Brewer Inc.
668 Mt Hope Avenue
Rochester, NY 14620-2731 USA
www.boydellandbrewer.corn

British Library Cataloguing in Publication Data
A catologue record for this book is available on request from the British Library

ISBN 978-1-84701-130-5 (James Currey paper)

The publisher has no responsibility for the continued existence or accuracy of URLs for
external or third-party internet websites referred to in this book, and does not guarantee
that any content on such websites is, or will remain, accurate or appropriate.

This publication is printed on acid-free paper

Typeset in 9/11 Melior with Optima display
by Kate Kirkwood

CONTENTS

LIST OF MAPS, TABLES & FIGURES

Maps

Tables

Figures

NOTES ON CONTRIBUTORS

Ward Anseeuw, a development economist and policy analyst, is a research fellow at the Agricultural Research Centre for International Development (CIRAD), seconded to the Post-Graduate School of Agriculture and Rural Development of the University of Pretoria. He is also the co-director of the Centre for the Study of Governance Innovations, University of Pretoria. He has conducted research for the last fifteen years in Southern Africa and the African continent on issues of agricultural and land policies, agrarian and land reforms, land conflicts and large-scale land acquisitions. He is a co-founder of the Land Matrix.

Joseph Ariyo is a retired professor of Geography from Ahmadu Bello University, Zaria, Nigeria. He undertook postgraduate studies in Canada at York University, University of Toronto and University of Waterloo. Joseph Ariyo served for four years as Provost and CEO of Kwara State College of Education at Oro and as a member of a group of consultants to the National Planning Commission to develop the environment sector of Nigeria's Vision 2020. Professor Ariyo's teaching and research interests are in rural development, land-use planning and resource management.

Michael Chasukwa is a senior lecturer and former Head of the Department of Political and Administrative Studies, Chancellor College, University of Malawi. He holds an MA (Political Science) and BA (Public Administration) from the University of Malawi. His research and teaching interests include the political economy of development, agricultural policies as they relate to development, land, youth and development, local government and decentralisation. He is currently a PhD candidate (Development Studies) at the School of Politics and International Studies, University of Leeds, UK.

Blessings Chinsinga holds a BA in Public Administration from Chancellor College, University of Malawi, an MPhil in Development Studies from the University of Cambridge, UK, and a PhD in Development Studies from the University of Mainz, Germany. An experienced academic, researcher and consultant, he is currently based at the Department of Political and Administrative Studies, Chancellor College, University of Malawi as an associate professor. He specialises in the political economy of development, public policy analysis, rural livelihoods and local level politics. He is also the deputy director of the Centre for Social Research at the University of Malawi, which is the research arm of the Faculty of Social Science.

Ruth Hall is an associate professor at the Institute for Poverty, Land and Agrarian Studies (PLAAS), University of the Western Cape, South Africa, and holds a DPhil in Politics from the University of Oxford. She has published four books on aspects of land and agrarian reform in South Africa, focusing on land redistribution, restitution claims and farm workers. Her current work focuses on land rights and 'land grabbing' and impacts on local people. She is co-founder of the Land Deal Politics Initiative, and coordinates the work of the Future Agricultures Consortium on land in Africa.

John Letai has over eighteen years work experience in the Horn and East Africa drylands on issues of pastoralists and other marginalised groups living in these areas. He has a wealth of knowledge in working with communities on natural resource management, insecurity or conflicts and other development issues. He has experience in policy formulation and implementation and policy advocacy. John has worked with different actors including governments, local and national NGOs, international organizations, among them International Committee of the Red Cross, Resource Conflict Institute, International Institute for Environment and Development and Oxfam GB.

Michael Mortimore is a geographer who taught and researched at Ahmadu Bello University, Zaria, Nigeria between 1962 and 1979, and was Professor of Geography at Bayero University, Kano from 1979 to 1986. Subsequently he carried out research studies as a senior research associate in the Department of Geography, Cambridge University, the Overseas Development Institute and as an Honorary Fellow of the Centre of West African Studies, University of Birmingham. His research and publications have focused on environmental management by smallholders in the drylands of Africa. He has advocated for taking small farmers' and pastoralists' knowledge and capacities fully into account in policies by governments, donors and practitioners and to create incentives to invest in drylands. He has written several reports for the IUCN, UNEP, UNCCD Global Mechanism, and other agencies.

Abdirizak Arale Nunow, from Garissa County in dry northern Kenya, has over twenty years' experience in development issues in arid and semi-arid areas in East Africa and the Horn of Africa. He holds a PhD in Environmental Science from the University of Amsterdam. His research interests include land deals and land-based investments, and conservation of threatened ecosystems such as the Tana Delta. He is currently a senior lecturer in the Department of Geography at Moi University, Kenya.

Gaynor Paradza holds a PhD in Law and Governance from Wageningen University and an MA in Rural and Urban Planning from the University of Zimbabwe. She has worked with PLAAS at the University of the Western Cape, the Future Agricultures Consortium, Zimbabwe's Ministry of Local Government and the University of Zimbabwe. Gaynor's recent publications include *Land Reform and Livelihoods Trajectories of Change in Northern Limpopo (co-authored with Aliber et al. 2012)* and *Single Women, Land and Livelihood Vulnerability in the Communal Farming Areas of Zimbabwe* (2010).

Marcel Rutten is a geographer at the African Studies Centre, Leiden University, and the Nijmegen School of Management, Radboud University, the Netherlands. He has been involved in longitudinal research on land tenure, water development, and food security in East Africa. Currently he is looking into conflicts over natural resources in semi-arid Africa linked to land acquisition and non-sustainable water mining by irrigated agriculture. His latest book is *Inside Poverty and Development in Africa – Critical Reflections on Pro-poor Policies* (2008; with Leliveld and Foeken). Forthcoming is a longitudinal study on the effects of eco-tourism initiatives in Kenyan and Tanzanian Maasailand.

Ian Scoones is a professorial fellow at the Institute of Development Studies (IDS) at the University of Sussex, UK and is director of the ESRC STEPS Centre. He has been joint coordinator of the Future Agricultures Consortium, and member of the land theme. He is a co-founder of the Land Deal Politics Initiative. He works on land, environment and agrarian change in Africa, particularly Zimbabwe. Recent books include: *The Politics of Green Transformations* (2015); *Carbon Conflicts and Forest Landscapes in Africa* (2015), *Green Grabbing: A New Appropriation of Nature?* (2012), *Dynamic Sustainabilities* (2010), *and Zimbabwe's Land Reform, Myths and Realities* (2010).

Maru Shete is a PhD researcher at the African Studies Centre, Leiden University, the Netherlands, and an Assistant Professor at St. Mary's University, Ethiopia. He holds an MA in Development Studies from Addis Ababa University, Ethiopia and an MSc in Development and Resource Economics from the Norwegian University of the Life Sciences, Norway. His main areas of research interest include land tenure, poverty, food security, impact studies, and economic development in Africa. He co-authored two chapters in *Beyond the Hype: Land Grabbing in Africa,*

(Zoomers and Kaag 2014) and *Digging Deeper: Inside Africa's Agricultural, Food and Nutrition Dynamics* (Akinyoade et al. 2014).

Rebecca Smalley has an MSc from the University of East Anglia, UK, and has previously conducted research on large-scale land acquisition in Kenya. In the past she worked for the United Nations Framework Convention on Climate Change secretariat and now works on corporate accountability, voluntary standards and smallholder initiatives in agricultural commodity supply chains.

Emmanuel Sulle is a researcher and PhD candidate at the Institute for Poverty, Land and Agrarian Studies (PLAAS), University of the Western Cape, South Africa. He has experience in both land policy and agricultural research in East and Southern Africa. His research focuses on understanding inclusive business models of land-based investments, land tenure and livelihoods in Sub-Saharan Africa.

Dzodzi Tsikata is an associate professor at the Institute of Statistical, Social and Economic Research (ISSER) at the University of Ghana. Her research is in the areas of gender and development policies and practices; land-tenure reforms and large-scale commercial land deals; informal labour relations and the conditions of informal workers, and her publications reflect these interests. Most recently, she co-guest-edited with Cheryl Doss and Gale Summerfield a special issue of *Feminist Economics* on Land, Gender and Food Security (2014).

Joseph Yaro is an associate professor of Human Geography at the University of Ghana, with a focus on rural development. He combines a rich background in development studies and rural geography with extensive rural research experience in northern Ghana. His specific research interests are sustainable development in rural areas; rural livelihoods; food security; climate change adaptation; land tenure and transnational land deals/grabs.

PREFACE

After the term 'land grabbing' captured headlines around the world in the late 2000s, researchers embarked on a spate of new studies to understand this dramatic new trend. Africa was the focus, but in Southeast Asia and Latin America too, researchers and activists started to document large corporate takeovers of community and state land. A great deal of attention at this time revolved around how much land was being acquired, where, by whom and for what. All this was important and helped to sketch out the contours of a new era of agrarian restructuring.

The research reported in this book was conducted under the auspices of the Future Agricultures Consortium's land theme (www.future-agricultures.org/research/land). Centred on a network of Africa-based researchers, our studies set out to investigate what these 'land grabs' actually meant to the people directly affected. Our work from 2010 to 2014 investigated 13 cases across 8 countries in Africa.

Our interest in writing this book was to ground the narratives of a 'land grab' and of 'agricultural investment' in detailed local studies that would illuminate how these are experienced on the ground. What did these deals look like? Why did they happen in the particular places and at the particular times that they did? What transformations in rural people's lives and livelihoods were being produced? And what were the implications for future trajectories of agrarian change across the continent?

Across the studies, we chose to adopt a political economy perspective. We were motivated by a conviction that large-scale land deals in Africa must be understood in terms of the economic interests that animate national politics, and that such investments – many of which did not materialise in practice – were best understood at the intersection of global drivers and local institutions, mediated through national politics and economy. We asked: what political conditions enabled and promoted big land deals? How did investors come to identify certain sites? Who were their intermediaries? To what degree did national law and policy facilitate or shape the deals? And through what processes did local people engage with proposed deals, what were their responses, what happened to them and what did they do?

We did not aim to assess the outcomes of the deals; indeed, most were in their infancy and it was too early to proclaim whether or not they had met their own goals or realised their promised benefits. However, we did have an ambition to understand these land deals more deeply, in their local and national contexts. Doing so required interviewing the full range of actors involved – the investors themselves, government authorities at national, provincial and district level, and not least the people directly and indirectly affected, including workers, outgrowers and smallholder farmers, displaced or otherwise. Our main challenge was to obtain accurate information about the terms of the deals, who provided permissions, and who paid what to whom. So much of this is opaque, and we were not able to overcome the predictable obstacles in all cases.

While working on these studies, we have also collaborated with the Land Deal Politics Initiative (LDPI – www.iss.nl/ldpi) to hold two international conferences on the Global Land Grab at the University of Sussex in April 2011 (www.future-agricultures.org/events/global-land-grabbing) and at Cornell University in October 2012 (www.cornell-landproject.org/activities/2012-land-grabbing-conference/).

These events and others spurred a mass of published material, particularly in a series of issues in the *Journal of Peasant Studies* but until now no collection has yet brought together case study perspectives on Africa. Case studies are important to build up our collective understanding of the profound changes being wrought across many countries across Africa, and draw out the key themes and implications. We hope that together the cases in this book tell an important story, but also serve as a basis for future research as these processes unfold over time.

The book shows that the actors getting large areas of land in Africa are diverse, yet the processes through which these deals come about show remarkable similarities, involving the intimate interplay of global and domestic private sector interests and state power. We aim to counter the caricatures about 'land grabbers' that see them as all-powerful and wealthy foreigners in cahoots with local politicians. Some elements of this reading are, of course, true, but our studies suggest the need to take a more critical stance, and to examine each case within its own context.

Our aim is to introduce students, researchers, activists, field practitioners and the general public to the politics of who controls Africa's land and agricultural futures. We hope that readers will sharpen their own understandings of the recent land rush and what this means for rural people, and see this in a more historical perspective than is offered in the media and policy reports. Our hope too is that the book will inspire students concerned with the realities of rural livelihoods in Africa to pursue their own studies and to help to enrich our collective understandings of the profound changes under way across so much of the continent.

Ruth Hall, Ian Scoones and Dzodzi Tsikata, June 2015

ACKNOWLEDGEMENTS

We would like to thank the many people we have interviewed and who have shared their time, knowledge and experience with us during the course of our research over the past four years. We are grateful to the UK Department for International Development which supported our work through the Future Agricultures Consortium in this period. Communications gurus Nathan Oxley in Brighton, Beatrice Ouma in Nairobi and Rebecca Pointer in Cape Town ensured that our various outputs leading up to this book were expertly published and widely disseminated. We are indebted to Nicole McMurray for expert copyediting, John Hall for producing helpful maps and Oliver Burch for on-going administrative support, to two external reviewers, and to our publisher, James Currey, commissioning editor Jaqueline Mitchell, managing editor Lynn Taylor, and copyeditor Margaret Cornell, with whom it has been an absolute pleasure to work.

ABBREVIATIONS

AAAK	Agricultural Auto-growers Association of Kenya
AfDB	African Development Bank
ADC	Agricultural Development Corporation
ADC	Area Development Committee
ADLI	Agricultural Development Led Industrialization
AISD	Agricultural Investment Support Directorate
BATUK	British Training Unit in Kenya
CAMEC	Central African Mining and Exploration Company
CSO	Civil Society Organisation
DCGL	Dwangwa Cane Growers Limited
DCGT	Dwangwa Cane Growers Trust
DRC	Democratic Republic of Congo
DUAT	Direto de Uso e Aproveitamento dos Terras, registered land use right
EEA	Ethiopian Economic Association
EEPCo	Ethiopian Electric Power Corporation
EIA	Environmental Impact Assessment
EPRDF	Ethiopian People's Revolutionary Democratic Front
ESIA	Environmental and Social Impact Assessment
ETB	Ethiopian Birr
EU	European Union
FAO	Food and Agricultural Organization
FAO VGs	Food and Agriculture Organization's Voluntary Guidelines on Responsible Tenure of Land, Fisheries and Forests
FDI	Foreign Direct Investment
FDRE	Federal Democratic Republic of Ethiopia
FGD	Focus Group Discussion
FISP	Farm Input Subsidy Programme
FPIC	Free, Prior and Informed Consent
GBI	Green Belt Initiative

GOG	Government of Ghana
GoM	Government of Malawi
GSU	General Service Unit
GTP	Growth and Transformation Plan
ITFC	Integrated Tamale Fruit Company
KHE	Agri-Fresh Kenya Horticulture Exporters
KSCL	Kilombero Sugar Company Ltd.
MAI	Massingir Agroindustrial
MGDS	Malawi Growth and Development Strategy
MoAFS	Ministry of Agriculture and Food Security, Malawi
MoARD	Ministry of Agriculture and Rural Development, Ethiopia
NAFDAC	National Agency for Food and Drug Administration and Control, Nigeria
NEMA	National Emergency Management Agency, Nigeria
NYS	National Youth Service
OI	Oakland Institute
SAGCOT	Southern Agricultural Growth Corridor of Tanzania
SAP	Structural Adjustment Programme
SIAL	Limpopo Agro- Industrial Investment Company
STFS	Settlement Transfer Fund Schemes
TARDA	Tana-Athi River Development Authority
TDIP	Tana Delta Irrigation Project
TISP	Tana Integrated Sugar Project
TLU	Tropical Livestock Units
TPC	Tanganyika Planting Company
TSB	Transvaal Suiker Beperk
WAMCO	West African Milk Company

1

Introduction ▊ The Contexts
& Consequences of
Africa's Land Rush

RUTH HALL, IAN SCOONES
& DZODZI TSIKATA

Africa is at the centre of a 'global land grab'. This is what critics have named the rapid growth in land-based investments or land deals since 2007, a phenomenon unmatched since colonial times. By some estimates, 70 per cent of the land transacted in large-scale transnational deals in recent years has been in Africa, often considered the world's last reserve of unused and under-utilised fertile and irrigable farmland (Deininger et al. 2011; World Bank 2009). It is this potential that has lured investors motivated by projections of rising food prices, by growing demand for 'green' energy, and by the allure of cheap land and water rights. But governments have often allocated to investors land that is occupied, used, or claimed through custom by local people, resulting in disrupted livelihoods and even conflict.

The case studies presented in this book depict the striking diversity of such deals: white Zimbabwean farmers in northern Nigeria, Dutch and American joint ventures in Ghana, an Indian agricultural company in Ethiopia's hinterland, European investors in Kenya's drylands and a Canadian biofuel company on its coast, South African sugar agribusiness in Tanzania's southern growth corridor, in Malawi's 'Greenbelt' and in southern Mozambique, and white South African farmers venturing on to former state farms in Congo. In all cases, acquiring land is intimately linked to gaining access to water: land and water 'grabbing' are thus inseparable (Mehta et al. 2012; Woodhouse 2012).

The book explores the investors and their interests, the processes through which these land deals were concluded, and analyses their outcomes for changing agrarian structure, rural livelihoods and food security. Analysis of emerging patterns of social differentiation focuses attention on who wins, who loses out, and what new dynamics of accumulation and marginalisation result, both within directly affected communities and the broader society. The case studies also investigate the political and policy narratives through which these deals are justified and understood, the contested views of land and property that underpin them, and the degree to which new agrarian struggles are emerging in response.

Table 1.1 Land deal case studies

	Nigeria	Ghana	Ghana	Ghana	Ethiopia (Oromiya)	Ethiopia (Gambela)	Kenya (Laikipia)	Kenya (Tana Delta)	Tanzania	Malawi	Mozambique (Maragra)	Mozambique (Massingir)	Congo
Location and ownership	New Nigeria Farms, Zimbabwe/South Africa	Integrated Tamale Fruit Company, Dutch & Ghanaian	Solar Harvest Limited, Norway	Prairie Rice Company, USA & Government of Ghana	Karuturi, India	Karuturi, India	Private owners, multinational companies	TARDA, Mumias Sugar, Kenya, Canada	Kilombero Sugar Company, Illovo, South Africa	Illovo, South Africa	Illovo, South Africa	TSB, South Africa and Mozambican investors	Congo Agriculture, Agri-SA, South Africa
Business model and labour regime	Family-run, large-scale farms, Seasonal employment peak of 3000, mostly women	Nucleus farm, with outgrower scheme	Plantation	Plantation, with processing plant and plans for outgrowers	Plantation; 200-300 part-time workers 75% women, 50 permanent staff, 22 expatriates	Plantation; 313 permanent and 735 casual workers, mostly men	Large-scale farms and ranches, run by families and companies	Estate, possible outgrowers. Projection of 20,000 jobs, currently none	Estate and outgrowers	Estate	Estate employing 4,857 workers, plus 1,625 outgrowers	Estate. Projection of 7,000 permanent workers and up to 45,000 jobs in total	Family-run, large-scale farms. 100 male casual employees during start-up
Size	13,000ha, in 1,000ha	552ha	13,800ha	1,250ha acquired; further 6,000ha possible	11,700ha	100,000ha (additional 100,000 ha possible)	Laikipia county is 9,462 square km	40,000ha; 16,000ha additional proposed, plus 4000 ha outgrowers	8,022ha (2 estates); outgrowers on 12,000ha	19,800ha (13,800ha at Nchalo and 6,000ha at Dwangwa)	6,500ha	31,000ha	80,000ha; possibly up to 200,000ha in future
Terms and investment	25 year lease (renewable); no rental; land set aside and compensation paid. State government loans offered	99 year lease; one-off payment. US$1m initial investment	25 year lease (renewable); land rental. US$2m initial investment	50 year lease, but no documentation; one-off payment US$2.25m initial investment held.	45 year lease; rental	50 year lease; rental	99 year lease; rental paid to government	45 year lease; payment to government. US$332.4m total investments	99 year lease; fees paid to ministry	99 year lease; compensation to villagers	50 year lease; annual fee	50 year lease; annual fee. US$740m total investment	30 years (renewable); annual rental to government

Table 1.1 cont.

	Nigeria	Ghana	Ghana	Ghana	Ethiopia (Oromiya)	Ethiopia (Gambela)	Kenya (Laikipia)	Kenya (Tana Delta)	Tanzania	Malawi	Mozambique (Maragra)	Mozambique (Massingir)	Congo
Prior tenure regime and land allocation authority	Customary land tenure. Kwara State Government under Land Use Decree	Customary land tenure. Yende chief	Customary land tenure. Tijo chief	Customary land tenure with individual usufructory rights. Government land, state land authority	Customary land tenure under Oromiya Regional State	Customary land tenure, under Itang district, and Federal Government of Ethiopia	Customary tenure. Government of Kenya (GoK)	Customary land tenure on Trust land, and state land. GoK Land Commission for title deeds.	Core state farm, later privatised, plus customary land. GoT Commissioner of Land, and village assembly	Customary land tenure. Government of Malawi	Customary land tenure. estate holds DUAT. Government of Mozambique	Unregistered and registered community DUATs. Government of Mozambique	State land, some occupied. Government, Ministry of Lands
Numbers displaced and affected	No settlements displaced, but 33 villages / farming settlements affected through lost land	15 households displaced; several villages affected	35 households displaced; several villages affected	Several small villages affected	No displacement; 3,317 households in five kebeles affected	No displacement; 1,239 households in five kebeles affected	Pastoralists displaced	Potential displacement of 25,000 people in 32 villages, but investor estimates 14 families	No displacement, several villages affected	Over 500 households displaced	Several families who had re-occupied the unused estate land after the war were evicted after Illovo's acquisition of the land	Displacements unknown; 13 villages affected	Several families displaced; four villages affected
Post investment land use, and prior use	Dairy and cassava, replacing bush fallow, mixed cropping and pastoralism	Mango, replacing bush fallow cropping	Biofuel then maize, replacing mixed cropping, fishing	Rice, replacing livestock production, and teff/ niger seed production	Planned for palm oil but currently maize, replacing mixed crop-live-stock farming system	Maize, sugarcane, palm oil, replacing mixed farming system	Game ranching, tourism, replacing pastoralism	Sugarcane and some maize, replacing crop production (Pokomo), pastoralism (Orma/ Wardei)	Sugarcane and food crops on outgrowers' farms, replacing rice, maize and millet	Sugarcane and maize, replacing mixed crop-live-stock farming system	Sugarcane, replacing mixed farming	Sugarcane planned, but no investment yet, would replace mixed farming	Maize and soyabean, replacing mixed farming
Water access	Close to River Niger, but no irrigation infrastructure. Rainfall, 1000-1500 mm/yr	Close to the White Volta River	Volta River close but agriculture is largely rain-fed; poor bimodal rainfall	Rainfed agriculture – no potential for irrigation as it is far from rivers	Adjacent to Akobo River and near Chibe River. Some irrigation; rainfall 1400 mm/yr	Near to Baro River. Irrigation of cane. Rainfall 1200 mm/yr	Limited water sources. Drylands area: 500-900 mm/yr	Tana River for irrigation. Some pans and boreholes	Ruaha Mkuu River part of Rufiji River basin. Irrigation and rainfed (1200-1600 mm/year rainfall)	Lake Malawi, Rainfall 770 mm/yr	Nkomati River for irrigation. Low rainfall (500mm/year)	Olifants River and dam	Small dams, old bore-holes and some streams. Rainfall, 1500 mm/yr

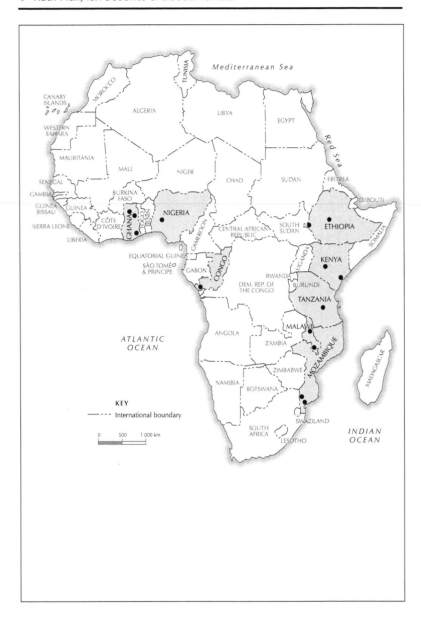

Map 1.1 Africa, showing the case study sites

While dramatic changes in landholding and land use are occurring, these case studies from West, East and Southern Africa suggest that some of the dynamics are not entirely new, but resonate with and even resurrect forms of production associated with colonial estates in the first half of the twentieth century and state farms in the early independence era. Complex directions of change are evident, with diverse implications for agrarian transitions (cf. Moyo et al. 2013; Akram-Lodhi and Kay 2009; Bernstein 2004; Byres 1991). As the chapters show, the patterns of change are varied, suggesting no simple resolution of the agrarian question, but a need to look in depth at both contexts and consequences. The land investments too have diverse implications for poverty and inequality in rural societies through the concentration of landholdings, growth of wage labour, new classes of accumulating elites, and rising landlessness.

The methods and logic of our investigations over several years starting from 2010 were shaped by a belief that to understand the textured variations in what is often contracted into the term 'land grab', multi-scalar research is needed. We therefore have conducted detailed local case studies, animated by local farmers, government agents and investors as the main protagonists. The case studies are embedded within specific localities, themselves shaped by sectoral, class, gender, race and ethnic dynamics, as well as regional contexts and national determinations (cf. Moyo et al. 2012). Table 1.1 offers a brief overview of the thirteen case studies we investigated across eight countries, in relation to a number of criteria.

The chapters pick apart the roles played by various interest groups, facilitators and intermediaries: local chiefs, district commissioners, agriculture ministries, national investment authorities and top-level government officials. In turn, our focus on the local dynamics of change can only be understood within the context of national and regional political economies, shaped by national, regional and wider geopolitical interests. It is these wider 'assemblages', beyond the 'grab', that become important in understanding the process, which is why one must go beyond a simple territorial focus (Sassen 2013). This recent phase of land enclosure and appropriation also has to be understood in historical context, with precedents being seen in earlier periods, notably the restructuring of economies and power through neoliberal structural adjustment, and the emergence of political and business elites (Moyo 2008; Amanor 2005, 2012), alongside long-term patterns of regional marginalisation and underdevelopment (cf. Amin 1972).

Africa's long-standing need for investment

Several factors have driven recent large-scale transnational land deals. The literature is replete with discussions of these, most notably the increasing financialisation of capital and its need for speculative acquisitions (Fairbairn 2014), combined with the global food, energy and financial crises of 2007 and 2008 (Cotula et al. 2014; Zoomers and Kaag 2014; Arezki et al. 2011; Cotula 2013; Anseeuw et al. 2012; White et al. 2012; Hall 2011; Borras et al. 2010; Cotula et al. 2009; among many others). Tied as it is to global processes of change in food, fuel and financial systems, the recent rush for land in Africa should be understood in a global, as well as an historical context. While Africa is often singled out as being at the centre of this global dynamic, data sources may be subject to various selection biases including better media attention in Africa, with the result that the extent to which this is a specifically African phenomenon may have been over-stated (Oya 2013b). While much commentary focuses on the scale and location of land grabs, in this book we focus rather on the underlying processes of land and agricultural commercialisation under way and their implications for livelihoods and agrarian systems through an in-depth case study approach.

Several important questions arise. In what directions is agriculture being commercialised? What institutional arrangements are becoming dominant? Are there good business models that could address some of the observed problems of large-scale land acquisitions? What roles are states playing? What is the significance of land becoming concentrated in the hands of transnational corporations and local capitalist classes? What new inclusions, exclusions and social differentiations are being created within countries experiencing land concentration? It is these questions that have animated our research, along with attention to the interests and considerations within Africa itself that are shaping governments' and citizens' responses to the land rush.

The long-term crisis in African agriculture and the failure of agrarian transitions have fuelled food insecurity, a large food import bill, rampant rural-urban migration and unemployment. The decline in state revenues has resulted in basic rural infrastructure being neglected, and in several countries state farms, irrigation systems and road networks are in varying states of disrepair. These have been serious long-standing concerns, exacerbated by the ravages of structural adjustment. In this context, many African states have welcomed investors and given, on preferential terms and sometimes for free, vast tracts of land to foreign governments, corporations and individuals. The idea that foreign direct investment in large-scale commercial agriculture would result in technology transfer – which benefits small farmers, provides much-needed food for local markets, creates decent employment for the youth, earns foreign exchange and forms the basis of industrialisation – has proven irresistible. Many governments have argued that they have large areas of empty, marginal, uncultivated or inefficiently-used lands that can be used more profitably for commercial agriculture (Nalepa and Bauer 2012). Such territories include customary lands as well as 'state' land in the form of abandoned, though sometimes occupied, state farms. Justifications for land acquisitions are thus frequently framed by narratives of scarcity and abundance at both local and global scales (Scoones et al. 2014).

African governments have, since the structural adjustment era from the early 1980s, adopted a range of investment, agricultural and land policies to create favourable conditions for the importation of private capital to drive agrarian transformation. For instance, policy and strategy documents such as Kenya's Vision 2030, Tanzania's Development Vision 2025, Ghana's Food and Agriculture Sector Development Policy, Ethiopia's Agriculture Development Led Industrialisation and Nigeria's Kwara State Back to the Land Programme have been put in place. There have also been major land reforms since the 1990s to promote land markets, titling and registration in several African countries, some of which are discussed in the case studies we present (such as Ghana, Tanzania and Ethiopia). Specific measures and institutional reforms such as federal land banks have sought to identify land that can be leased for foreign direct investment in Ethiopia (see Chapter 4), and investment promotion centres and special land courts have been established to improve the efficiency of administrative and legal processes in Ghana (see Chapter 3). These developments marked a shift in focus from smallholder agriculture to medium- and large-scale agriculture (such as in Tanzania and Mozambique – see Chapters 7 and 9) or the refinement of long-standing policies privileging large-scale agriculture (such as in Kenya – see Chapters 5 and 6).

The drive for foreign direct investment in agriculture has in some cases been related to sub-regional priorities, an example being the emergence of sugar as one of the most significant commodities in Southern Africa, where the crop is having profound economic, environmental, political and social effects (Chapters 7, 8 and 9). Tanzania's bid to benefit from this through sugar estates and outgrower schemes echoes and builds on South African agribusiness efforts to establish sugar plantations in Malawi, Mozambique and Zambia. While governments may have national goals in mind, the regional context matters – not least to the investors who are seeking to disperse risk by distributing their operations across multiple countries in order to take advantage of different conditions conducive to profitable production.

The dynamics of enclosure and agricultural commercialisation

The chapters in this book seek to examine the extent to which large-scale commercial agriculture and its land acquisitions have benefited local communities and their own farming – whether in the form of technology transfer, employment, food security, new opportunities for smallholders or the transformation of rural economies. This builds on an increasingly influential literature that is raising questions about the strategy of agricultural commercialisation as it unfolds through extensive land acquisitions and enclosures in Africa (Ansoms and Hilhorst 2014;

Cotula 2013; Peters 2013; Wolford et al. 2013; Anseeuw et al. 2012; White et al. 2012).

Several chapters also seek to analyse the inter-linkages of land, state and politics through a *longue durée* approach, demonstrating that it is not only proximate developmental considerations that are driving the pace of land commercialisation and concentration in Africa, but rather that the current land rush is the latest instalment, distinct without being unique, in a long history of enclosures, acquisitions and dispossessions (Alden Wily 2012). Both past and contemporary enclosures have provoked struggles over resources by people who currently control political, social and economic power at national level, and their counterparts in the countryside (see Chapters 4, 5, 6 and 10).

To what degree are experiences of land investments and agricultural commercialisation similar across the continent? Our studies suggest that, despite enormous differences in systems of land holdings, levels of land concentration, contributions of agriculture to employment and to gross domestic product and levels of food imports, there are remarkable similarities in experiences of agricultural commercialisation across African countries. The implications for the direction of rural change are strikingly similar. In all our case studies, even where the land acquired is not community land or held under customary tenure, the process is towards privatisation of land rights, commodification of land and natural resources and towards social differentiation. Almost all investments have faltered, with some halting entirely while others have restrategised, regrouped and continued on a new path (see Chapters 2 and 10 in particular). The best laid plans have come apart, and some of the plans were not that robust in the first place.

There is an emerging consensus on the need to define more rigorously what is meant by land grabbing, and to be careful when interpreting data on land investments (Oya 2013b; Scoones et al. 2013; Anseeuw et al. 2012). This should not be restricted only to large-scale acquisitions, or to transnational deals. Several of our chapters shed light on a range of processes of land concentration occurring in rural localities across Africa, into which larger and transnational deals are inserted and which compound land scarcities and land conflicts. In the study of the Laikipia area of Kenya, where much of the concentration is driven by local elites, but exacerbated by the growth of foreign-owned ranching, four different processes are identified: the consolidation of smallholder farms for sale; the selling off of sections within large ranches; the consolidation of smaller ranches and the conversion of farms for horticulture. Each of these processes has particular implications for local farmers and pastoralists, but their cumulative effects are the observed changes in land ownership and land use patterns, and an overall intensification of land concentration (see Chapter 5).

Various chapters also speak to the debate about business or institutional models of land acquisitions, particularly the suggestion that contract farming or nucleus outgrowing models are to be preferred over large plantations, as a 'win-win' solution that could provide the missing link between smallholders and agribusiness investors (Cotula et al. 2009; von Braun and Meinzen-Dick 2009; World Bank 2008). Three chapters broach this issue directly (see Chapters 7, 8 and 9), while others compare outgrowing with other models of commercialisation (see Chapter 3). This is clearly an issue in need of more consideration in future studies of agricultural commercialisation.

Most of the chapters are about land transactions that are mature enough for discussion of their impacts. However, a few chapters are devoted to planned acquisitions, deals in progress and acquired lands not yet in use, but enclosed or not yet enclosed (see Chapter 6); or deals which have collapsed or been restructured or taken over by new companies (see Chapters 3 and 10). As well as documenting the impacts of large-scale land acquisition, our work also draws attention to the real impacts of deals that do *not* happen: those where production gets under way and soon stops, those where only a small fraction of the land acquired is ever used and those where land is acquired but investors never take occupation of it. In each case, enormous impacts and losses might be felt by the 'host' communities. As the experiences in Kenya's Tana Delta show, what might be worse than a land grab to enable commercial farming is a land grab in which land is enclosed for investments that fail to materialise (see Chapter 6). While planned, new and failed deals do not yield much detail on the question of investment impact, they are important for mapping developing processes, the key actors and their positioning, resistance and other responses to deals.

While the international response to 'land grabs' has taken the form of varied attempts to regulate the processes through which they take place (Margulis et al. 2013), we focus not only on processes but also, more substantively, on the terms of the deals, their early outcomes and the processes of social change that they instigate. We draw a distinction between corporate social responsibility initiatives for self-regulation by corporate investors and multilateral agreements such as the Food and Agriculture Organization's Voluntary Guidelines on Responsible Tenure of Land, Fisheries and Forests (FAO VGs). While the former entail unaccountable forms of self-regulation by corporate investors, the latter were negotiated by states with extensive civil society participation. The former are less likely to find purchase due to a lack of enforcement mechanisms, while the latter, 'anchored in existing international human rights obligations' (Seufert 2013) constitute a new tool in struggles by rural social movements – even though they are 'voluntary' (McKeon 2013). Civil society perspectives are divided between those seeing 'transparency' and governance reforms as having some merit, while others emphasise the danger of these deflecting from the direction of agrarian change being promoted. As the former UN Special Rapporteur on the Right to Food, Olivier de Schutter (2011), observed, governance frameworks that aim to make large-scale private investment in agriculture more responsible can be seen as a manifesto to dispossess the global peasantry 'responsibly'. Whatever the governance frameworks, the outcomes of 'land grabs' are as diverse as the contexts into which they are inserted. We highlight how land deals articulate with pre-existing politics, populations and economies, rather than presuming that they involve the creation of entirely new production systems in an environment that is economically and politically inert. Thus the chapters that follow are all concerned with explaining the outcomes of large-scale land acquisitions, and how and why they have often received mixed or dismal reviews, setting these insights into local, national and regional contexts. The themes emerging from the chapters include the role of the state; institutional arrangements and changing land relations; livelihood effects and their implications for rural differentiation and class, gender and kinship relations; responses and conflicts arising and, last but not least, implications for agrarian transformation in the long term. These themes are discussed in the subsequent sections of this chapter.

The state as actor and referee in land deals

A recurring theme in our and others' research is the pivotal role of African states in large-scale land transactions and how this is influencing change in local agrarian systems. Debates about land grabs and land deals inherently involve profound questions about state authority and governance (Wolford et al. 2013). And as Boone (2014) observes, property relations are not only acted on by states, but property relations are constitutive of politics and state authority at local and national levels. Regimes in Africa involved in land deals differ in their antecedents, democratic credentials, strategies for attracting foreign direct investment and the level of land concentration they preside over. Yet these post-colonial states display some common characteristics in how they have managed foreign direct investment and what they are prepared to do to keep investors coming; how they exercise their powers of eminent domain in situations of legal pluralism, institutional weaknesses and capacities, and their close relationships with particular interest groups in society.

While foreign investors may be seen to be 'grabbing' African land, the growth of domestic capital means that local elites, too, are acquiring land with state support for a variety of purposes. This can be understood in terms of state-capital alliances (Harvey 2003). Our cases show that the national state, while often pivotal in conceding to deals, is joined by a spectrum of local state authorities, national and local business elites – what Peters (2013: 537) terms the 'accelerating process of appropriation by national agents'. Thus both 'state' and 'capital' are heterogeneous and differently situated in relation to processes of enclosure, commercialisation and accumulation. There has been in many cases a convergence of externally-

and locally-led commercialisation, with the latter ranging from micro-level 'bottom-up' land grabs within communities to national business interests, often in partnership with the state (Wolford et al. 2013). Various chapters in this book show that strong support from state officials and traditional leaders for large-scale commercial farming represents another instalment of the elite consensus to privatise communal and state property for its own benefit, creating new struggles over scarce resources, inclusions and exclusions and changes in class, gender and kinship relations (see Chapters 3 and 5; also see Doss et al. 2014; Englert and Daley 2008; Tsikata and Yaro 2014; Verma 2014).

Not all the states discussed in this book were champions of free land markets. Most had nationalised all land after independence, with some reintroducing private forms of title or other formalised land rights in the 1980s and 1990s. At the very least, there have been contestations about whether state or private ownership is the better approach to land management. Mozambique, for example, is widely held to have the most progressive land law in Africa, recognising customary and informal tenure as constituting a property right, whether registered or not, and yet it promotes large-scale land investments that involve land enclosure and commodification (see Chapter 9). The Ethiopian government has been concerned that encouraging the flourishing of land markets would result in land concentration through the dispossession of poor farmers (see Chapter 4). Other states have evidently been less ambivalent about creating land markets and encouraging private ownership, and have actively pursued these through their land reform programmes.

Some regimes (Congo, Ethiopia, Nigeria and Tanzania) actively sought foreign direct investment, offering land, bank loans, infrastructural support and favourable terms of investment (see Chapters 2, 4, 7 and 10). Specific strategies include targeting particular groups of farmers from other African countries (Zimbabwean farmers in Nigeria and South African farmers in the Congo) or targeting capitalists from 'emerging' economies (such as Indian and Middle Eastern businesses in Tanzania, Kenya and Ethiopia) (see Chapters 2, 4, 6 and 10). Strategies for promoting foreign direct investment include so-called 'public-private partnerships', centred on local capitalists and states elites, while making some provision for the inclusion of local communities, but on vastly different terms from the foreign investors (see Chapters 2, 6 and 7).

Although national sovereignty has been invoked by governments to defend their plans to transform agriculture and protect food security, our studies add to the evidence that state sovereignty is regularly undermined by the demands of commercial agriculture projects and the conditions they have secured in contracts. Demands for policy reforms on genetically modified organisms to accommodate commercial farmers; demands for changes in investment laws to protect the repatriation of profits and demands for special tax status are all examples of this challenge to state sovereignty (see Chapters 2 and 10).

What if these commercial deals had not emerged, or if alternative investments had focused on existing farmers instead? Several authors have posed the counterfactual question and explored the outcomes of similar investments in Nigeria or Ethiopia; for instance, those that were directed at smallholders (see Chapters 2 and 4), or how commercial agriculture would fare without the strong state support afforded to it, which smallholders do not receive in any consistent fashion. In this context of chronic under-investment in farming, state officials in Ethiopia either ignored or intimidated local communities into submitting to terms unfavourable to them (see Chapter 4) and, in Tanzania and Kenya, consistently took sides with foreign investors in disputes with local communities (see Chapters 5, 6 and 7).

State participation in land transactions has been further complicated by federalism and the decentralisation of land administration systems. In some countries, arrangements have been made to devolve certain powers from the federal to the state or provincial level. Similar processes of power devolution have involved decentralised authorities and traditional leaders. For example, in Nigeria and Ethiopia, the power of state governments to shape land acquisitions and land policy is under constant negotiation. The federal state in Ethiopia has stronger control over land transactions than the regional states (see Chapter 4), while in Nigeria, federal laws enabled the governor of Kwara State to commandeer large tracts of land already used by citizens, for the use of Zimbabwean farmers (see Chapter 2). In Kenya, the devolution of power and financial resources to counties produced an important shift in power to the local level, enabling county authorities to negotiate with investors (see Chapters 5 and 6). Within federal systems, the division of landholding power between federal and state authorities has created ambiguities about who has the power to deal with which aspects of land management. These shifts in power and control have ambiguous implications for local people and their land rights. While the principle of subsidiarity might suggest that these levels are closer to people and therefore their influence, it is also at the local level that resource contests between the local elite and small farmers are most intense. Do more centralised or decentralised systems enable greater accountability of states to existing landholders? Our studies point in different directions on this question.

Institutional weaknesses also account for some of the confusion about powers and responsibilities and the failure of state institutions to regulate land deals effectively. This is evident in cases where land has been nationalised, implying a strong state with clarity about its land interests, but state ownership of land has not extinguished the claims of those who live on and work the land. In Ethiopia, Kenya, Tanzania, Mozambique, Congo and Nigeria, the claims of land users, who depend on the land for growing food and grazing animals, have been mishandled by state officials under the guise of state ownership. In many cases, land users are considered squatters and are either denied compensation for their losses or have claims ignored on the grounds that they lack titles (see Chapters 4, 6 and 9). In other situations, there is confusion (and buck-passing) over who should pay them compensation: the state or investors (see Chapter 10). In several of our cases, large tracts of land have been allocated in ways which flouted laid-down procedures for land alienation (see Chapters 2 and 4). The situation in systems dominated by customary law and communal lands is not much better, as land users have been dispossessed by traditional rulers, with the state acting as a referee, and often the same people working within the state also hold traditional office or have strong connections within these structures (see Chapters 3 and 6).

The establishment of legal modalities for large-scale acquisitions appears to lag behind policies and other measures. The land tenure reforms of the 1990s did not anticipate the acquisition of large areas of land or make specific provisions to regulate this. Thus questions about the nature of customary land interests – who has the power to negotiate land deals and to grant title; who should be paid for ownership and compensated for the loss of land use; what amounts would constitute reasonable payments for land and what length of lease would be uniformly given – are all left to the negotiators of deals to address on a case-by-case basis. The result has been wide divergences in the deals even within any one country (see Chapter 3). An outcome of these large land investments is that unregistered customary land interests are in a state of flux and insecurity, with enduring questions about whether they can be recognised as property rights (Peters 2013). Processes of privatisation and individualisation of such interests are in full gear, and the outcomes nearly always undermine the tenure security of smallholders. On the other hand, we see a strengthening of the power of traditional land authorities as landowners rather than trustees for people who occupy and use the land through custom.

One outcome of the renewed intensity of land acquisitions is that many transactions are not recorded in official statistics. In the case of Kenya, which has had a long tradition of land registration, one study found that, although several large ranches have been consolidated and fenced as single units, this is not reflected in the database of the Ministry of Local Government. While this may be a deliberate strategy by land owners to enable them to pay lower property rates, it keeps the state out of new land transactions, with the result that the extent of land concentration is not known (see Chapter 5).

Land deals are often either done in secret or without consultation of local communities and even, in some cases, local leaders. In the Congo case, opposition Members of Parliament and local councillors were not aware of a significant land deal involving 80,000ha in their constituencies until after it was concluded (see Chapter 10). Some have attributed such ignorance among local actors to the technicality of deals, low levels of literacy and the absence of technical support for land-holding communities (see Chapter 5), while others have attributed this to a lack of transparency, accountability and participation (see Chapters

3, 4 and 10). The failure to involve local communities in negotiations has meant that communities only respond to deals when their effects become real, and the window of opportunity to negotiate terms when transacting community land is long gone.

Livelihood impacts and their implications

The policy turn to large-scale commercial farming is creating conditions that develop or deepen the dualism of agrarian structures. In many respects, the land rush has revived the large- versus small-farm debate, and proponents and critics of land deals rely heavily on old, established discourses to support their arguments (Baglioni and Gibbon 2013). These distinct perspectives shape our understandings of the impacts of Africa's land rush. Oya (2013c) urges those researching land grabs to engage with the long-standing debates in agrarian political economy. Specifically, does the land rush herald the return of the agrarian question of capital, and the potential development of capitalist agriculture at scale in Africa? Or does it foreground the agrarian question of labour, the crisis of rural reproduction and the creation or absorption of 'surplus labour'?

With regard to impacts, Cotula et al. (2014) note the difficulty of assessing socio-economic outcomes in the absence of baseline studies, while Oya (2013c) explores the reasons 'why we do not know very much' about the impacts of the land rush, despite all that has been written about it. Where large plantations are established, Cotula et al. (2014) found in their comparative study that the promised benefits were not realised largely due to the limited number of permanent and even temporary jobs created, and the poor and insecure forms of employment that emerge. Both caution against the unrealistic projections on which land deals are usually premised. In the absence of longitudinal studies to grapple with changes in economies and society over time, and research that expands beyond case studies to demonstrate cumulative macroeconomic effects at national level, methodologies for investigating the impacts and implications of the land rush are constrained. Negative impacts at local level may enable benefits at other levels, although the available data prevent any rigorous assessment as to whether or not this is the case.

Our studies in this book show the lack of a well-defined approach to the smallholder sector, and a lack of measures to promote synergies between the small- and large-scale sectors. This issue is discussed in terms of the livelihood impacts of land transactions, focusing on three aspects: loss of resources; implications for livelihood activities and employment opportunities, and the distribution of social benefits. The studies provide valuable detail on these issues.

Investments have had variable success. For example, in the case of Zimbabwean farmers in Nigeria, efforts at chicken-rearing have been more successful than dairy, which in turn have been better than their efforts to cultivate crops (see Chapter 2). Interestingly, commercial farmers found themselves experiencing challenges similar to those faced by smallholders, though to a lesser degree, including chronic difficulties in securing adequate finance, energy and infrastructure (see Chapter 2). A common finding is that only a fraction of the land that smallholders and pastoralists lose to commercial investment is placed under cultivation, especially in the shorter term (see Chapters 3, 4 and 10). This finding echoes a shocking statistic presented in a study by the UN Food and Agricultural Organization: only 1.7 per cent of land that had been recently acquired through large-scale leasing for agriculture was under production (FAO 2013).

Farmland investments have produced some permanent employment in Nigeria, Ghana, Ethiopia, Tanzania and Mozambique, although not enough jobs have been created directly – in all cases far below initial projections – and the majority of these jobs are casual and seasonal (see Chapters 2, 3, 4, 7 and 9). In general, the pay on offer has been poor, even when compared with similar jobs in the locality (see Chapter 10). In some cases, wages much lower than the local average have been introduced, thus creating employment that captures the most desperate in the area (see Chapter 4) or migrants (see Chapter 3). In some cases, full-time employees have lamented their loss of land to continue to engage in farming activities to supplement their low wages, while those in seasonal employment have noted the incompatibility of their wage work with their own farming activities and therefore food security (see Chapters 7 and 9). Last but not least are the immense challenges for the planning and execution of social and reproductive activities, particularly for migrant workers. This issue is particularly challenging for women who have tended to benefit least from employment opportunities (see Chapters 3, 4, 7, 9 and 10).

Projects have often led to the loss of water, farmlands, rangelands and the commons, which were used by landless people and especially people already marginalised in terms of resource access and resource tenure, such as women, young people and migrants, for farming and harvesting of natural resources (see Chapters 2, 4, 5 and 7). Some of our studies have made efforts to compute these losses through surveys (see Chapters 3 and 4). However, such losses are often incalculable and represent a ratcheting-down of livelihood assets for poor communities. After losing the resources on which they survive, they may simply not be able to recover. This is because livelihood strategies involve multiple activities dependent on social and economic relationships and ecosystems that, once disrupted by land deals, cannot be revived and are seldom if ever adequately compensated for (see Chapter 3).

In the case of contract farmers and outgrowers, several chapters provide a reality check for the generally positive attitude in policy circles toward such arrangements. In Ghana, Malawi, Mozambique and Tanzania, the outgrower model was found to have several weaknesses. These include the rigidities in the terms of contracts which favour companies over outgrowers; lack of transparency in the weighing and measuring of products; the fixing of prices of inputs and products, harvesting delays; broken guarantees of a ready market for products, and the loss of time for growing food. As a result, earnings have been generally disappointing in that they are lower than expected and are often delayed (see Chapters 3, 7 and 9). Even more fundamentally, the outgrower model exposes farmers to the vicissitudes of the global trading system, while tying them to the bottom of the value chain. These findings echo the critical discussions of contract farming in the literature (cf. Smalley 2013; Oya 2013a; Little and Watts 1994). The most successful outgrowers are those who have been able to maintain their own farming activities while participating in the outgrower schemes, but this is only feasible for larger landholders and excludes many smallholders, particularly women.

Failures of expected technology transfers also undermined envisaged livelihood improvements. In the case of the Nupe farmers in Nigeria, local smallholders adopted new crops along with better crop management following the arrival of the Zimbabwean farmers, but the effects on overall production were negligible (see Chapter 2). Local farmers thought real improvements would come if they could also secure credit, tractor hiring services and good prices for their crops. Compounding their frustrations were ongoing contestations around land tenure. When they lost land to the commercial investors, the land set aside for a community-model commercial farm had not been allocated to any local farmer. In the same vein, some pastoralists were learning new techniques from the Zimbabwean dairy farmers and had been rewarded with a steady market for their milk. However, there were contestations around grazing on uncultivated land allocated to commercial farmers, raising questions of the scale of technology transfer and its sustainability. In Tanzania, by contrast, a few farmers acquired title deeds and were putting their individually-owned farms together to form block farms to grow sugar on a larger scale, with the support – including the transfer of technology – of the sugar transnational Illovo. In some cases, they have been able to use these title deeds to secure loans from the bank (see Chapter 7).

These examples notwithstanding, the predominant message across the chapters is the failure of technology transfer, with few positive linkages between large-scale commercial agriculture and smallholder farming or pastoralism. The reasons include the character of the capital-intensive monoculture plantation business model itself, which is a production system incompatible with smallholder farming in that it uses technologies that cannot easily be adopted by local farmers because of costs and differences in the scale of operations. Also, the cash crops that are grown on commercial farms are often different from the staples grown by local farmers. In other cases, investors and locals are in different lines of business that conflict with one another; for example where investors take over land for crop production in areas used by pastoralists (see Chapters 3, 4 and 5). Investors' desire to grow a wide variety of commodities in order to determine what would be most profitable, with little of the infrastructure needed for successful commercial production, means that technology transfer is a secondary consideration (see Chapters 2 and 10). Even outgrowers often do not benefit much from technology transfer, and are not offered access to irrigation and other technologies used in the nucleus farms of investors growing the same crops (see Chapters 3, 7 and 9).

Our studies also expose some of the differences within groups of smallholders who are experiencing land concentration. One of the Kenya studies identifies three groups of smallholders – those who bought and settled on land as a result of land pressure in their regions of origin; those who bought land for speculative purposes and were mostly absent from the locality, and those who bought land to use as collateral to access bank loans (see Chapter 5). These contrasts are important because a process of consolidation of smallholdings is taking place, where land brokers in collaboration with state officials are consolidating small parcels and selling them to foreigners, who only later discover the contested nature of the land they have acquired. The Ghana study found differences between migrants and people living in their natal communities, and a group of medium-scale farmers who commuted from a nearby regional capital to farm who had lost their farmlands to a *Jatropha* plantation.[1] This resulted in losses of employment for women who had previously worked on the farms, who in turn became the main protagonists in protests against the project (see Chapter 3).

Several studies have focused on the situation of pastoralists, highlighting their neglect in agricultural policies that privilege sedentary farming and farmers. Studies from Kenya and Ethiopia found that their already-precarious livelihoods were under severe strain with the consolidation and enclosure of both ranches and smallholder farmlands (see Chapters 4, 5 and 6). Lands that are common property resources used regularly by pastoralists, or lands they migrate to in times of drought, are no longer readily available. In the cyclical droughts that have followed this recent period of enclosures, pastoralists have suffered heavy losses to their herds. This current instalment in long-term processes of dispossession is reshaping pastoralist livelihoods, entrenching vulnerability with uncertain outcomes in the long term (cf. Catley et al. 2013).

What are the long-term environmental effects of land pressures created by enclosures of community lands? In some situations, pastoralists are engaging in continuous rather than rotational grazing because of constraints on their mobility, or exploiting forests for fuelwood and other resources. In other situations, people have had to migrate to seek new farmlands, pasture and water. The result has been overcrowding, causing

---

[1] *Jatropha curcas* is a Latin American plant from whose seeds oil can be extracted and refined into bio-diesel.

soil degradation and a loss of biodiversity, making both productive and reproductive activities more difficult. Paradoxically, these degraded areas abut areas of plentiful resources that have been enclosed. This juxtaposition of plenty and scarcity side-by-side is an important factor in the resource conflicts identified in Laikipia in Kenya, for example (see Chapter 5, also cf. Scoones et al. 2013). But in Nigeria, synergies are evident, as the emergence of commercial dairy operations has enabled pastoralists to access new markets (see Chapter 2).

Land acquisitions have complicated effects in sensitive ecosystems that have multiple uses and support diverse and already-fragile livelihoods. The chapter on Kenya's Tana Delta (Chapter 6) explores this in relation to the thousands of hectares of land in this poverty-stricken and conflict-ridden region being leased out to investors for industrial-scale farming, including sugarcane cultivation and biofuel production, as well as for mining. These deals are expected to result in the eviction of thousands of smallholders from their villages. In addition, Orma pastoralists and their hundreds of thousands of cattle will potentially lose critical dry season pastures. Because of land-use competition between farmers and pastoralists, this was already an area of endemic dry season conflict. As the Tana acquisitions are still in progress, their effects are not yet fully felt, but they have already prompted violent protests that have cost lives.

Across the chapters, efforts are made to identify winners and losers in land transactions. In addition to the usual suspects – commercial ranchers, transnational agribusiness, foreign and local elites, politicians and senior civilian and military government officials – a few studies have found that within disadvantaged groups such as pastoralist communities, new elites are emerging as participants in and beneficiaries of large-scale land acquisitions. Often these groups are able to benefit from land acquisitions by controlling local branches of state land institutions, such as the District Land Boards in Kenya (see Chapter 5) or the Regional Land Commissions in Ghana (see Chapter 3), or by taking up the few business opportunities that come with these projects (see Chapter 7).

The burgeoning literature on large-scale land acquisitions has debated whether the nationality of those acquiring large tracts of land is important (cf. White et al. 2012; Zoomers 2010; Cotula et al. 2009). The dominant focus on foreign investors ignores the involvement of local interests in large-scale land acquisitions, an issue addressed in a number of chapters. These show that local interests can counteract the move towards privatisation. For example, the Tana Delta study observes that, while the private ranches owned by foreign investors were enclosed, those that had been acquired by pastoralist elites were not, implying that they could be used by land-hungry pastoralists. Some pastoralist elites worked with the poorer segments of pastoralist society to organise themselves to acquire group ranches (see Chapter 6). This difference in access to privatised grazing land could provide a safety valve in times of drought and crisis, and could be important for avoiding land-use conflicts in the future. In other cases, commercial farming by local elites has not been so land-intensive and has not created the kinds of tensions caused by larger foreign acquisitions (see Chapters 3, 4 and 5). Apart from smaller landholdings, where there are gradual endogenous processes of commercialisation there may be clearer opportunities for technology transfer and synergies with smallholder farming than in big transnational investments.

While these instances may suggest that foreign investors and their local commercial farming counterparts have contrasting sensibilities and behave differently, not all local acquisitions are in this cooperative tradition. Further, local elites and state officials have in some instances worked closely with foreign interests, pursuing the same purposes.

The dispossession and disruption of the lives of local communities arises in part because, in the rush to promote agribusiness, not enough policy and political support has been given to how countries might benefit from more of the value chain of the various commodities being promoted. In Tanzania, the promotion of sugar farming has not included local enterprises in sugar processing and distribution (see Chapter 7). In the same vein, the land rush has seen little being done to promote the processing of horticultural products, refining of biofuels and value addition to other commodities that have seen a boom in this period. This raises the spectre of the trajectory of commercialisation currently under way replicating the commodity dependence of many African states evident from colonial times through independence, rather than a route to capturing more of the gains across more lucrative value chains. Whether or not this will turn out to be the case depends on the decisiveness among policy makers in each country to leverage investment for the greater good.

Responses, resistance and land-related conflicts

Communities have responded to changes brought about by the expansion of large-scale commercial farming in different ways. Responses have varied from support to outright hostility and resistance. In some cases, initial support for investment and the promise of development has turned to hostility in the face of disappointments. Within communities, certain groups have found new opportunities for employment or for enterprises linked to new commercial operations. But across our studies, many have been locked out of these new opportunities, while also shouldering the costs of losing land, water and common property resources. This explains the widespread resort to various acts of resistance including theft, destruction and acts of vandalism. How communities respond depends on a number of factors: the pre-existing tenure system and local land interests; the intensity of existing land-use conflicts; the range and viability of alternative lands and economic activities; the transparency and smoothness of land acquisitions; what promises are made; the landholding practices and business models of investors; the extent of new livelihood opportunities created and how broadly these are shared, and state and investor attitudes and responses to community concerns. Responses to new investments may be seen as a continuum, ranging from support to extreme hostility (Borras and Franco 2013). Many people who once welcomed a new investment later changed their minds as events unfolded. Investors, too, have in several instances had their initial optimism dashed by the complexities of conducting commercial operations, leading in some cases to the contraction of initial plans to less ambitious scales or methods of production (Hammar 2010). The Congo study is a case in point. Given the staggeringly high levels of food importation (95 per cent), the enthusiasm for the South African commercial farming interests on the part of government officials is to be expected. This does not preclude tensions in the future, given the differing expectations among parties and the evident collapse of much of the investment (see Chapter 10). The situation in Nigeria unfolded in a similar manner, with high expectations on all sides, which were soon tempered by realities on the ground (see Chapter 2).

Resistance has taken many forms. In Ethiopia, mutual aid groups were organised to send representatives to the President of the Regional State, and farmers signed petitions to the District Assembly. There have also been thefts, abductions and death threats directed at foreign employees of investing companies. That it has not been possible to prosecute anyone for these acts is an indication of the strength of community feeling and also distrust of the state (see Chapter 4). In Kenya, resistance to the loss of pastoral grazing lands has been quite comprehensive, involving court cases, demonstrations, illegal night grazing, open resistance and violence resulting in the loss of life and property. Here, the situation has been compounded by drought and the enclosure of lands that were used as emergency grazing grounds. The number of violent episodes in Laikipia is significant, with four private ranch invasions occurring between 2002 and 2009 (see Chapter 5). This conflict, which is not between land uses, but rather between ownership regimes, signals the deep divisions that are being created through processes of land and agricultural commercialisation.

The parties to conflicts arising from large-scale land acquisitions are quite well identified in the literature. Studies have identified conflicts between the state and local communities; between new land holders and local communities; between different groups within local communities; between local leaders and community members, and between communities – with all of these conflicts relating to losses, gains and the sharing of opportunities (Ansoms and Hilhorst 2014; Wolford et al. 2013; Cotula et al. 2009). The case studies in this book provide further insights into the complicated nature of these conflicts and the shifts in their contours over time. In Kenya, alliances within communities to respond to the loss of land were altered when the state and the political elite, using ethnicity to prosecute a national election dispute, played off pastoralists against smallholder farmers with devastating effects (see Chapters 5 and 6). Several of the studies point to how these current tensions around land acquisitions and the land scarcities they engender are creating conditions that could produce further tensions and violence in the future (see Chapter 2).

State strategies for managing complaints, violence and other forms of resistance have included ignoring claims and petitions by asserting the state ownership of land; the siting of police posts in the area; the creation of buffer zones around villages to avoid community land losses; agreements to allow communities to use portions of acquired land both for farming and for harvesting of natural resources until commercial farmers are ready to cultivate, and compensation and financial support for livelihood activities (see Chapters 2, 4, 5 and 6). In other cases, community members have been detained and threatened by a coercive state apparatus. While some of these strategies have been effective, others have not succeeded in stemming resistance. In most cases, conflict is not directed at the companies themselves, but at state authorities or local elites, although the case of Illovo in Malawi is an exception (see Chapter 8).

Rural development and agrarian transformation

What are the new trajectories of agrarian transformation being established through large-scale land acquisitions and what does this mean for rural development? Processes of commercialisation arising from land-based investments, often coupled with changing market conditions for local producers, have varied pace and outcomes. But the direction of change is clear: towards commercial production by medium- to large-scale local farmers alongside larger estates, now owned not by colonial powers but by foreign companies or by multinational companies, often in partnership with domestic capital. As with previous moments of enclosure and commercialisation, Africa's recent land rush is already sparking resistance and counter-movements.

Our chapters show that activities related to commercial agriculture have in several instances created new employment and demand for services, improvements in infrastructure, improved incomes and new patterns of consumption, particularly in nearby urban areas where processing activities and sales take place. We have identified several new boom towns that have emerged as a result (see Chapters 2, 3, 7 and 9). While these improvements were welcomed in these locales, they were not necessarily the same people or areas that had suffered the biggest losses of land. Expanded economic opportunities were often not significant enough for setting in motion processes of rural development.

The introduction of large-scale commercial farming in regions where smallholder family farming predominates has the potential to create a dualist agrarian structure (see Chapters 2 and 10). However, commercial farming is still more of a small fragile enclave in the smallholder-dominated system than a fully-fledged system in its own right in most countries. One dimension of commercialisation initiatives that has not made much headway in the cases we studied is the creation of a successor generation of small- and medium-scale commercial farmers. This raises questions of whether accumulating farmers will be able to transfer their enterprises to the next generation – rather than lose these to big corporate investors – and what the new young farmers will need in order to flourish and to adapt to changing circumstances.

A central message of the book therefore is that the challenges facing commercial farmers and agribusinesses that have acquired large areas of land are dimming the vision of large-scale commercial farming as the best approach to agrarian transformation. At the same time, the political and policy narratives about pro-poor development and slogans about agriculture as a priority notwithstanding, smallholder farmers continue to face enormous challenges to their survival, while the rapid pace of land concentration is uncovering and reinforcing the social differentiation often masked by kinship systems in rural Africa (Peters 2013). The implications are acute for young people and their transition either into family farming or out of agriculture entirely, and therefore for the next generation of farmers in Africa (cf. Sumberg et al. 2014).

Debates on land and African agriculture: continuity and change

Not all this is new. Indeed, African agriculture has a long history of attempts at commercialisation, introducing large-scale farming alongside or in some value-chain relationship with small-scale farming (Oya 2013a; Smalley 2013; Little and Watts 1994). What is also not new is the way in which such processes underline existing contours of social differentiation in rural Africa (Berry 2002, 2009; Peters 2004). Agricultural policies are often presented as technical solutions to problems of food insecurity, fluctuating global markets and unpredictable weather, but at heart they are shaped by politics, both national party politics and the political significance of classes of farmers in regional and national economies (Poulton 2014; Bates 1981).

Our contribution builds on this literature by locating both existing farming classes and new agribusinesses within the national political economy. We identify four major debates in the existing literature from which our research draws inspiration, and to which we contribute insights from fieldwork and analysis.

First is the debate about the status of customary tenure: how robust local institutions are in the face of commercial interests, and how to secure tenure rights (Alden Wily 2011; Peters 2009; Okoth-Ogendo

2008). Among the varied approaches to resolving this problem have been formal private titling (Kenya), enabling low-cost certification of rights (Ethiopia), certification through devolved institutions (Madagascar), alternatives to titling through *de facto* recognition of rights (Mozambique) or vesting land in villages (Tanzania) and, most recently, innovations in 'community titling' through state-governed legal demarcations (Mozambique) and bottom-up certification processes driven by non-governmental organisations (Zambia). Pre-existing tenure systems, and attempts to recognise and formalise rights, are crucial factors shaping how land acquisitions are conducted, and the leverage that local people can exert to determine the forms and terms of investment on land they hold or claim. Formalising land rights is complex in tenure systems based on non-exclusive uses and 'nested' systems of rights to different land-based resources (Lund 2008; Cousins 1997; Bassett and Crummey 1993). Formalisation may not have a positive impact on agricultural productivity (Lawry et al. 2014), but can provide a basis for people to contest, refuse, or leverage improved terms from potential investors, and from their own state. Without this recognition of land rights, the principle of 'free, prior, and informed consent' is likely to be unrealisable (Vermeulen and Cotula 2010b). Serious investments in consultation and accountability mechanisms are needed to give effect to the array of guidelines and policy frameworks promoted by the UN (FAO 2012b) and the African Union (Land Policy Initiative 2014; AU/AfDB/UNECA 2009).

A second debate is the relationship between large-scale and small-scale producers, the factor and commodity market conditions that shape who wins and who loses, and the roles of state institutions in shaping these outcomes through regulation (Lipton 2009; Binswanger et al. 1995). This was of central importance during the years of 'developmentalism' in the early post-colonial era (Heyer et al. 1981). Agriculture in Africa has long been constrained by scarce capital and also labour, especially skilled labour. Large-scale estate farming is not the only possible answer to the long-standing challenge of intensifying agricultural production (Berry 1993). Smaller farms are often both more labour-intensive and more land-intensive, despite being capital-constrained. As Sara Berry (1993) found in four detailed studies in Nigeria, Ghana, Kenya and Zambia, rather than a linear process of 'development' or 'modernization', there have been cyclical moments of 'expansion and contraction' in agricultural commodity markets, each associated with the changing fortunes of particular rural classes. In recent years, the 'large versus small' debate has re-emerged (Balgioni and Gibbon 2013) as the search is on for the holy grail of a 'win-win' solution in the form of an 'inclusive business model'. Such a model, it is argued, could enable a synergistic relationship between private investors securing land for industrial agriculture – often monocropped landscapes producing for global markets – and smallholders producing food and, increasingly, cash crops on their own land (Vermeulen and Cotula 2010b; Cotula et al. 2009). This embeds contract farmers, or outgrowers, in processes that can be described as commercialisation *without* dispossession (Berry et al. 1988).

Can what appear to be contradictory interests be reconciled and harmonised in such a way? The studies included in this book have found few such synergies, despite several of them focusing on partnerships between agribusinesses and smallholders. Exploring the potentials for connecting large, intermediate and small-scale farms to generate prosperous and inclusive rural economies, requires further comparative research,[2] and should stimulate a debate about what configurations of land holding, what labour regimes and what economic linkages result. To date, this discussion has become mired in an unhelpful debate about the assumed relative pros and cons of large- versus small-scale farming, with often entrenched views dominating (cf. Deininger et al. 2014; Baglioni and Gibbon 2013; Collier and Dercon 2014; Deininger and Byerlee 2012; Deininger 2003), and without a broader analysis of how different configurations of capital and labour could be integrated in particular contexts.

A third and related debate is about the implications of big land-based investments for social differentiation and class relations. We address questions of class, but also look at what this means for kinship networks, families and homesteads, gender and generational differences in how people perceive opportunities and threats from large-scale land investments, how they are affected and how they respond. Much of the 'land grab' literature, notably from activist organisations, has focused on 'investors' and their impacts on 'local people', suggesting a dynamic in which the rich and powerful reshape and remake local environments in which local people feature either as passive beneficiaries of 'development' or victims of 'dispossession' (GRAIN 2008; ILC 2011; Oxfam 2011). However, in order to get to grips with processes of accumulation, dispossession, incorporation or exclusion, our understanding must emerge from a more sophisticated analysis of such processes, and a more rigorous definition of terms (Hall 2012a, 2013). Our case studies suggest that something more complex is under way than the simple narratives often relayed, as investors encounter enormous difficulties with initiating production, and various local people resist or collaborate, or move between the two, in ways that advance their diverse interests and that subvert investors' plans.

Almost everywhere, 'local communities' are divided and over time become more economically differentiated as a result of the articulation between local production systems and economies, and new production systems introduced by state-backed investors (Wolford et al. 2013). Further, we find patterns of accumulation, incorporation and new emerging class structures – all forms of differentiation among 'host' communities that are

---

[2] See the study, Land and Agricultural Commercialisation in Africa, conducted in Ghana, Kenya and Zambia by several of the authors in this book, and others (www.future-agricultures.org/laca).

shaped by pre-existing relations of class, gender, generation and ethnicity. These are refracted through the newly-created agrarian labour regimes that produce differentiated classes of labour, including casual, seasonal and temporary forms of employment, and those eking out a living on the margins of commercialising rural economies – what Bernstein (2002) calls 'fragmented classes of labour'. All this shows how, while some might experience losses and scarcity of land and other natural resources, in fact what we are seeing is the political redistribution of scarcities at multiple scales, within communities, at the national level, and in global circuits of capital (Scoones et al. 2014).

A fourth debate is the connection between the creation of large-scale commercial farms and the rural non-farm economy.[3] As Berry (1993: 74) observed, commercialisation involves the expansion of intermediaries and traders alongside farmers. These new actors might be able to sustain a livelihood and build a commercial enterprise out of brokering agreements, or buying and selling on, between farmer and buyer, on the basis of loan finance and market information. While this pattern, in previous moments of endogenous commercialisation, saw the emergence of farmers' marketing cooperatives, this is not the case in the most recent period. Far less influential in negotiating terms and prices are the outgrower associations now emerging to organise contracts and block farming to supply nucleus estates and processing facilities, such as in Tanzania, Malawi and Mozambique (see Chapters 7, 8 and 9). Positive spin-offs into the rural non-farm economy are the most common form of development observed across the chapters (cf. Haggblade et al. 1989), benefiting residents of rural towns and service centres, rather than smallholder farmers who might compete with incoming investors, lose their land or be unaffected. Cases from Nigeria, Ghana, Tanzania and Mozambique show how growing small towns and satellite industries provide goods and services linked to agribusiness enterprises (see Chapters 2, 3, 7 and 9). However, the costs and benefits are distributed across different populations. Such processes create a pull of young people to urban centres and small towns, and produce remittance economies. Whether such income streams can be reinvested in production depends on whether some family members are able to retain access to land. If so, secured land tenure alongside small 'boom towns' could potentially see rising cash incomes and expenditure among rural populations.

Each of these four debates has been long-running and highly contested. The recent 'land rush', and associated processes of commercialisation that have emerged, add a new complexion to these debates. Yet the basic features remain very much the same. Agrarian economies are forever undergoing change, with new configurations of land ownership and use. As the chapters in this book show, the impacts and outcomes for different people very much depend on the context, which is why a detailed case

---

[3] See the study, *Space Markets and Employment in Agricultural Development*, conducted in Malawi, South Africa and Zimbabwe (www.future-agricultures.org/smead).

study approach looking in detail at what happens over time is needed. Moving beyond the simplistic caricatures of the 'land grab', as either catastrophe or opportunity, is essential.

Conclusion

Since its peak following 2007-08, Africa's 'land rush' seems to have slowed, as the real implications of investment and production have become more apparent, as opportunity costs in other investment destinations have changed and as drivers such as spiking food and oil prices have abated, even if temporarily. The 'revaluation of land' (Borras et al. 2011b) under way globally was rapid but it was not linear. Today, investors are far more cautious in their prognoses for profits: several 'bubbles' have burst, not least the hype surrounding biofuels. Since then, many *Jatropha* projects in Africa have been abandoned, some before production even started, and others after just a fraction of the expected land-clearing and planting had been achieved (Locke and Henley 2013; Sulle and Hall 2015). However, while the land rush may have slowed, it has not stopped. All indications are that global demand for food, fuel and feedstock will continue to drive demand for fertile land and water into the future. Growing African economies and consumer demand in urban centres compound this demand in conditions rendered ever more uncertain by extreme weather events and changes to the climate.

Large-scale land acquisitions are thus shaping profound change in African agriculture and in African rural societies and economies. Such annexation of territory and the changes it instigates are not without precedent. Indeed, historical cycles of commercialisation are evident and are associated, in different places and at different times, with processes of colonial dispossession, state nationalisation, villagisation or privatisation (Edelman et al. 2013). Most recently, commodification of land and natural resources through the growing influence of financial institutions and 'offset' schemes has altered the politics of natural resources significantly (Fairhead et al. 2012). The (re)creation of agrarian dualism through land deals is taking place in an age of globalised, corporatised and financialised agriculture (Fairbairn 2014; Clapp 2014). This may accelerate inequalities of class and other forms of differentiation already evident and growing in post-liberalised African agriculture (Moyo et al. 2012), and fundamentally shift the balance of interests in agrarian economies.

All this raises doubt concerning the claims made about the benefits of large-scale land deals, and the patterns of investment associated with, for example, the G8's New Alliance for Food Security and Nutrition[4], state-supported development corridors across the continent, as well as the array of deals by private corporations, often with state and elite backing,

---

[4]   http://new-alliance.org/

such as those documented in this book. The assumptions that large land-based investments will create an emerging, entrepreneurial, middle-farming class, hooked into commercial value chains and benefiting from infrastructure, technology and expertise from these large investments need to be questioned. The evidence for this is slim indeed. Rather, land deals appear to be short-circuiting existing farming systems and creating enclave investments, with limited employment and often requiring significant state subsidies to remain viable. Where local farmers are incorporated, as in the cases of contract farming, this is often on adverse terms that have profound implications for gender relations and women's access to and control of productive resources and cash incomes. With these links to large investments, such farming populations are now part of particular commodity chains – in the cases in this book, sugar is a major feature – within an increasingly globalised and financialised agro-food system (Fairbairn 2014). This system is undergoing major corporate restructuring, as firms seek profit in highly-constrained circumstances, fuelling commercial imperatives to grab cheap land and exploit labour (McMichael 2012).

So what is the fate of the small-scale African farmer within this scenario? Ultimately, this hinges on processes of negotiating with capital, and with allied political elites, on the terms of incorporation (cf. McCarthy 2010) into diverse forms of commercial agriculture and different value chains. This may be more significant for such farmers than the outright grab of land that has been the focus of the outcry over the past few years. As Peluso and Lund (2011: 668) observe: 'What is new is not only land grabbing or ownership, but also new crops with new labour processes and objectives for the growers, new actors and subjects, and new legal and practical instruments for possessing, expropriating, or challenging previous land controls.'

As our book shows, a range of processes of enclosure is occurring, located within diverse trajectories of agriculture commercialisation, driven by different dynamics. The role of labour and the terms of employment are crucial (Li 2011), as people are incorporated as labourers and out-growers and as suppliers in complex agribusiness arrangements. As the cases illustrate, there is no simple process of rural proletarianisation, but more the emergence of hybrid classes of labour engaging with new commercial endeavours. There are, however, clear winners and losers who become evident as processes of social differentiation unfold locally. How this will all pan out will depend heavily on local contexts, and particularly the political alliances that are forged between local elites and international capital. In some settings, a new form of dualism between corporate and family farming is emerging, replicating patterns not seen since the establishment of the settler economies of the colonial era. But this time, as then, the creation of a large-scale commercial farming sector is not straightforward, and will require massive state support and finance, which is very often absent in the cases we have examined. This explains the far-from-linear process of commercialisation with many setbacks and returns to the drawing board.

An alternative trajectory may be a˙ move by external investors to integrate with aspects of local agrarian economies more firmly, realising that an enclave model is not feasible, economically or politically. Various forms of integration are possible, from outgrower arrangements to joint ventures to other value chain links, for example in trading, processing and so on. The chapters show how, as only some people will benefit, processes of inclusion and exclusion will inevitably fuel social differentiation. The terms of incorporation therefore become crucial. External investment may yet find better and safer returns through working with large- or medium-scale local farmers, potentially organised as blocks, where risks of land disputes are minimised, and other costs are transferred to local producers. While relatively small currently, such groups of medium-sized commercial farms may become an increasingly significant feature in many African contexts, as entrepreneurs and urban elites invest in acquiring and consolidating land, which once was part of the 'communal' smallholder sector (Jayne et al. 2014; Smart and Hanlon 2014). In time, this incremental process of land acquisition by local elites, backed by capital, may be cumulatively more significant than the more dramatic large-scale 'grabs' seen in the recent past.

What then is the future for the smallholder sector, the core of most of Africa's agrarian economies? Despite frequent declarations of the end of the peasantry, and the resolution of the agrarian question through urbanisation and industrialisation (Bryceson 2004), the peasantry – in now increasingly diverse forms – is remarkably persistent, with some scholars observing a resurgence of peasant styles of production (van der Ploeg 2009). The peasantry is far from being a single class, if ever it was, and is highly differentiated by age, gender, ethnicity, as well as occupation, with many relying for their livelihoods on various forms of labour, often highly uncertain and fragile (Bernstein 2010b). Poor infrastructure, high transport costs, poorly functioning markets, a lack of credit, growth in demand from local markets, and agroecological conditions have made skilled local labour essential. Yet smallholder farming has many advantages, as it is rooted in family labour, but also, as petty commodity production, involves various forms of hired labour (Peters 2013; Lipton 2009). Such family-based farming is unlikely to disappear any time soon. Indeed, when large-scale farm enterprises set up alongside such smallholder production systems, the smallholder areas are often more productive, entrepreneurial and vibrant, despite the massive financial and political support that prestige investment projects attract.

The key question, we argue, then becomes less about the land rush as a distinct phenomenon, but more how new forms of capital, crops, production systems, labour regimes and expertise become inserted into – or resisted by – existing political-economic configurations, and in turn how this affects agrarian structures and patterns of social differentiation, and with what distributional consequences. As we have emphasised in this chapter and is demonstrated throughout the book, the land rush is best seen as one of a number of processes of commercialisation of agriculture, involving particular forms of financialisation and commodification, not all of which result in the appropriation of land, although all result in various dynamics of social differentiation. Thus not all investments see a process of 'accumulation by dispossession' (Harvey 2003), or a simple incorporation into globalised capitalism, involving 'a savage sorting of winners and losers' (Sassen 2010). The processes of change on the ground are more subtle, context-specific and variegated than such sweeping assessments permit.

For more effective understandings of the land rush, therefore, we argue for a switch of emphasis to understanding the multiple processes of enclosure and commercialisation and the terms of incorporation of different groups. This highlights the wider issues of labour, technology, expertise, markets, as well as land, and processes of incorporation into new forms of market economy. As the chapters that follow show, it is in this way and with these questions in mind, that the contexts and consequences of Africa's land rush can be better understood.

2

State, Land & Agricultural Commercialisation in Kwara State, Nigeria

JOSEPH A. ARIYO & MICHAEL MORTIMORE

Introduction

The World Bank has identified Africa's Guinea Savanna agro-ecological zone as the world's largest under-developed agricultural resource (World Bank 2009). Kwara State, part of Nigeria's 'Middle Belt', lies within this zone. It has a relatively low population density and extensive rotational fallow-farming systems are used. Kwara has in recent years been the site of experimentation in large-scale commercial agriculture, involving Zimbabwean and local farmers, in a project known as the Shonga Farms, named for the location at Shonga Town in the district of the same name. The initiative is driven by the Kwara State government, as part of a policy to modernise agriculture and to contribute to national food security as well as creating employment. This chapter examines the experience gained from the Shonga experiment, and assesses its implications for agricultural policy.

History of land appropriation by government in Nigeria
The state has been directly involved in land matters since the creation of modern Nigeria, which brought together incumbent land tenure structures and subjected them to the ultimate suzerainty of the state. Pre-existing forms of land tenure include the Muslim Maliki code of law (in Northern Nigeria), traditional Family Land (in the south of the country) and other pre-Islamic and traditional forms. The result of suzerainty was a dualistic tenure system in which a distinction was made between *statutory* and *customary* law, where the state recognised customary rights of use, but reserved for itself the right of appropriation of urban and 'development' land. This right was devolved to the state governments and compensation was paid only for loss of economic crops and 'betterment' (meaning buildings and other fixed investments).

In the 1970s, faced with the difficulty of acquiring land for public purposes – especially in southern Nigeria where family land rights were strongly upheld – and following a high-powered national review of land issues (Mabogunje 2009), the (then) military government issued a Land Use Decree (now the Land Use Act of 1978). Intended as a means of ensuring easier access to land for government and (ostensibly) for individuals, the Act forms part of the Constitution, meaning that it cannot be easily amended or discarded. The Land Use Act nationalised land by vesting control of all land in the state governors. This gives the states the power to appropriate land from families and communities and to issue long leases (certificates of occupancy) to statutory holders. Governors in many states have exploited this provision of the Act to allocate tracts of rural land much larger than the stipulated maximum of 500ha, ostensibly for agricultural and infrastructural development.

Nigeria's long-standing agrarian policy has been based on transforming the smallholders into modern farmers producing for export (initially of the 'colonial' crops: palm oil, cocoa, cotton and groundnuts) and later for national food security (rice, yams, cassava, maize, sorghum and millet). Nigeria's continuing food import burden is now changing the agricultural policy orientation in favour of large-scale commercial agriculture. The small-scale sub-sector is considered by many to have failed, notwithstanding the fact that imports are largely made up not of the traditional food staples grown by smallholders, but of wheat and rice, in response to changing preferences among the urban population.

The new policy strategy (especially in Kwara State) is to make access to land and credit easier for individuals or corporations using industrial/commercial farm technologies. The necessary subsidies and privileges can be managed better where there is a 'bankable' agricultural project that forms part of the formal sector of the economy. Much faith is placed in the technologies of commercial agriculture spreading across the country from the enclaves being created now.[1] There is a range of requirements if commercial agriculture is to be successful, none of which can be taken for granted in Nigeria. First is secured tenure on available land. Second is a regular and timely flow of adequate and cheap funds for farm infrastructure, machinery and working capital. Third is a regular supply of high-quality inputs including fertilisers, agrochemicals and seeds. Fourth is a pool of skilled labour, including equipment operators, builders, plumbers, electricians, mechanics and low-wage labourers at harvest. Fifth is basic infrastructure, including adequate and regular electric power and efficient transportation to link with equally well-developed product markets. Sixth is a stable policy environment to encourage medium- and long-term investment. These requirements, in the Nigerian context, mean that the state has a pivotal role to play in the growth and sustainability of commercial agriculture (Daramola 2010).

[1] Large-scale farming is not new to Nigeria, however. Individuals (including a former President) and corporations (such as breweries) have been acquiring land grants from State governments and accumulating land through purchase for many years.

Map 2.1 Nigeria, showing the location of Shonga Farms in Kwara State

This study relies primarily on in-depth interviews carried out in 2010-11 with key players in the New Nigerian Farms run mostly by white Zimbabweans – what we call the 'Shonga experiment' – and with local farmers (Map 2.1).[2] In Shonga District, those interviewed included four senior government officials, seven commercial famers, eight local farmers who lost some of their lands to the commercial farmers, three pastoralists, three community leaders, six service providers and twelve farm workers. The interview data used in this chapter were supplemented by on-farm observations.

New Nigerian Farms, Shonga: the story of an experiment

The pursuit of large-scale commercial agriculture by the Kwara State government is predicated on the notion that a key pathway to socio-economic development is creating a class of commercial farmers who will utilise the large expanse of arable land and equitable climate with which the State is endowed. It all began with the election campaign promise made by Dr Bukola Saraki in 2003 during his successful run for Governor. In his first year of office, he initiated a 'back-to-the-land' programme in an attempt to address youth unemployment. This involved setting aside large tracts of land in many locations across the State, and the provision of loans for land clearance and procurement of improved seeds, fertilisers and agrochemicals. Of the targeted youth, only 13-15 per cent took advantage. Instead, a few farmers and many non-farmers took the package of incentives and re-sold them outside the State.[3]

The coming of Zimbabwean farmers
Following farm occupations in Zimbabwe in the early 2000s, dispossessed white Zimbabwean farmers became an alternative group whom Governor Saraki targeted to save his faltering policy of socio-economic development through commercial agriculture. In 2004, with political support from the Federal Government of Nigeria and diplomatic support from the British Government, he invited a five-man delegation drawn from the Commercial Farmers Union of Zimbabwe and their counterparts from Agri-SA in South Africa for a one-week fact-finding visit to Kwara State. The visit, which was paid for by the Kwara State Government, led to the signing of a Memorandum of Understanding (MoU) between the state and the (mostly) Zimbabwean farmers.

---

[2] Later enquiries updated the story to 2013. For comparison, surveys were conducted on three privately owned indigenous commercial farms (of 19 large tracts of land allocated by the Kwara State Government) in 2012 in Asa and Moro Local Government Areas (to be reported in Ariyo and Mortimore 2014).

[3] Communication by the Kwara State Commission for Agriculture, October 2010.

The MoU committed the State Government to provide suitable land close to the Niger River for year-round irrigation, infrastructure (including access roads and electricity), access to credit as the farmers were not able to bring any capital of their own, and federal pioneer status, which brings exemptions from import duties on agricultural equipment and from taxes on turnover. The obligations of the commercial farmers were to incorporate each farm enterprise with US$80,000 of share capital, contribute 1 per cent of their gross turnover to a community trust fund, and provide instruction at least once a month in the state farm training institute. Under these terms, thirteen farmers arrived in Shonga District and commenced farming operations in 2005.

State support for New Nigerian Farms
The State Government invoked the provisions of the Land Use Act to appropriate 13,000ha, and allocated 1,000ha to each of the thirteen commercial farmers on a 25-year lease, which is renewable and at no cost to the farmers. In addition to providing electricity and access roads, the State Government built an additional block of classrooms in a local secondary school, resurfaced roads in Shonga township and improved the road leading to the state capital of Ilorin in an attempt to placate the local community.

Although the initial requirement in the MoU was for each farm to operate as an independent company, the commercial farmers did not come with any money of their own to invest in the farms. They relied solely on the Kwara State Government to fulfil its financial obligations in the agreement to enable their farming to take off. The State Government provided interest-free loans in 2005 for this purpose. In addition, and to facilitate access to bank credit, the farmers formed a partnership with the State Government in the form of a consortium named Kwa-Zimbo Enterprises. The consortium took a US$5 million loan from the Federal Government-owned Agricultural, Cooperative and Rural Development Bank.

To ensure access to credit, the thirteen farms were first reorganised into three syndicates – dairy, poultry and crops – and then, through the influence of the Governor, a consortium of five commercial banks was drawn in to invest a further US$6.6 million as equity in Kwa-Zimbo Enterprises. Kwa-Zimbo Enterprises was renamed as Shonga Farms in 2008, and then as New Nigerian Farms in 2010. As of 2014, it consists of sixteen enterprises: thirteen farms, one milk processing plant (Shonga Dairies), one feed mill and chicken abattoir (Valentine Chicken) and one planned cassava processing plant (Shonga Fufu). The equity distribution is: the five banks (45 per cent), the thirteen commercial farmers (40 per cent) and the State Government (15 per cent), with the latter acquiring its equity share through its spending on farm infrastructure. An entity termed 'Shonga Farm Holdings', consisting of representatives of the banks, the farmers and the State Government, has been established to manage the finances of the commercial farms and to perform the function

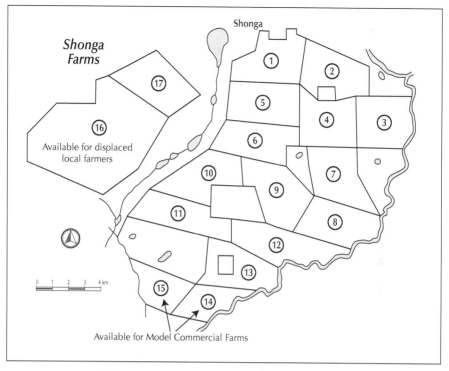

Map 2.2 Detailed map of Shonga Farms, showing commercial farms and farms for displaced local farmers

of a clearing house between the lending banks and the farms. Individual enterprises were required to source credit through Shonga Farm Holdings and the five participating banks.

The political support of the State Government was as crucial as its financial support in enabling commercial farming to develop in Kwara. The Governor mobilised state resources – money, personnel and machinery – and put them at the disposal of the farmers during the take-off period. The farmers also had direct access to him – a rare privilege – and he accorded their problems priority attention. Political support was also given for the use of state resources to manage local opposition to the allocation of the land to the Zimbabweans and to beef up security in the area. The Governor exploited his position as chair of the national Governors' Forum to secure preferential treatment on matters concerning the commercial farmers that fall within the purview of the Federal authorities, especially in the period up to 2007, when Chief Olusegun Obasanjo, himself a large-scale commercial farmer, was President of Nigeria.

Performance of the Shonga experiment

Prior to the arrival of the farmers, in the area earmarked for their commercial farms, 33 farming settlements were practising rotational ('bush') fallowing. Cultivated farms and economic trees were scattered amongst fallow lands. In addition to the thirteen commercial farms (Map 2.2), two 'community model commercial farm sites' (around 600ha each) were to be allocated in units of 5ha to youths from the locality, nominated by the Emir of Shonga, while 3,540ha were set aside as compensatory land for farmers whose fields were appropriated. About 120 people who desired more land have sought and been provided with some (Farm 16 on Map 2.2). No settlements had to be relocated.

The farmers have invested heavily from their loans in land clearing, residential buildings and farm infrastructure, including on-farm roads, storage facilities, workshops, equipment, boreholes to supply water for household and farm uses, electricity generators and, in the case of the poultry and dairy farmers, chicken and livestock pens. Each has developed 50 per cent or more of the 1,000ha allocated. One farmer estimated the fixed investment on his farm to be US$1.6 million, an achievement made possible through the loan guaranteed by the Kwara State Government. Clearing of the land was carried out jointly with the State Government, which undertook the felling of large trees using heavy machinery from the Ministry of Works, while the farmers employed local people to dig up the roots and level the land for farm machinery.[4]

Poultry farming is the most successful enterprise at Shonga, and is viable in Nigeria, given adequate capital for own production of feeds. Four farmers specialise in chicken production, with an integrated feed mill and abattoir under a company named Valentine Chicken. All were tobacco growers in Zimbabwe, and started out in Shonga growing only crops, such as maize, rice, cassava and soybeans. The decision to diversify into poultry farming and processing was a means of overcoming the logistical and marketing constraints confronting them. The chickens are raised under very modern conditions (with air conditioning) such that they are table-ready much earlier than the six weeks broiler chickens usually take, although an erratic power supply affects the maintenance of correct climatic conditions in the pens and the abattoir. The farmers compound the chicken feed themselves from crops they grow, ensuring its superiority over feed available in the market. By late 2012, 100,000 chickens were being slaughtered per month. They are dressed for delivery to eateries in Lagos and Abuja.

All the four dairy farmers use Jersey cattle, imported from South Africa in 2008. Maize silage, cowpeas, soybeans, sorghum and cassava

---

[4] This is at variance with media reports that the State Government directly cleared the land leased to the farmers, built residential houses for them and sank boreholes for their farms and homes.

are grown in Shonga for feed. All four farmers have increased their herds. The average daily milk output per cow is in the order of 15-20 litres, depending on the resources available to produce (or buy) feed. In order to add value to the milk produced, the four dairy farmers established a milk processing plant named Shonga Dairies to homogenise milk from the dairy farms, and also milk from the cattle herds of the local pastoralist Fulani. About 10 per cent of the milk supplied to Shonga Dairies is converted into yoghurt and pasteurised milk. Kwara State Government used to buy some of the pasteurised milk for its school feeding programme, but this has since stopped. The main market for the yoghurt is Ilorin, as well as other large towns in Oyo and Osun States. The remaining fresh milk (about 90 per cent) is supplied to West African Milk Company (WAMCO) in Lagos, a subsidiary of Friesland Campina of Holland. The dairy farmers would like to embark on expanding their herds and dairy operations in order to achieve the scale they deem necessary for economic viability. The inadequate and irregular flow of funds remains a constraint. Frustrations over a shortage of funds and failures by the state to deliver the promised irrigation infrastructure caused two dairy farmers to leave Shonga, with other farmers taking over their livestock.

Field crop production so far has been influenced by internal market opportunities or failures, experience with the new growing conditions, and shortages of finance. The crops so far tried include soybeans, cassava, maize, sorghum, and rice. Soybeans have done well, but maize was dropped by several farmers because of either drought or the sandy soil conditions. Cassava – originally seen as a strong market performer because of its use by the brewing industry – has suffered from a shortage of working capital and a depressed market. Rice cultivation was seriously held back by unfinanced plans for irrigation equipment. Fluctuations in funding that the farmers received from year to year resulted in fluctuations in the area they cultivated.

Three cases illustrate these experiences:

Farmer 2 achieved about 350 tonnes of rice and sorghum in 2010 and 180 tonnes in 2011. Maize was not very successful on account of inadequate rainfall in 2011, and the yield was only 120 of the expected 300 tonnes. Having experimented with many crops in Shonga, Farmer 2 would like to concentrate on rice, which he considers to be suited to the area and commands a good price. By 2011 he had almost completed and test-run a pivot sprinkler irrigation system supported by a pump from the banks of the River Niger, but this has remained idle due to a lack of working capital.

Farmer 6 had 45 years farming experience, growing tobacco in Zimbabwe. He started out as a member of the dairy syndicate, but switched to cassava and soybeans and then replaced cassava with maize in 2011. He experienced an increased output of soybeans from 300 tonnes in 2010 to nearly 500 tonnes in 2011. Maize output was not so impressive in 2011 due to an unexpected short spell of drought. Commercial boreholes were too few for supplementary irrigation. No new infrastructure or machinery was purchased in the 2011 farming season.

Farmer 9 had 47 years of farming experience in Zimbabwe with seed crops, soybeans, barley, peas and vegetables. In 2005, he tried maize and cassava, but the maize was a disaster in the first year, due, according to him, to the sandy nature of the soil. Since then he has stuck to growing cassava only. In his view, he needed to cultivate a minimum of 300ha annually to make a decent profit, and could actually plant on a lot more land if more funds were available. By 2011, this farmer had nearly 400ha of cassava in the ground ready for harvest, though some planted as far back as 2009 was rotten or had turned into useless woody tubers. In 2011, he signed up as an outgrower of new cassava varieties developed by the International Institute for Tropical Agriculture in Ibadan and planned to plant 80ha of the new varieties, but had capital enough for only 25ha and a weak cassava market undermined his capacity to repay his loan. Since then, he has tried without success to obtain approval from the National Agency for Food and Drug Administration and Control (NAFDAC) for cassava processing.

The future of the crops-only farms hangs in the balance. By 2012, farms were not making profits yet. The land had been cleared but there was insufficient capital for operation at the planned scale. Bankruptcy was a possibility for some. In early 2012, four of the Zimbabwean farmers left Shonga, with another following in 2013. They did not consider the financial environment to have improved sufficiently to make large-scale farming profitable. On the positive side, the Federal Government's efforts to develop a cassava value chain began to pay off towards the end of the 2012 farming season, in the form of increased demand for the crop both within and outside Nigeria.

Financial and other constraints to commercial farming
The most debilitating constraint faced by the commercial farmers at Shonga is inadequate operational funds. Access to bank credit is difficult and slow and, when granted, the credit is always far below what is required each farming year. The farmers complained that Nigerian banks do not understand agricultural loans and that no agricultural economists were sent to appraise their operational plans. Dairy farmers received more funding than the 'crops-only' farmers in the 2010 and 2011 farming years. Nevertheless, in 2011, poultry farmers received more funding than the other two groups, and were able to increase broiler chicken production while some dairy farmers could barely keep their cows above starvation level.

The underlying cause of these funding constraints is a major crisis in the Nigerian banking sector. In 2011, the Central Bank of Nigeria classified four of the five participating banks in the Shonga Farm Holdings as 'distressed' and ordered them to divest from their non-banking subsidiaries. The farmers hoped that Stanbic Bank, which was to become a participating bank in Shonga Farm Holdings, would improve the flow of credit, but this did not make any significant difference in the flow of capital to them in 2012.

Finance has also frustrated plans for irrigation. The main reason for the choice of Shonga for the 'experiment' was its proximity to the River Niger, the irrigation potential this offers and the promise by the State Government that irrigation infrastructure would be built. However, this is still at a very early stage. Farmer 2, mentioned above, could not wait any longer for the completion of the irrigation project promised by the State and built his own, on which he intended to grow rice several times a year, but he left Shonga in 2012 having failed to raise the working capital needed.

Irregular public power supplies and the poor state of the Nigerian roads are also problems facing the farmers. Until power became available from the national grid in 2011, farmers relied on diesel-powered generators and, even now, power cuts ensure that the generators are still used several times a day and at considerable cost, especially in the poultry pens and processing plant, which require 24-hour service provision. Poorly-maintained road infrastructure and long distances to markets also add to logistical costs.

In the long term, the remaining farmers would like to be able to produce for domestic and export markets. A lot, they opined, depended on how the constraints facing them are managed, especially the constraints posed by the lack of access to adequate funds. However, in contrast to their earlier bright hopes, discouragement had set in amongst the farmers, especially those growing only crops. They expressed the fear that the whole 'Shonga experiment' might fail if the bank loan problems were not sorted out quickly. At the point of our research in 2013, the finance problems had not been resolved and seven of the initial thirteen farmers had left Shonga.

Immediate effects of the Shonga experiment

The appropriation of such a large expanse of land by the state (13,000ha for the thirteen farms and 4,656ha for compensation) was greeted with protests, sometimes violent, by local people who claimed it as their own. For these local farmers, it has restricted the land available to them for rotational bush fallowing, a main feature of their farming system that lessens dependence on chemical fertilisers. The appropriation of land has also reduced the rangeland available to settled pastoralists and visiting nomads. A total of fifteen communities, totalling 1,990 people, have been identified as being affected and paid compensation.

Contradictions abound between official and local views on land and property, not only in Kwara State, but throughout Nigeria. Whereas the official view is that land held by the state under the Land Use Act (1978) is abundant and largely idle, especially in the Middle Belt where Kwara State is located, the local view is that communities (and not individuals) have owned the land from time immemorial, and moreover that it is not abundant. Local land uses consist of arable farming under the bush fallow system, open range for livestock rearing and collection of natural resources from woodland. These conflicting views are at the root of local agitations against the alienation of large tracts of land by the state for the purpose of establishing the New Nigeria Farms at Shonga.

The State Government managed local resistance to land appropriation with several strategies. A new police post was sited within the commercial farm area at the height of the agitation, although this was abandoned by December 2010, an indication of a growing rapprochement. The state created 'buffer zones' around each village that were excluded from the Shonga experiment, with the result that allocation to the commercial farmers did not entail the immediate uprooting of local people. Agreement was reached with the commercial farmers to allow local people to plant crops in the commercial farm areas that were allocated to them but were not yet being used for commercial farming, and to access wild fruits, grasses and firewood in these areas. Compensation equivalent to US$58,000 was paid in cash to 1,990 out of the 2,771 local people who claimed to be affected by the appropriation either of farmland or of fallow land. The remaining 781 people had their claims annulled as false, according to the State Ministry of Agriculture and Natural Resources. A monetised agricultural incentive package was also presented to the affected people, which consisted of US$73 per hectare for land preparation, up to a maximum of one-third of the land area lost. If a person gave up 30ha, for example, s/he would be paid $37 per hectare up to a maximum of 10ha (i.e. one third of the 30ha they had lost), amounting to $370. Each farmer was also given a bicycle and US$20 for procurement of new inputs, such as fertiliser and improved seeds. Many people who had lost no land also received these benefits.

The emergence of commercial agriculture at Shonga has substantially increased the demand for labour, generating a significant income multi-plying effect on the local economy. Employment on the farms is close to 3,000 at peak periods. Except for the farm managers, who came from Zimbabwe, most of the workers are from the local communities and amongst them are a few return-migrants, lured back from the cities by the prospect of a steady job. There are also some artisans and technicians who provide services and live in Shonga or as far away as Ilorin.

We interviewed a sample of eight part-time female employees, including field workers and abattoir workers, about their perceptions of the benefits and challenges of the Shonga experiment. The main benefit was their additional cash income and the greater respect their incomes earned them in their families, although they wished that employment was not seasonal. With this independent income, they can meet small financial needs independently from their husbands. Against these benefits, they regretted being unable to attend the market when farm duties take precedence, and the absence of any leave, as the farms operate a 'no work no pay' policy. They also noted the improved electricity supply that followed the commercial farmers to Shonga, which enabled these women to use grinding or other drudgery-reducing machinery in their homes, and improve communications through mobile phones.

A sample of male farm employees recognised the commercial farms as a source of substantial additional income that supported their other livelihood activities. Part-time workers as well would have liked to work full-time. Some have been able to diversify their livelihood activities through additional income earned from the farms, such as by entering the commercial motorcycle business. They also recognised the direct and indirect benefits of the infrastructure that came with the commercial farms: electricity, borehole water, upgraded inter-urban and township roads, and mobile phones. Against these benefits, they had less time to work on their own farms, and thus had to hire labour, which was unsupervised and created some problems. In addition, they often missed or were late to attend the weekly market, festivals and Friday prayers at the central mosque.

The main visible effects the commercial farmers have had on local farming practices are the wide adoption of soybeans by the local Nupe farmers, better crop management – especially keeping to the right seed population – and timely weeding. Local farmers also reported increased production of maize and sorghum, which are in high demand by commercial dairy and poultry farmers. Some have been assisted by the commercial farmers to harvest their soybeans.

The Nupe farmers said that they would like the same agricultural assistance given to them 'as to the white farmers'. Suggestions for longer-term agricultural development assistance from the state included: an effective tractor hiring service that would enable them to operate larger farms, cheap and timely credit to buy inputs, good quality seeds 'like soybean seeds we get from the white farmers' and 'good prices for our crops'.

A 'community model commercial farm' scheme that was intended to facilitate the transition from small-scale farming with manual labour to large-scale mechanised operations has not taken off. None of the 1,200ha set aside for this purpose has been allocated to anyone. Off-the-record comments among state officials imply that there are no interest groups at the state or local level pushing for the implementation of the programme. This failure undermines the stated goal of the Shonga experiment in agricultural modernisation.

Effects of the Shonga experiment on pastoralists have been mixed, with new opportunities opening for market access while access to grazing is lost. One of the commercial farmers has been working with a pastoralist who has a large herd to develop better milk-producing cows through selection over several generations. Promising results have been achieved and the pastoralist hopes to establish his own dairy outfit. Other local pastoralists have shown interest in cattle breed improvement. The number of 'experimental cattle' increased from fourteen in 2010 to 22 in 2011. These animals were kept in a field close to a commercial dairy farm.

Some pastoralists have been visiting two commercial farms regularly, and are being exposed to the preparation of different combinations of cattle feeds, as well as artificial insemination. They have also been exchanging ideas with the white farmers on the recognition and treatment of different livestock diseases. Another positive impact on local pastoralism is through the provision of a steady market for milk. Shonga Dairies purchases approximately 150 litres of milk daily from the local Fulani herders at 100 Naira/litre, which translates into a daily income of US$100 between the ten to twelve local pastoralist women identified at the time of the survey.

However, rights to grazing on uncultivated commercial farmland are contested, and pastoralists contest the accusation by white farmers that local cattle have transmitted foot-and-mouth disease to the dairy cows. They claim that nomadic herds from elsewhere were responsible. Some pastoralists have argued that converting their production into a modern dairy operation with crop production, though a good idea, will run into problems: who among their numerous children should be selected to venture into modern dairying? What will be the future relationship of the beneficiary with the rest of his siblings? How will they source capital to buy the types of machinery that the white farmers have? Raising capital by selling off some of their numerous cattle is out of the question, they said. Would the government give them land as it has given it to the white farmers?

Eight local farmers, who had lost some of their lands to the commercial farms, were interviewed. The average holding was 4.5ha, distributed in three plots, and with no more than 2ha cultivated in any year. With an average family size of ten, smallholders grew rice, maize, sorghum, yams, cassava, melon and groundnuts. Four have adopted soybeans. All of them have secondary incomes. All said that the compensation received for the land was insufficient. Reasons given included: 'money is never enough', 'farm inputs are too costly' and 'I prefer my land to monetary compensation'. However, additional land was offered to them (Farm 16 in Map 2.2). The local farmers are divided between positive views of this land (it is a fertile 'virgin' land, cleared for them by the state, and with space to practise rotational bush fallowing) and negative ('too far from our residences' and 'vulnerable to thieves').

All of the respondents reported that they had been denied access to natural resources such as wood, wild fruits, grasses and rangeland on lands allocated to commercial farms but not yet cleared, even when the agreement reached with government was that they would be given access to un-cleared land. However, the respondents considered the commercial farms as having had a generally positive impact on the area (employment, infrastructure, mobile phones, water from boreholes, and the upgrading of Shonga Township Road). They considered the long-term prospects for development to be good, on condition that the State Government continues to invest in infrastructural development. Community leaders in Shonga Town and two nearby villages also cited employment, infrastructure and expanded markets as benefits, while complaining of inadequate compensation and lack of direct consultation with leaders such as village heads, religious leaders, youth leaders, and leaders of the pastoralist group, before lands were appropriated for commercial farming.

The most uniformly positive response to the commercialisation under way came from actors in the wider economy who had not lost land, but had gained from increased economic activity. Male service providers in the vicinity (a mechanic, motorcycle 'taxi', welder, mason, plumber and carpenter) pointed to more regular and higher incomes than before the Shonga development, and improved personal and family welfare. Natives of villages outside Shonga, however, could not identify any benefits for themselves, and those travelling from Ilorin or even Lagos to provide services complained of the costs of travel or of relocation. Female service providers (shopkeepers, market traders and vendors) also pointed positively to new employment (including of their own children) and higher volumes of sales, access to electricity (grinding, sewing, refrigeration of water and soft drinks for sale) and mobile phones, and the success of a new product – yoghurt made on Farm 3 – that is of high quality and sells well. Their assessment was entirely positive.

Conclusion

The Kwara Government's initiative to promote commercial agriculture on the springboard of thirteen white farmers mostly from Zimbabwe has drawn considerable attention in the media, and Shonga Farms are reputed to have played host to over 50,000 visitors between 2005 and 2010. The results that Shonga Farms have achieved in the short time of their existence, the constraints confronting them notwithstanding, testify to the role of the state in creating the enabling environment that is required for commercial agriculture to thrive (Mustapha 2010).

There is the possibility of the emergence of a dualistic agrarian structure in Kwara State represented, on the one hand, by Shonga Farms with heavy state support and other large-scale commercial farms in other parts of Kwara with less state support, and smallholder peasants and pastoralists, on the other. Dualism could become a reality and a permanent feature of rural Kwara if the tempo of implementation of the state agricultural commercialisation policy is significantly stepped up. At the moment the commercial farms are too few, poorly funded and without enabling infrastructural support to bring about a lasting and deep change in the agrarian structure of the state. Despite the several failings and shortcomings of the Shonga experiment, the Federal Government remains committed to the development of a commercial agriculture, based on a dualistic agrarian structure.

In terms of local impacts, the Shonga Farms have spread a few new farming practices to local farmers and popularised soybean production; spread livestock improvement methods to local pastoralists; created employment for local people, and expanded the market for local products. These achievements notwithstanding, lack of affordable credit in sufficient amounts for operation and expansion, and the failure to develop the irrigation infrastructure promised by the state have severely curtailed production on the Shonga farms, which forced some of the commercial farmers to leave. Evidence in Shonga and other areas of Kwara State where large-scale commercial agriculture has been introduced (Ariyo and Mortimore 2014), points to the existence a highly-privileged class of commercial farmers subsidised by the state and a class of peasants and pastoralists with only a modicum of state support. The social differentiation in rural Kwara could also be viewed as comprising an emerging class of capitalist resource owners and a class of formerly-independent producers-turned-wage-labourers on the commercial farms. These are signs of the type of social transformation that could happen in rural Kwara if agricultural commercialisation is intensified across the state.

The Shonga experiment raises a fundamental policy issue about the role of the state in funding commercial agriculture. The pattern of investment that characterised Shonga Farms relied heavily on state funds. The farmers neither brought any foreign investment capital into the country directly nor fulfilled the MoU obligation that required them to incorporate each farm enterprise with US$80,000 share capital. The pattern of investment that brought Shonga Farms into being suddenly became unsustainable and not replicable in the face of competing demands on the state's meagre resources.

The Kwara State experiment in commercial agriculture raises several important questions for policy.[5] How, for example, do the majority smallholder peasants feature in this policy shift towards large-scale commercial agriculture? Kwara State is pursuing three models of agricultural development, all calling for financial resources it cannot adequately muster. These are the high-profile, large-scale and capital-intensive commercial farm model in Shonga; a model aimed to produce successive generations of commercial farmers, through training and empowerment, to replace the ageing farming population in the rural areas (Ariyo and Mortimore 2013), and the long-standing model of providing a modicum of incentives to smallholder farmers and leaving them to their own devices to move agriculture forward.[6] The presumption in these approaches to agricultural development in the state is that strong symbiotic relationships

---

[5] See Forrest 1993; Mustapha and Meagher 2000.

[6] The World Bank now favours investing in small-scale agriculture (World Bank 2008).

would develop between the technologically-advanced Shonga Farms, the local peasantry, young farmers and the financial system to revolutionise the agricultural sector. This has not happened and the initial achievements of Shonga Farms are highly vulnerable.

Another major policy issue in relation to the emergence and possible expansion of large-scale commercial farms in Kwara State is the long-term impact it might have on land sufficiency for local farmers who need it in abundance to accommodate their rotational bush fallow farming system. When land becomes constrained and 'buffer' areas are encroached upon, the relationship between the locals and the white farmers may turn sour. Often neglected in considerations of land availability in Kwara State and the Middle Belt of Nigeria in general is a recent increase in the sedentarisation of previously-mobile pastoralists (Abbass 2013; Adisa 2009). This will definitely change the calculus of land sufficiency to support the diverse livelihoods of different stakeholders in Kwara State.

The case study points to an agrarian political struggle unfolding in the area. The first dimension is represented in the confrontations, sometimes violent, that ensue between communities and the state when the latter uses its power of eminent domain to appropriate, 'for public good', lands that the people consider to be their own and on which their livelihoods depend. The second is latent competition between mobile pastoralists and sedentary farmers. The resistance to the Shonga experiment on the part of local farmers coincided with sporadic confrontations between the commercial farmers and pastoralists, who discovered that lands on that they had grazed their livestock for generations suddenly became out-of-bounds. These struggles over land and resources are not mediated by any inclusive decision-making process, and land deals continue to be arbitrary, non-transparent and not subject to proper democratic scrutiny.

The Shonga experiment in commercial agricultural development – along with the other similar, less-subsidised and lower-profile initiatives – is unsustainable and therefore not reproducible. More importantly, these projects are inequitable, when juxtaposed against the meagre agricultural budgetary allocations accorded to the smallholder farmers and pastoralists who produce the bulk of the food and meat consumed in the state. The critical question to be addressed is: what form of agricultural land policy would be fair and equitable against the backdrop of the possible long-term impacts we have observed where large-scale commercial agriculture enters an area dominated by bush fallow agriculture, and with a growing population of mobile pastoralists?

3

Recent Transnational Land Deals & the Local Agrarian Economy in Ghana

JOSEPH AWETORI YARO
& DZODZI TSIKATA

Introduction

Contemporary large-scale transnational land transactions in Ghana are occurring within a context of agrarian stagnation, the failure of agrarian transformation and on-going livelihood crises in Ghana's countryside. Land tenure systems are also in a state of flux, the subject of aggressive reforms to strengthen the liberalisation of land markets. This has become a platform for the take-over of agricultural lands by the rural elite with the support of the state and urban elite. Indeed, there is an on-going long-term process of land concentration and dispossession of small-scale farmers. More recent transnational land deals, which accelerated in the 1980s as a result of increased foreign investment in mining and logging, deepen this process (Agbosu et al. 2007). While these developments are occurring across Ghana, their specific manifestations are determined by the nature of the customary land tenure systems of particular areas.

Ghana as a site of transnational land acquisitions is interesting not for the size of acquisitions, but for their significant cumulative effects on the agrarian political economy. Unlike other African cases, agricultural lands are mainly held and transacted under customary land tenure systems in Ghana, which has a long history of smallholder-based agriculture, even for export farming. This chapter examines three recent commercial land deals for agribusiness projects in rural Ghana: the Prairie Volta Rice Company Ltd based in the Volta Region, Solar Harvest Ltd (formerly Biofuel Africa Ltd) and the Integrated Tamale Fruit Company (ITFC), the latter both based in the Northern Region (see Map 3.1). All three transactions are mature enough for their livelihood outcomes to be examined.

The data presented are from a mix of research methods, including in-depth individual interviews with 24 local male and female farmers in the three communities most affected by the land deals; focus group discussions with all-male and all-female groups in the three communities; key informant interviews with traditional authorities and their officers

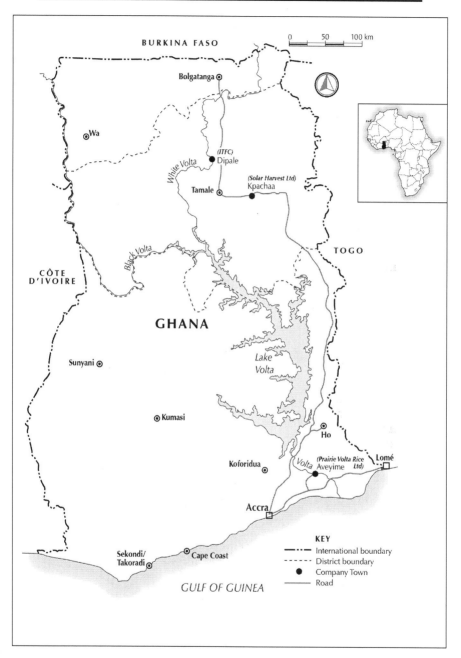

Map 3.1 Ghana, showing the location of Integrated Tamale Fruit Company (ITFC), Solar Harvest and Prairie Volta Rice company

and company officials; and a survey of 300 individuals in the three project sites.

The chapter examines the three case studies in terms of three broad areas of change in the agrarian structure: land tenure and commercialisation; livelihoods and food security; and agrarian struggles. It offers some conclusions and recommendations for reforming the governance of commercial land transactions in Ghana.

The context of land deals

In spite of decades of economic growth, agriculture still supports more than half the population in Ghana. However, agricultural stagnation over several decades - exacerbated by a global economic crisis and local factors such as population growth, environmental stress and governance problems – has resulted in crises in rural livelihoods (Adjei 1999; Al-Hassan 2007; Boni 2005). The collapse of the economy in the late 1970s and early 1980s resulted in the adoption of structural adjustment programmes, which effectively introduced neoliberal policies with an export-biased model of development (World Bank 1984). Rural areas in Ghana with favourable conditions for the cultivation of export crops received considerable investments in infrastructure, technology and technical services, while food crop areas were neglected (Puplampu 1999; Rimmer 1992; Rothchild 1991). However, from the 1990s, local demand arising from rising urban incomes led to a new impetus for food crops, especially the major staples such as maize, cassava, yam, millet and plantains. Criticisms of the export bias of economic policy resulted in fresh initiatives to develop new improved crop varieties, targeted fertiliser subsidies, mechanisation services and improvements in feeder roads nationwide. This resulted in substantial increases in the production of food crops and new commercial crops such as cashew nuts and mangoes. However, these developments did not change the market-friendly, export-oriented strategy, which stressed the importance of non-traditional exports as a new solution to rural poverty (Tsikata and Yaro 2013; UNDP 2007; Tsikata and Yaro 2011).

Agriculture has been affected by land market liberalisation promoted by the World Bank since the 1980s, which has accelerated land concentration and tenure insecurities. This has gone hand-in-hand with state efforts to encourage Foreign Direct Investment (FDI) in agriculture and other sectors as a strategy of modernisation and growth. The establishment of the Ghana Investment Promotion Centre, special commercial and land courts and the granting of concessions to FDI can all be seen as part of the strategy to promote large-scale commercial agriculture. In 2000, land market liberalisation culminated in a National Land Policy and the Land Administration Project, a fifteen-year land tenure reform project. Its main features are a reformed Lands Commission, including a one-stop-shop for land registration, the consolidation of land laws, a titling and registration programme and the establishment of customary land secretariats (Aryeetey et al. 2007). Neither the land policy nor the agricultural policies prioritised the interests of smallholder farmers, although over the years, there have been some smallholder-friendly measures such as fuel and input subsidies.

The dominant land tenure system in Ghana is the customary system controlled mainly by chiefs, *tendamba* (land priests), lineage heads, and family heads, legitimated by the 1992 Constitution and overseen with legislation and judicial processes by the state land institutions. The customary land tenure regime has undergone rapid changes since the colonial period under pressure from domestic and external factors. These include the transformation of communal lands to private property with state support as shown by the granting of land titles backed by the 1986 Land Title Act. In peri-urban areas, former agricultural lands have been converted to industrial and residential development (Yaro 2012), while in rural areas, the state machinery has allocated mining concessions to companies under the mining code, with the state determining appropriate compensation to farmers for the loss of crops and royalties to chiefs. This, together with the increasing commercialisation of agriculture, is deepening a process of land concentration, while newer cash tenancies are replacing sharecropping systems. These changes have altered the rules of engagement in customary tenure relations and call into question the image of customary land tenure systems as 'relatively open, negotiable and adaptive' (Peters 2004: 270). Instead, the landscape of land transactions reveals processes of exclusion, deepening social divisions and class formation (Peters 2004).

Rural Ghana is currently experiencing a new form of agrarian crisis that is qualitatively different from past agrarian crises caused by the collapse of production systems. This current crisis is characterised by processes of growing inequalities and the strangulation of small producers by their location in global commodity chains. There is a continuous decline of agricultural productivity, rising food insecurity, increasing poverty and intensified emigration from deprived regions, especially northern Ghana (Channar 1999; ODI and CEPA 2005; Songsore and Denkabe 1995). The expansion of the export economy in the forested south of Ghana has led to in-migration and local investment in modern commercial farming.

There have been increasing contradictions among state, capital and smallholder farmers, a situation worsened by climate change, land degradation, population growth and market-based pressures of production (Puplampu 1999). Social groups in Ghana whose conditions of living worsened following the neo-liberal reforms included rural women in food crop areas and marginal environments, displaced people from mining concessions and people in areas with poor basic services (Konadu-Agyemang 2000; Obeng-Odoom 2012).

Three periods of large-scale land deals are important in Ghana. The first involved the colonial acquisitions in mining, palm and infrastructure development. The second was the 1970s and '80s acquisitions in mining and commercial agriculture, specifically rice in northern Ghana, and palm and the so-called non-traditional exports such as fruits, vegetables, nuts and spices, in the south. The third, and most recent period, includes acquisitions for biofuels, food and horticulture, as well as for mining and oil and gas, happening since 2000.

In this third wave of acquisitions which involves biofuels such as *Jatropha curcas,* a tree crop which is said to thrive on marginal lands, the rural commons that survived the first two cycles of large-scale land deals have become an important source of land. The major transnational companies with active operations in Ghana include Scanfuel, Kimminic Estates Ltd, Natural Africa Diesels, Central Supercare Company, B1 Ghana Ltd, GoldStar Bio-Diesel Company, Biofuel Africa Ltd, and Northern Sugar Resources Ltd. These companies use plantation-based and outgrower-production-based systems. There have also been land acquisitions for mango, bananas and other fruits in the Volta, Eastern and Northern Regions; rice in the Volta Region; pineapples in the Eastern Region and bananas in the Greater Accra and Eastern Regions. There are inconsistencies in the reported sizes of these acquisitions. However, one estimate has put the recent acquisitions at 907,000ha (GRAIN, 2011). The three cases that are described below were selected from these third cycle acquisitions for biofuel, rice and horticulture.

The three cases

Integrated Tamale Fruit Company (ITFC)
The export company Integrated Tamale Fruit Company (ITFC) was established in 1999 as a joint effort between the Dutch company Komma BV (30 per cent) and Ghanaian partners. In the Savelugu-Nanton District, the company has its 83ha headquarters at Gushie, but its 552ha nucleus farm is at Dipale. The company operates a nucleus-outgrower model thereby combining the advantages of plantation agriculture with involving local people in a global agribusiness enterprise. It focuses on the cultivation of mangoes, but its processing plant at Gushie processes other fruits (mainly drying) for export. The company has obtained various fair trade and organic certifications, and its established market is the Netherlands-based Agrofair Company. The ITFC nucleus farm has 202ha under mango cultivation and the remaining area of 350ha is used for biodiversity conservation. There were 1,200 outgrowers in 2010. The people in these communities come mainly from local Dagomba communities, with a few migrants, mainly Ewe fisher-folk from the Volta Region operating on a tributary of the Volta River. Rain-fed agriculture and other natural resource-based activities constitute the base of the rural economy.

Prairie Volta Rice Ltd
This is a rice project owned by a limited liability company, a joint venture between the Government of Ghana (GoG) and an American company called Prairie Texas. It is located in the Central Tongu District of Ghana, and the project farms on land belonging to the community of Mafi-Dove and the offices and processing mill are at Aveyime, one of the larger communities in the district. The company has four tracts of land: one of 5ha for its offices and mill; 15ha for a helicopter landing strip, and two fields for irrigated rice of 1250ha and 2000ha. The business model is a large-scale mono-crop plantation using mechanised production techniques and hired labour. The rice is then processed and sold exclusively within Ghana. The Central Tongu District is in the Lower Volta, inhabited by the Tongu Ewe, who have a long tradition of river fishing and flood-plain agriculture. The damming of the Volta at Akosombo in 1965 disrupted their livelihood systems and led to the mass migration to other parts of the country, particularly along the Volta Lake and tributaries of the Volta River, while some diversified into urban activities and farming in ecologically favourable forest regions of Ghana. The majority of the people remaining in the study area now earn a living mainly from farming and the harvesting of resources from the commons.

Solar Harvest/Biofuel Africa
Solar Harvest Ltd, formerly known as Biofuel Africa Ltd, was established in 2007, and had its operations in the Yendi District in the Northern Region. The initial investor went bankrupt in 2009 following the global financial crisis and the subsequent loss of investor confidence in the economic viability of biodiesel. The company was reorganised in October 2010 and renamed Solar Harvest. It abandoned *Jatropha* and took up food crop production, notably maize. The original company leased 10,600ha of land for 50 years, of which 400ha were planted with *Jatropha* and 220ha were used for maize in 2011. The company operated a mono-crop plantation business model, which involved clearing large tracts of land of vegetation to enable the use of modern technologies. Its projects are now defunct as a result of crop failures over two seasons of maize cultivation, although the land remains in its name. The Ghana Irrigation Authority and the Millennium Development Authority awarded the company the management contract for the Botanga Irrigation Project in the Tolon-Kumbungu District in 2012. The surrounding communities are predominantly rural with farming as their main livelihood activity. The village of Kpachaa is a migrant Dagomba settlement. Before the company's land acquisition, rich non-resident farmers from Tamale were already cultivating large tracts of land, mainly with maize. Thus there was already a process of land concentration and commercial agricultural production taking place in this area, a feature which sets this case apart from the other two cases discussed in this chapter.

Changes in agrarian structure

Land tenure and commercialisation

The land tenure systems in the project communities are 'skin' systems for Dipale and Kpachaa, and family systems for Dove/Tademe. Under the 'skin' systems, the chiefs hold the land in trust for the people, while under the family system, the lineages have direct control over the use of their land. The growth of the land market has led to rental agreements and conversion of sharecropping systems to monetary payments, especially in the forest zone of Ghana. Scarcity is the main driver of change as old ways of accessing land and other natural resources are altered in ways reflecting both opportunities and constraints. Table 3.1 shows the increasing inadequacy of land and the strategies adopted by households in response to land acquisitions: 79.3 per cent of respondents who reported inadequate land sizes had made some adjustments. These included the intensification of production on existing land, especially in Kpachaa where scarcity has been created due to long distances to areas of available lands. Where alternative lands are abundant, people simply acquired new lands, as in Dipale which has land in the northern sections. In Tademe, where most of the land has been taken by the Prairie acquisition, the community has had to negotiate with the next village for land. The Prairie Rice communities have the largest number of respondents with inadequate land holdings (Table 3.1). This is because of the already relatively small landholdings per household and the return-migration due to the hope for jobs following the establishment of the company. However, many people are leaving again, as shown in Tademe where a male participant in the men's focus group discussion reported 'We are idle. We do not have any work to do. Because of that people have left for Praso, Yeji, Krachi and other places'. Similarly, Biofuel Africa's arrival in the Kpachaa area was likened to 'scattering of guinea fowls in the bush when their space is invaded' (participant in men's FGD, Kpachaa).

In the case of Dipale, where more respondents managed to acquire land within the community (Table 3.1), the capacity of people to access land was premised on their ability to invest in virgin lands further away from their villages and original farmlands. This caused additional constraints on the poorest villagers, especially women, who are only able to access small parcels of lands near their settlements. Furthermore, in Dipale much of the land is of poor quality and cannot be used for certain crops. These 'unusable lands' became the impromptu refuge for women and the most marginalized in the communities due to their inability to access fertile lands because of scarcity and the cost involved in commuting and clearing woodlands far from the villages.

The majority of people in Dipale and Kpachaa now borrow land from neighbours, whereas as in Dove and Tademe, sharecropping contracts

Table 3.1 Adequacy of land holdings and adjustments made (%)

	Dipale (ITFC)	Dove/Tademe (Prairie Volta Rice)	Kpachaa (Solar Harvest)	Total
Land size inadequate	43.4	97.2	51.3	67.2
N	**53**	**106**	**39**	**198**
Adjustments made				
More intensive use of land	9.5	22.0	19.4	19.7
Acquired more land within community	85.7	35.0	25.0	39.5
Acquired land in another village	4.8	15.0	2.8	10.8
Diversified to non-farm	0.0	11.0	0.0	7.0
Landless	0.0	9.0	0.0	5.7
Acquired less land than lost	0.0	5.0	0.0	3.2
Backyard gardening	0.0	2.0	0.0	1.3
Did not lose land	0.0	0.0	52.8	12.1
N	**21**	**100**	**36**	**157**

* The size of the sample (N) varies for each question either due to some respondents not answering all questions or questions being inapplicable to some respondents. This applies to the samples/totals in all tables in this chapter.

Source: Field Survey 2012

have become a new strategy for accessing land. Moreover, the old practice of clearing new land, which gave one the status of *kagsogu* owner (land user with primary rights over land), is dominant in Dipale and Kpachaa. In Dove and Tademe, *nudufe* (usufruct rights inherited from the ancestors) was the main means of accessing land. Productive land is becoming more difficult to access and this scarcity has implications for migration patterns: in the Kpachaa case, a quarter of the village out-migrated, a pattern similar to Dove and Tademe where this has been a historical reality. An important implication of land scarcity is the inability of migrants to acquire land without paying for it. Also, indigenes can no longer just clear uncultivated lands at will. In Dipale, the activities of sand extraction and fishing positively contribute to the local economy and have created diversified labour sectors, including water melon farming along the banks of the White Volta. Here, the lack of compensation has prevented affected people from expanding their economic activities, and has therefore impeded social mobility.

The extent of crop change has been considerable, reflecting mainly the amount of adequate farmlands with specific agronomic qualities suitable for particular crops and wider market considerations. However, commercial farming operations have had minimal influence on the process. Many people in Dove changed crops (44.8 per cent), followed by Dipale (26.2 per cent) and only 12.8 per cent did so in Kpachaa. Since *Jatropha* is neither a food crop nor locally familiar, the community members have not adopted it. However, the cultivation of crops varies according to the nature of the soil and topography of the new land to which farmers relocated. In Kpachaa, there are no valleys in the northern sections close to the national forest reserve where many relocated, hence the decline in the cultivation of rice. On the other hand, in Dove and surrounding villages, farmers boosted their own rice production due to the cultivation of long-grain rice by the Prairie Company. The surge in demand for long-grain rice was made possible by the reputation of the variety grown by the company, which has spurred local replication in production. In Dipale, the initial adoption of organic mangoes was short-lived because of bush fires; however, the collaboration between ITFC and agricultural NGOs to provide fertiliser, credit and other input subsidies led to an increase in maize output.

Incomplete proletarianisation and disruptions
in agrarian livelihood activities
The conversion of farmers into workers is the most far-reaching socio-economic change under way in the study areas. The lure of a monthly cash income as opposed to the long wait for harvest in an unreliable subsistence farming system made the prospect of proletarianisation initially acceptable. Table 3.2 indicates the high proportions of the population employed by the companies in Kpachaa and Dipale. This contrasts with the much smaller numbers employed at Dove and Tademe.

There were more casual workers than permanent workers, with many perceiving their wages as being inadequate. The majority of workers combined their company job with other activities such as farming. This process of change is described as one of partial proletarianisation (Byres 1981; Harriss 1992). This was necessitated by farmers needing to continue procuring their own food from family farms and filling shortfalls in income. The casual nature of much of the employment on offer was a disincentive for some while for others it was an advantage, depending on the availability of land and possibility for household members to diversify their livelihoods. In Dipale and Dove, where virgin lands existed, casual work gave people the flexibility to determine when to work on their own farms. In the case of Kpachaa where there was scarcity of fertile land, casual work was a source of income and employment insecurities. In addition, when people got used to formal wage employment, it became difficult to re-adjust to subsistence farming, as seen in the Dipale and Kpachaa cases.

The scale and types of employment created, and how employment combined or conflicted with people's own farming activities, varied across the three cases. Biofuel Africa Ltd employed 75 individuals from Kpachaa, out of a total of 280 employees. The employees stopped

Table 3.2 Employment levels, wages and activities

	Dipale (ITFC)	Dove/ Tademe (Prairie Volta Rice)	Kpachaa (Solar Harvest)	Total
Have you been employed by the company?				
Yes	26	6	20	52
	40.60%	5.10%	54.10%	23.70%
No	38	112	17	167
	59.40%	94.90%	45.90%	76.30%
Total	**64**	**118**	**37**	**219**
Is it permanent or casual employment?				
Permanent	15	1	4	20
	57.70%	16.70%	20.00%	38.50%
Casual	11	5	16	32
	42.30%	83.30%	80.00%	61.50%
Total	**26**	**6**	**20**	**52**
Are wages adequate?				
Yes	3	0	6	9
	11.50%	0.00%	30.00%	17.30%
No	23	6	14	43
	88.50%	100.00%	70.00%	82.69%
Total	**26**	**6**	**20**	**52**
Combined company employment with own economic activities				
Yes	26	2	13	41
	100.00%	33.30%	65.00%	78.80%
No	0	4	7	11
	0.00%	66.70%	35.00%	21.20%
Total	**26**	**6**	**20**	**52**

Source: Field Survey 2012

meaningful subsistence farming and cultivated only between 0.4 and 0.8ha, which were under the care of their wives and children as they were only free at weekends. However, the collapse of Biofuel Africa Ltd led to retrenchment of hired labour. Prairie Volta Rice company employs over a hundred permanent staff, and between 50 and 60 casual labourers. There were limited employment avenues available to the local people at Tademe and Dove due to mechanisation and the location of the mill in another community. However, self-employment among innovative business-minded community members is gaining ground in Aveyime where the rice mill is located. Transport operators, carriers, market women, rice wholesalers and retailers, food vendors and many other service providers have emerged in response to the demand created by the rice mill's multiplier effects on the local economy.

The ITFC had a total of 255 employees drawn from surrounding communities of which 24 per cent were women. Women were engaged for grafting, mulching, cutting, packing and selection of mangoes. Male employees, on the other hand, worked as technical field staff and farm hands or in the processing plant handling the crates of mangoes. In addition, villages participating in the outgrower scheme had 100 outgrowers cultivating 0.4ha of organic mangoes each. Unfortunately, savannah fires burnt down the farms of the outgrowers at Dipale in 2010. In addition, once the nucleus farm was established, the number of employees from Dipale fell to less than ten workers in 2011. In the meantime, the benefits of continued employment went to Gushie and the surrounding villages which were closer to the processing plant. The earnings from the mango scheme for outgrowers in the other participating communities have been disappointing; far below projections of earnings rising from US$150 in the third year to as much as US$3,000 in the tenth year of cultivation (Osei, 2007). For example, Yakubu, one of the few farmers with 0.8ha of mango – twice the average of 0.4ha at Gushi – harvested mangoes worth US$59 in 2009 (the third year), US$78 in 2010 and US$312 in 2011. Few farmers in his group earned that much from their mangoes in 2011. While there was some progression in earnings, it was too gradual to fulfill the assumption that the ITFC project would earn outgrowers much more than their food crop farming. This is especially true considering that the initial investment made by the ITFC for 0.4ha of mango is US$5,000. Several generic benefits accrued to the communities as a result of corporate social responsibility investments, employment and multiplier effects. Communities listed these as including infrastructure such as dams, a clinic, boreholes, a palace for the chief and schools. In addition, youth employment, payment of school fees for selected children through scholarship schemes and provision of inputs such as fertilisers improved the lives of some community members in these spheres.

The cultivation of crops for the local market creates more economic prospects downstream than those for exports due to the value chains spawned. For example, the multiplier effects of the rice mill on Aveyime were not replicated in the case of Gushie because the products of the ITFC were for export and were not locally sold or consumed. This confirms the findings of Dufey et al. (2007) on the benefits of locally oriented production systems.

Implications for livelihoods and food security

The acquisition of land encompassing common property resources resulted in a decline in the availability of medicinal plants, thatch, firewood and wild foods in all the research communities (see Table 3.3). People now needed to travel longer distances to access these on other communities' lands, thus increasing distance, time and costs for procuring these goods and also increasing the risks of inter-community conflicts. While travel times to these resources was much longer for Kpachaa than for Dipale or Dove, at Dove the physical barrier of the river rendered the new commons inaccessible. According to the Environmental Protection Agency's guidelines and promises by Biofuel Africa and ITFC, shea trees – prized by women for shea nut butter, an important source of income – were not to be cut, but left standing on the new farms. This was not feasible since they are numerous and would impede the mono-cropping of mangoes and *Jatropha*. Only a few old trees of socio-cultural significance were left by ITFC on their nucleus farm.

In general, access to the commons in an environment characterised by seasonality has implications for food and livelihood security, as resources are perceived to be on the decline and scarce. First, the creation of large farms has meant that the direct benefits people gained from wild fruits, wild life, herbs and naturally-growing crops used for food were lost. Second, the incomes they could earn from selling these products, as well as fuelwood, thatch and other non-food products, were also lost, especially by women and the poor. Income from these activities was previously used to buy food, pay medical bills, procure educational materials and ensure a thriving community.

One result of these losses is that new patterns of negotiation are emerging for access, household time allocations and competition in the face of scarcity in all communities, albeit in different ways. What is common to all the communities studied is that powerful members of the community who negotiated the land deals had not considered these livelihood activities based on common property resources as major sources of income and survival. The role of power underpinned by the institutional dimension of these deals explains the changing dynamics of land use and access.

Table 3.4 shows that a majority of respondents perceived household food security to have declined after the land acquisitions, while overall wellbeing improved for a minority who were gainfully employed by the

Table 3.3 Access to common pool resources

	Dipale (ITFC)	Dove/ Tademe (Prairie Volta Rice)	Kpachaa (Solar Harvest)	Total
Access to medicinal plants				
Declined	30	35	16	81
	93.80%	92.10%	72.70%	88.00%
Remained the same	2	3	6	11
	6.20%	7.90%	27.30%	12.00%
Access to thatch				
Declined	34	57	32	123
	94.40%	98.30%	88.90%	94.60%
Remained the same	2	1	4	7
	5.60%	1.70%	11.10%	5.40%
Access to firewood				
Declined	58	120	39	217
	95.10%	100.00%	100.00%	98.60%
Remained the same	3	0	0	3
	4.90%	0.00%	0.00%	1.40%
Access to shea nuts				
Declined	53	1	9	63
	91.40%	100.00%	81.80%	90.00%
Remained the same	5	0	2	7
	8.60%	0.00%	18.20%	10.00%

Source: Field survey 2012

companies or did not lose land, or both. Tademe in the Prairie Volta Rice concession reported the biggest reduction in food security because they lost most of their lands. Some improvement in wellbeing was reported only in communities where employment and social facilities were provided such as at Kpachaa where a dam, grinding mill and access to a vehicle for ferrying expectant mothers to the hospital were provided. Dove and Tademe had not been provided with any community development because the Prairie Volta Rice company dealt with the government and did not feel obliged to provide corporate social responsibility. Hence the communities of the Prairie project recorded the highest level of deterioration in wellbeing, as the benefits of the project were largely enjoyed by other communities and urban consumers of rice.

Table 3.4 Household food security and wellbeing before and after acquisitions

	Dipale (ITFC)	Dove/Tademe (Prairie Volta Rice)	Kpachaa (Solar Harvest)	Total
Did your household have sufficient food before acquisition?				
Yes	61	119	33	213
	95.30%	98.30%	89.20%	95.90%
No	3	2	4	9
	4.70%	1.70%	10.80%	4.10%
Total	64	121	37	222
Does your household have sufficient food now – after acquisition?				
Yes	40	8	13	61
	62.50%	6.60%	33.30%	27.20%
No	24	113	26	163
	37.50%	93.40%	66.70%	72.80%
Total	64	121	39	224
Has your overall wellbeing improved after acquisition?				
Improved	11	0	6	17
	17.20%	0.00%	15.40%	7.60%
Remained the same	25	6	12	43
	39.10%	5.00%	30.80%	19.20%
Deteriorated	28	115	21	164
	43.80%	95.00%	53.80%	73.20%
Total	64	121	39	224

Source: Field Survey 2012

Lareba (a 31-year-old woman) previously earned about US$80 per annum from fuelwood alone, which enabled her to procure food and take care of small expenses for her children. Now, the family experiences food shortages for between four and five months of the year due to clearance of vegetation, including fuelwood sources, by the company. This reinforces the more general point that rural dwellers greatly depend on the availability and proximity of natural resources in relative abundance so as to prevent over-exploitation. Ease of access to these resources is only possible when large tracts of unused land are accessible to people. It is a mistake to define such commons as 'abundant', 'wasteland' or 'idle' as the basis for agricultural investments in land.

Agrarian struggles and social differentiation

In Ghana, as elsewhere, the processes of large-scale land acquisition and the modernisation of agriculture have not been without contradictions, struggles and conflicts. These processes trigger contestations between different interests and class groups. As these land acquisitions are not well regulated, they result in different arrangements and terms. The acquisition by Biofuel Africa involved negotiations with the divisional chief of the area, detailing the benefits the project would bring and the rent payable to him. The communities were involved only via a campaign to win their support. Resistance from within these communities to the land acquisition was minimal, despite NGO activism against the deal at the national level. Promises of employment, social development and the general transformation of the area enabled this initial peaceful outcome. The company fulfilled several of the promises it made to the village in the first year of its operations, thus cementing its relations with the communities.

In the case of ITFC, the chief of Dipale village was involved in the initial negotiations, which enabled the people to also take part in expressing their views and negotiating outcomes that would benefit them. However, this was truncated as ITFC decided to by-pass the village chief and deal directly with the paramount chief who gave out the land without reference to the local community. This led to a silent revolt against the company's activities and the company reneging on its promises. Relations have improved following steps by the company to provide social development as compensation for their initial mistakes.

The case of the Prairie Volta Rice company exemplifies the government's shortfalls in their development interventions involving the seizure of lands for national development without compensation. The transfer of land by the government to Prairie Volta Rice sparked several disputes about the ownership of the land. The company therefore decided to deposit the cost of the land into a special account to pay off whoever was declared the true owner of the land by the courts. The lamentation of the people and chiefs at the limited involvement of the community and its effects on benefit streams is captured in this statement by a village elder at a men's focus group at Mafi Dove:

> There should be a negotiation and the right compensation paid. The government alone should not decide on the value of the land. We were thinking that the project would take off so the youth of this town

would be employed. We have not been treated fairly at all. We gave out the biggest tract of land but the project headquarters is on a different land (Aveyime). We will ask for the head office to be moved to Dove, and if not, the project will not take off. We would also ask for the name to be changed to Dove rice. We want our name to be heard.

Table 3.5 shows that the Prairie Volta Rice concession dispossessed more people compared to the investments in the two cases in the North. However, none of the communities affected by the ITFC and Solar Harvest investments were compensated because the chiefs hijacked the process and the proceeds. In contrast, in the Prairie Volta Rice area, there has been some compensation for the loss of crops even though conflicts have arisen over how to share the money. Inadequate or lacking compensation means the inability to engage in alternative livelihoods. Also, where compensation was paid only to landowners, those who historically used, but did not own, the land lost out.

Table 3.5 Land lost to acquisition and compensation

	Dipale	Dove	Kpachaa	Total
Did you lose any land?				
Yes	20	118	17	155
	37.00%	97.50%	43.60%	72.40%
No	34	3	22	59
	63.00%	2.50%	56.40%	27.60%
Total	54	121	39	214
What compensation did you receive?				
Poor	0	29	0	29
	0.00%	24.60%	0.00%	18.80%
None	19	89	17	125
	100.00%	75.40%	100.00%	81.20%
Total	19	118	17	154

Source: Field Survey 2012

Thus in situations where the processes of land acquisition have a direct bearing on who gets included and excluded from the activities and benefits of the company, existing land tenure systems dictated the payment of compensation to male usufruct owners, even if women cultivated those lands, as typified in the Kpachaa and Dipale cases where women received no support for their losses. In the case of Dove, compensation for the land was given to mainly family heads who decided how to share the proceeds. Members of the communities were deprived of the direct monetary benefit due to the existence of these traditional power structures defining receivers of 'cola' money to be only those in ordained positions. With regard to crop compensation, in the case of Dove, however, both men and women were paid one-off amounts ranging between 15 and 20GHC (US$8-10) for their crops, but not for their loss of the common resources such as palm trees, mango, velvet tamarind and other fruit trees (focus groups in Dove).

The chiefly class in the Dipale and Kpachaa deals benefited from the compensation paid for the land and subsequent courtesies of the companies such as free fertilisers and gifts for occasions and requests for help whenever the need arose. These were at the expense of families for whom compensation would have been useful in diversifying family income sources. The ability to engage in company activities (such as outgrowing) was only possible when people had large farmlands. Since women did not own land in the 'skin' tenure systems, few women had the economic resources to participate in these ventures. Social differentiation among different classes of people is on the increase due to the processes of inclusion and exclusion from the benefits of modernising agriculture.

In all cases people had been involved in conflicts, with the highest number of people indicating involvement at Kpachaa (76.9 per cent), followed by Dipale (57.2 per cent), with Dove showing the least involvement in conflicts amongst informants (49.2 per cent). The conflicts related to: loss of farmlands, inter-community disputes over land, arguments over who was entitled to compensation, and disputes between the youth and elders due to poor consultation. Also, land deals have ignited long-standing land disputes between neighbouring communities.

There were also struggles among different levels of chieftaincy for the right to lease out land, such as between the chiefs of Dipale, Savelugu and Yendi, in which the Yendi chief used his powers to extinguish the interest of the lower chiefs. Struggles between dispossessed farmers, chiefs and companies typify resistance to deals that exclude ordinary farmers from the negotiations. Farmers and former workers of Biofuel Africa occupied sections of the unused land in the concession on their own initiative. There has been open criticism against the leasing of the land to ITFC and the compulsory acquisition of Dove lands. This has led to a decline in the respect for chiefs in these places. Also, struggles between neighbouring competing communities such as between Dipale and Gushe have centred on who can garner the benefits of company employment and socio-economic amenities. The same struggles and resentments exist between Dove and Aveyime because of the location of the rice mill, which is not benefiting the Dove community whose lands were acquired for the project.

The main group of farmers to resist the land deal in Kpachaa were rich urban migrant farmers from Tamale. Their exit from the area led to a reorientation in the social and agrarian structures. Their modernising influence on local farming through mechanisation, exchange of labour for ploughing, fertilisers and employment avenues was lost and replaced by Biofuel Africa's *Jatropha* plantation. Also greatly affected were women labourers who worked for the urban farmers during sowing, weeding and harvesting periods.

Similarly, access to employment was important in creating new patterns of economic differentiation. Criteria for employment followed both technocratic and traditional protocols in order to meet the company needs and also appease traditional structures. People who were able to demonstrate their loss of substantial pieces of land at Dipale and Kpachaa had better chances of being employed than those who did not have much land to start with. Local recruiters for the projects were selective, especially as jobs were scarce. A new emerging class comprised those with the skills to access jobs and the assets to take advantage of new opportunities. These observations support Byres' (1981) assertion that modernisation of agrarian systems hastens the process of social differentiation by consolidating the rich peasantry as a powerful and dominant class. The sometimes silent and inarticulate resistance to large-scale land acquisitions is mainly due to the hijacking of processes by powerful actors who represent the community, but whose positions and practices do not fully capture its interests.

Conclusion

The outcomes of different transnational land deals in Ghana have been remarkably similar, whether they have involved investments in food crops or non-food crops. They included unfulfilled expectations of alternative employment, land dispossession, the loss of the commons and increasing inter-community tensions. Thus far, their benefits have been meagre, while their disadvantages have been significant.

A key finding from our study was that the livelihood strategies of small peasants involved multiple sources, which were dependent on social, political and environmental relationships, and these tended to be destabilised by land deals. In addition, some deals threatened bio-diversity as a result of their monoculture practices. Furthermore, the projects generally failed to generate the levels of employment needed as alternative livelihood activities for the displaced people, particularly women. In the cases examined, the returns on the investments made by the companies were modest, partly because of unfavourable local conditions and changing global trends.

Local traditional rulers and intermediaries of the state have facilitated land deals. The state as a player in transnational land deals has compounded their negative outcomes. Institutional failures manifested in the lack of regulation and attention to community problems have occurred alongside conflicts of interest in the role of the state and ambiguities in the role of state officials, as noted with failures of land tenure policies by the Ghanaian state in the past (Antwi and Adams 2003; Aryeetey et al. 2005; Awanyo 2003; Berry 1997). Often, state officials are members of local elite groups made up of chiefs and their elders, community leaders, technocrats and local partners of foreign investors. The elite consensus on the privatisation of state and communal resources leaves small farmers and rural families vulnerable to expropriation and livelihood insecurities.

The privatisation logic of structural adjustment policies (World Bank 1981, 1984) is being played out in the countryside, through the privatisation of rural lands for the benefit of transnational companies and big local farmers, a process which is disenfranchising poor farmers. Transnational land deals are changing the traditional dynamics and arrangements of power and resource access systems (Abdulai and Ndekugri 2007; Alden Wily 2008; Amanor 2001, 2005). Competition for inclusion in the benefit streams accentuates class differences, which are normally camouflaged by kinship systems in rural areas. Emerging differences within the ranks of communities affects the social relationships needed to assure sustainable livelihoods.

Agribusiness as currently organised is exacerbating social inequalities and resource conflicts within and between communities in rural Ghana. The problems of governance at all levels of society make equity and respect for human rights peripheral to the business of large-scale land acquisitions for commercial agriculture projects.

4

Large-Scale
Land Acquisitions
in Ethiopia

MARU SHETE
& MARCEL RUTTEN

Implications for
Agricultural
Transformation &
Livelihood Security

Introduction

Land, the state and politics are intimately interlinked in the political economy of Ethiopia and land has been central to the political debates between the ruling government and opposition political parties. Since 1992, more than 2.1 million hectares of land comprising nearly 4,700 separate projects have been leased to mainly foreign agricultural interests, with a peak of investment activity in the period from 2007. The amount of land transferred so far is much less than the target based on the government's estimates of 'available land'. Yet the country has received a lot of media attention and criticism for the rush to transfer huge tracts of farmland to foreign and domestic capital.

This chapter explores the unfolding of two major land deals, both investments by the Indian company Karuturi Agro Products plc. Karuturi Agro Products plc is the Ethiopian operating name of the Bangalore-based cut-flower company owned by Sai Ramakrishna Karuturi. It operates in two Ethiopian states, Oromia and Gambela, and one case study from each is presented. See the map of the study area (Map 4.1).

The chapter is based on primary data collected through fieldwork conducted between March 2012 and May 2013. Data were collected through household and employee surveys, interviews with key informants, affected people and communities, group discussions and systematic observations. In addition, secondary data were collected from various government offices (at federal, regional and district levels) and from the large-scale farms to substantiate the primary data.

Political and policy narratives around land in Ethiopia

Commercial farming is not new to Ethiopia. It dates back to the Imperial era (1930–1974) when a few foreign companies, such as the Dutch sugar

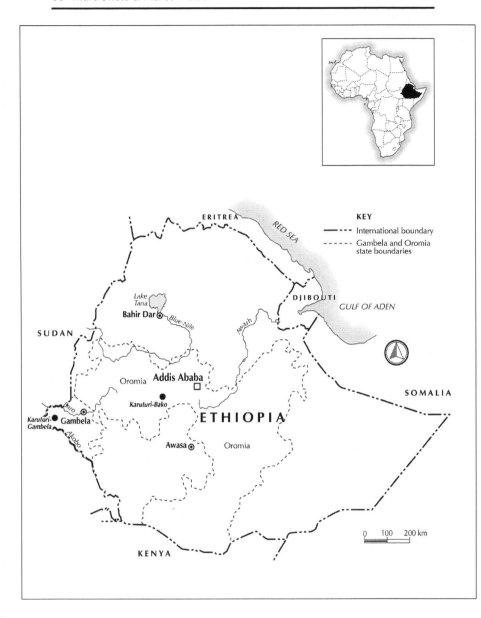

Map 4.1 Ethiopia, showing location of Karuturi-Bako and Karuturi-Gambela

giant HVA, cultivated high value crops including sugarcane, cotton and sesame in the Awash valley (Zewde 2008; Rahmato 2009). A push to large-scale farms existed in this period, guided by the ideology of transforming 'traditional' agrarian societies into 'modern' societies in the Western style (Abbink 2011).

The overthrow of Emperor Haile Selassie's government in 1974 by the Derg (a committee of the armed forces, police and territorial armies that opposed the emperor) resulted in changes to land and property relations between the state and the peasantry. The Derg regime (1974–1991), guided by the socialist ideology of 'redistribution with growth', nationalised all privately owned farms from the Imperial period and transformed them into state farms. The 1975 land policy brought all land under state control and gave usufruct land rights to the peasantry, with a relatively egalitarian distribution of land (Ministry of Land Reform 1975). During this period, capitalist farming stagnated, while state farming and producers' cooperatives were promoted.

The agrarian crisis and widespread famine and poverty of the 1980s contributed to the resolution of the long-standing civil war and a change of government in 1991. The Federal Democratic Republic of Ethiopia (FDRE) was formed by the Ethiopian People's Revolutionary Democratic Front (EPRDF), which continues to rule the country. The major economic policy shift of the EPRDF government from the Derg regime was the adoption of a series of economic reform measures based on the philosophy of free-market policy (TGE 1991). The market liberalisation reforms, *inter alia*, removed the embargo by the former regime and established private capitalist agriculture. In terms of land ownership, however, there were no changes (Belay and Manig 2004). The government further developed the Agricultural Development Led Industrialization (ADLI) strategy in the mid-1990s, which served as a framework to develop the country's poverty reduction strategy programmes. The ADLI considered smallholder farmers as key players in propelling economic growth for the poverty-stricken nation (MoFED 2003).

However, a strategic shift from a purely smallholder-oriented agricultural policy has been witnessed since 2010 with the Growth and Trans-formation Plan (GTP). The GTP underlined the need to establish greater complementarities between smallholder peasant farming and large-scale commercial farming. This is premised on the expectation that large-scale commercial farms facilitate the transfer of improved farming technology to smallholder farmers, contribute to local-level food security by increasing the availability of food from large-scale farms and increase the purchasing power of local people through wage employment, generating additional revenue[1] and much needed foreign currency and contributing to infrastructure construction. Although some private investors acquired large-scale farmlands as early as 1992, following market liberalisation, the

---

[1] Revenue in the form of land lease fees and income tax from firms and company workers.

amount was not significant before 2007, when renewed interest among wealthy nations, transnational corporations and new portfolio capital emerged to acquire farmlands in the developing South.

The government justifies the transfer of large-scale farmlands to investors by claiming the presence of vast tracts of 'unused' land that are suitable for large-scale commercial farming. Identification of 'unused' land was done through satellite images without rigorous ground-testing by the Agricultural Investment Support Directorate (AISD),[2] making the notion of 'available but unused' land in Ethiopia problematic. It includes lands occupied by pastoralists that are assumed to be insufficiently productive but are not necessarily 'empty' (Galaty 2012; Lavers 2012a). Also included are lands that form part of pastoralists' seasonal herding systems (Borras and Franco 2012) and lands used by local people for sideline economic uses, such as collection of honey, wood or other forest products (Abbink 2011). Additionally, it includes lands that are assumed to be marginal, but have cultural and ecological significance, and some lands that overlap with national park boundaries (Nalepa 2013).

Magnitude and trends of agricultural investment in Ethiopia

In 2008, the FDRE established what is called the 'Federal Land Bank' under the AISD of the Ministry of Agriculture and Rural Development (MoARD)[3] and issued a directive that gave the mandate to transfer farmlands amounting to more than 5,000ha to the AISD (FDRE 2010). Regional governments still retained the mandate to transfer farmland less than 5,000ha. Close to 3.6 million hectares of land were identified from Gambela, Benshangul Gumuz, Southern Nations, Nationalities and Peoples (SNNP), Afar, Oromia and Amhara Regional States and reserved under the Federal Land Bank (Rahmato 2011). Except for Oromia and Afar Regional States, the other regions 'voluntarily' transferred the land identified by the AISD to the Federal Land Bank. Since there was no clear demarcation of the land under the mandate of the regional states and the AISD, there have been cases where the regions and the AISD have transferred the same parcel of land to different investors.

This created a source of conflict and inefficiency in the administration of large-scale farmlands. In early 2012, economically emerging regions such as Gambela and Benshangul Gumuz were prevented from making any land deals, even of less than 5000ha, for reasons of corruption and mismanagement of land resources (Interview with an expert at the AISD, 15 March 2012).

---

[2] The AISD was restructured in late 2013 and renamed the Agricultural Investment and Land Administration Agency (AILAA).

[3] The MoARD is now renamed the Ministry of Agriculture.

Up to July 2013, the amount of land transferred to investors from the land reserved under the Federal Land Bank was only 447,803ha. This, however, does not necessarily mean that the balance from the Land Bank is still available, since regional governments were also handing out farmlands from the Land Bank. While it is clear that large areas of land have been acquired by investors, estimates of the magnitude of the investment are inconsistent – largely due to poor access to reliable information. The Oakland Institute (OI) (2011: 18), for example, estimated that close to 3.6 million hectares of land had been acquired in Ethiopia. Lavers (2012b: 114) reported close to 5 million hectares under pre-implementation and 656,000ha already implemented in Ethiopia. The World Bank, on the other hand, reported that 1.2 million hectares of land had been transferred to large-scale investors (World Bank 2011: 62). The various figures are difficult to reconcile as they cover different time periods and are derived from different data sources (see Locher and Sulle 2014 and Scoones et al. 2013 on problems of data discrepancies).

To arrive at a more accurate estimate, information was collected from different government agencies responsible for maintaining records, such as the Federal Investment Authority, the AISD, the Regional Environmental Protection and Land Administration Bureau and Regional Investment Bureaus. As Table 4.1 illustrates, the results show that more than 2.1 million hectares of land were transferred to agricultural investors between 1992 and 2013, to a total of 4,698 projects under different phases of implementation. This estimate is equivalent to 3.8 per cent of the total agricultural land (56 million hectares) claimed by the Ethiopian government (MoARD 2009) as suitable and 'available' for crop production. Analysis shows that the regional states with the largest proportion of the total land transferred in Ethiopia are Benshangul Gumuz (28.3 per cent of the total land transferred), Oromia (21.6 per cent) and Gambela (18.8 per cent). Foreign investors have received 52.8 per cent of the total land transferred to date. The average amount of land acquired by a foreign investor[4] is 3,688ha, compared to 479ha by a domestic investor.

Considering Rahmato's (2011) definition of a large-scale farm (greater than 2,000ha) and the average estimated land size acquired by foreign investors (3,688ha), most foreign-owned farms in Ethiopia are likely to be large-scale. Indians, followed by Saudi Arabians, dominate land acquisition in the country. Investment projects in Ethiopia showed a rapid rise in the period 2007–2009, in which 69 per cent of all the project licenses were issued (Figure 4.1). This trend was most distinct in Gambela and Benshangul Gumuz regional states where 85.7 per cent and 82.3 per cent of the project licenses, respectively, were issued over the period 2007–2009. The global food price hike was argued to be one of the drivers for the renewed interest in farmlands by capital-rich countries in

---

[4] Foreign investment projects in this paper include projects owned by Ethiopians by origin but foreigners by nationality, projects owned by foreigners by origin and by nationality and those projects that are joint ventures (Ethiopians and foreigners).

Table 4.1 Farmland acquired by investors in Ethiopia (1992–2013)

Region	Land size transferred (ha)	No. of projects	No. of projects by foreigners	Land acquired by foreigners (ha)	FDI Proportion of total (%)	Regional distribution (%)*
Afar	47,744	48	8	25,150	52.7	2.3
Somali	22,762	16	9	13,400	58.9	1.0
Tigray	109,318	397	36	57,030	52.2	5.2
Amhara	171,772	1290	28	34,720	20.2	8.1
SNNP	311,502	1408	50	207,316	66.6	14.7
Benshangul	600,254	306	41	243,350	40.5	28.3
Gambela	399,491	304	14	225,012	56.3	18.8
Oromia	458,292	929	85	193,432	42.2	21.6
Total	2,121,135	4,698	271	999,410	52.8	100

Sources: authors' compilation of government datasets of AISD, Ethiopia Investment Agency, Regional Investment Bureau, Regional Environmental Protection and Land Administration Bureau.
* Calculated as land transferred in each region as proportion of total land transferred to investors in the country

Figure 4.1 Food price index and proportion of investments projects in Ethiopia (1992–2010)

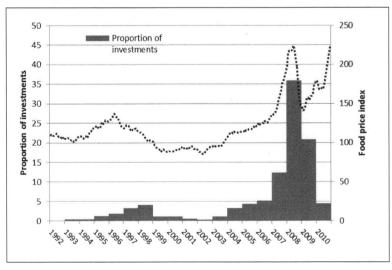

Source: Schoneveld and Shete (2014)

the developing South (Rahmato 2011; World Bank 2011). Due to pressure from various human rights groups, donor agencies and researchers who criticized the rush in land transfer as 'land grabbing' and a threat to local food security, there is some indication that the Ethiopian government has become more cautious regarding investment.

Contested views of land and property rights in Ethiopia

Historically, land and the state have been inseparable and this is also true in contemporary Ethiopia. Land is used as an instrument to control the peasantry and as a mechanism to incorporate the periphery into the centre. The EPRDF government, like its predecessor, regards all land as state property. Under state ownership of land, regional states in Ethiopia are given considerable autonomy by the Constitution to develop their own land administration policy while complying with the general law developed at federal level.[5] Article 40(8) of the Constitution states that landholders are entitled to compensation payments commensurate with the value of the land when it is expropriated for public purposes (FDRE 1995). However, peasants and pastoralists can only seek compensation when they have land registration certificates confirming their claims to the land. Those on the periphery are at a disadvantage as they have not received such certificates for their farmland. In the periphery, pastoralists and agro-pastoralists make use of land through the customary system and so are not entitled to compensation when the land is transferred for large-scale farming. To date, these transfers have targeted communal land, very often grazing areas (Makki 2012).

While the EPRDF government argued that privatisation of land brings about its concentration in the hands of the rich through distress sales and fosters the eviction of poor farmers (Crewett and Korf 2008), the Ethiopian Economic Association (EEA) argued that ownership of land by the state undermines efficiency and the development of a land market (EEA/EEPRI 2002). Peasants and pastoralists in Ethiopia experience 'land dependency' as opposed to 'land sovereignty', which is a source of insecurity, and they can be expropriated from their land at any time with the justification of its being needed for greater 'public purposes' (Rahmato 2011: 6).

To examine these issues in more detail, the following two sections present case studies of farms belonging to Karuturi Agro Products plc, one in each of the two regional states where they operate. Karuturi Global, an Indian company, is a major cut-rose producer and exporter, operating in Ethiopia under the company name of Karuturi Agro Products plc. It entered the Ethiopian flower production and exporting business in early 2000 with a 50ha flower farm under the Ethiopian Meadows

---

[5] Four regions in Ethiopia such as Amhara (ANRS 2006), Southern Nations, Nationalities and Peoples (SNNP 2007), Oromia (ONRS 2007) and Tigray (TNRS 2006) developed their own land administration legislations and gave land certificates to smallholder farmers.

plc company, and acquired large-scale farm plots in both Oromia and Gambela Regional States.

Case 1: Oromia Regional State
In 2008, the company received an offer from Oromia Regional State to acquire farmland in Bako Tibe District. The regional government played a key role in facilitating the land transfer to the investor, while the district- and zonal-level roles were limited. The 11,700ha[6] land deal agreement was signed at regional level with a lease rate of Ethiopian Birr (ETB) 135 (US$ 7.04)[7] per hectare per annum for 45 years, with a rent-free window for the first six years as an incentive for the investor. The agreement allows cultivation of different crops,[8] and the company is producing maize. By 2013 the company had developed close to 3,000ha of land along the banks of the Akobo River and on the relatively better drained part of its concession.

Although the general procedure to acquire farmland for investment before the changes in land policy in 2009 required investors to identify potential farmland for investment, negotiate with community members and submit the consent of the community together with a business plan, an environmental impact assessment and other documents, this deal did not pass through all these processes. Free, Prior and Informed Consent (FPIC) of the community in Bako Tibe District was not obtained by either the investor or the government. The land transferred to the company was assumed to be vacant following the survey of the Ethiopian Electric Power Corporation (EEPCo) which had identified the Bako plain as a potential reservoir for a hydroelectric dam in 1984.

In reality, however, there were 3,317 households in five villages using the land for different purposes such as cultivation of teff (*Eragrostis tef*) and niger seed (*Guizotia abyssinica*) and grazing of livestock. About 20,000 cattle owned by these households depended on the land as a feed source (Schoneveld and Shete 2014). As one respondent observed, 'Although the households have been cultivating the land for the production of food crops and grazing of cattle, they don't hold land certificates and they are not officially recognised as owners of the land' (Interview with Bako Tibe District Administrator, 20 March 2012). There were also some households with land certificates whose parcels of land were transferred to the Karuturi farm in Bako, but because these households were not compensated in accordance with the law, the concession to the company had not yet been demarcated. The amount of land might therefore decrease to 10,700ha so as to avoid displacement of these households

---

[6] The soil type is predominantly black soil (Vertisol) with water-logging problems, and is suitable only for some crops and grazing of livestock.

[7] The exchange rate between Ethiopian Birr and US$ on 14 February 2014 was: 1US$= ETB19.179

[8] The contractual agreement is for the cultivation of oil palm and other food crops. The company is cultivating maize although the soil type (Vertisol) is less suitable for maize production.

within the company's concession (ibid.). Conflicts have been common. While these disputes are not yet resolved, the company has constructed a runway for aeroplanes on a parcel of land owned by a nearby smallholder farmer who has a land certificate. In addition, it has dug boreholes on the plots of farmers who have land certificates, although these farmers are reportedly not permitted to draw drinking water from these boreholes (Interview with five older farmers in Goromitti village on 3 April and five in Oda Gibe village on 3 March 2012).

Case 2: Karuturi Agro Products PLC in Gambela Regional State
Karuturi received a similar invitation from Gambela Regional State in 2008 to discuss the possibility of acquiring a large parcel of land for agricultural investment. A team composed of an expert from the public relations department of the company, Karuturi's father Surya Rao Karuturi, and the company's lawyers travelled to Gambela in April 2008. The regional government offered them 300,000ha of land at a rate of ETB20 (US$1.04) per hectare per annum and when Karaturi heard about the attractive land deal, he instructed the team to sign the agreement before the government changed its mind (Dubey 2012). The land deal was first signed in 2008 for the full 300,000ha of land in Itang and Makuey (formerly Jikawo) districts, for the cultivation of oil palm, cereals and pulses.

Again, the procedures of land acquisition for agricultural investment that existed before 2009 were not followed. As explained by the manager of the Karuturi farm in Gambela, the company did not consider the suitability of the land for agricultural production or the challenges of flooding in the area (Davison 2013), and community-level negotiations between the company and the community, as suggested in the procedure, had not been carried out before the company acquired the land. The land deal was re-signed with the AISD in 2010, following the regulation that gave the mandate to transfer land amounting to more than 5,000ha to the federal government. The new contract agreement retained the same terms as the first deal, but reduced the size of the allocation to 100,000ha. It was agreed that the 200,000ha remaining should be released upon satisfactory performance of the company on the initial 100,000ha land. The company developed a much more modest area of close to 5,000ha, where it was predominantly producing maize before it withdrew from production entirely in 2014.

The land transferred to Karuturi in Gambela is inhabited by the Nuer (Makuey district) and the Anuak (Itang district) ethnic groups. The Nuer are agro-pastoralists who practise extended livestock production and small-scale crop production following the seasonal overflow of the Baro River. Land is a key source of pasture for their large number of cattle and a source of agricultural plots for crop production. The Anuak also practise small-scale food production and complement their livelihoods with fishing and gathering of wild foods from the bush and the forest. The concession of Karuturi is composed of pastureland, forest and bush land, and is part of the *Duma* wetland that is a unique habitat for insects and birds. Free, Prior and Informed Consent of the community was not obtained before the land was transferred to the investor. Equally, the land identification process by a team of experts was carried out hastily through satellite imagery with little effort at ground-testing.

Outcomes of the land deals

This section explores the outcomes of the land deals in the two case study sites. Major changes in land use and access have taken place, with impacts on livelihoods. The expected benefits of land investments in terms of employment, technology transfer and spillovers into the local economy have been limited. The impacts were also highly gendered, with additional accusations of abuse of female employees on the farms. Overall, the type of business model adopted – an exclusive plantation arrangement disconnected from the local area, and reliant on the importation of wage labour from within but also from outside the area – is, it is concluded, inimical to the positive outcomes envisaged by advocates of land investments, including both the company and the government.

The case of Karuturi in Oromia
The local people in Bako Tibe District in Oromia, on average, own 1ha of land but they cultivated about double this amount prior to the Karuturi investment, the difference being accounted for by the loss of customarily-owned land which is now transferred to Karuturi. A significant proportion of landless youth used to generate income by cultivating teff and niger seed in the rich soil that is now part of the company's concession. Focus group discussions held in Goromitti village with five landless youths on 2 April 2012 and five older farmers on 3 April 2012 revealed that the cultivation of teff and niger seed on parts of the land transferred to the company not only complemented the households' food supply but also brought in additional income to settle expenses such as school fees and tax, and to buy food oil, salt and clothing. With the loss of this land, there is a significant decline in their living standards, which they called 'starvation on native lands for the benefit of a foreign company'.

In addition, the customary land had been used as grazing land for livestock. Prior to 2008, households owned an average herd size of thirteen Tropical Livestock Units (TLU),[9] although this declined to ten TLU in 2012 due to a shortage of pasture after the land was leased to the company. Due to the shortage of pasture, some households sold their cattle while others lost them as a result of feed shortages and disease.

Focus group discussions (FGD with five farmers on 3 April in Goromitti village and five in Oda Gibe village on 3 March 2012) indicated that

[9] Domestic animals owned by households are converted to Tropical Livestock Units (TLU) using the conversion factors suggested by Storck *et al.* (1991).

the Bako Plain was known for its huge livestock production potential. Farmers from other highland regions bring their cattle to the area under a shared benefit arrangement that entitles the local farmers free access to milk and milk products and ownership of one cow for every five managed. With the loss of the grazing land due to the transfer of the land to the company, the shared benefit arrangement has been discontinued, which has affected their food consumption and incomes negatively. It was also explained that the company had dug deep trenches around its estates that resulted in the death of cattle due to unknown diseases after the animals had drunk the water collected in the trenches.

Karuturi dug 22 boreholes and started to irrigate from the Akobo River. Previous access to water for livestock from the Akobo River has been completely blocked for downstream users since the company started using the river for dry-season cultivation. Shortage of water for cattle was mentioned as a serious problem for the livelihoods of the local people (FGD held with five youths on 2 April and five farmers on 3 April 2012 in Goromitti village, and five farmers in Oda Gibe village on 3 March 2012). The members of the focus groups explained that farmers in the villages used the Aboko River as a source of water for their cattle before their access to the river was completely blocked by Karuturi. Now, they trek their cattle three hours every day to the Gibe River which has resulted in not only body weight loss of the animals, but also the farmers spending fewer hours on farming, both of which have had negative effects on their agricultural production and overall livelihood. The rush for African farmland is reported by Olanya (2012) to have a hidden strategy of securing water access for large-scale commercial agriculture.

The loss of cultivation plots for teff and niger seed, grazing land and access to drinking water for cattle, as discussed above, has brought hardship to the local people's livelihoods, and food insecurity has increased, according to informants. Analysis of households' consumption expenditure and coping strategy revealed that 26–30 per cent of the households in Bako that have lost access to land have become food-insecure. They have adopted different coping mechanisms, such as eating less preferred but not necessarily less nutritious foodstuffs, even when cheap, skipping eating for a whole day, borrowing food from neighbours (which is considered a loss of dignity in the community) and consuming seed stock that has been set aside for cultivation in the following season.

Although investment creates employment, the amount and quality of the employment generated and its contribution to the livelihoods of the local people can be questioned. In an interview with employees working at the farm, it was stated that women in the Bako villages have very limited opportunity to earn cash income, regardless of performing different activities as housewives. The company has now created employment opportunities for women but the amount of income is too small to change their lives (Interview with two women and two male youths on 8 April 2012 at Karuturi farm). Indeed, wage employment on the Karuturi farms is highly insecure and seasonal. During the survey period, there were between two and three hundred casual workers, thirteen security guards, seven supervisors, nine tractor drivers and helpers and five machinery operators. Wage rates are comparatively low. The rate paid to daily labourers was ETB7 (US$0.36) per day during the first three years of operations before it increased to ETB12 (US$0.63) in late 2011, despite the going rate in the surrounding area being ETB20 (US$1.04) per day. However, during pre-implementation engagements, the company committed to paying up to ETB30 (US$1.56) a day. Even for skilled workers, wage rates are low. For example, the company pays ETB 800–1200 (US$41.7–62.6) per month for tractor operators, while the going rate in the district ranges between ETB 2000 and 3000 (US$104.3–156.4) a month. For this reason, the most desperate people are those who have taken up jobs at Karuturi.

Community members predominantly participate in low-skilled employment, for example as security guards and plantation workers, despite having the potential to perform more skilled duties. Data from the district revenue office showed that between 30 and 44 Indian expatriates in the 2010–11 period were engaged in on-farm employment. During our field research, thirteen Indian expatriates were working as tractor operators and field supervisors. Employment for local people is menial and seasonal. Interviews (with two women and two male youths at Karuturi farm on 8 April 2012) revealed the lack of clear procedures of hiring and firing, illustrated by the firing of fourteen employees in 2012 for no known reason. The employment is at low wages and lasts for three to four months a year, and the employees receive only a short break for a midday meal. They are often mistreated by their Indian supervisors. They explained that the wage employment is not life-changing but they now have no other options, having lost the land that they used to use to produce food and generate income.

Women were found to work as domestic servants and in other manual jobs but were reported to be abused by Indian supervisors. Two women (interviewed on 26 March 2012) reported that they were fired without receiving their wage income because of their rejection of sexual advances by an Indian supervisor. They also reported that another woman who used to serve as a housemaid was raped by an Indian supervisor and then fired. She became pregnant and dependent on her family. It was alleged that the Indian who abused her travelled back home before the woman received any justice. In general, the Indians and the youth with better technical skills received most of the benefits generated from the limited employment by the company and the rest of the local people have generally lost out from the land transfer.

The field survey showed limited technology spillover from large-scale commercial farms to smallholder farmers in the vicinity. The company achieves low yields, and poor farm management is widely commented upon. If the value of the maize produced by Karuturi is compared with the value of the teff that was previously produced by the smallholder farmers on the same parcel of land, the smallholder farmers generated a far more valuable crop. Reacting to the misuse of the land by Karuturi, the five FGDs (held with farmers in Goromitti, Oda Gibe, Chittu and Worabile villages on 3 April 2012) revealed that smallholder farmers achieve maize yields of around six tons/ha on the red soils that are suitable for maize cultivation as compared with the company that achieves low maize yields on the black soils with poor drainage. The farmers are of the opinion that they have very little to learn from the poorly performing large-scale farm, and believe that the company has misused the black soils which are suitable for teff and niger seed cultivation and grazing of cattle.

In Bako, Karuturi converted grazing land scattered with fig and acacia trees to maize cultivation. The perception of the local people was that the clearing of the trees brought significant changes to the micro-climate of the area. Participants of the five FGDs in the four villages mentioned above said that the fig and acacia trees scattered over the grazing fields were used for ritual purposes, shade for humans and cattle and for community gatherings. After the trees were cleared by Karuturi, the local people experienced a rise in day temperature and lost shade for ritual and community gatherings. The negative effects of large-scale farming are also reported by Shete (2011).

The case of Karuturi in Gambela
In the case of Karuturi in Gambela, the land acquired by the company has been a source of pastureland and wild products for the local people. The limited jobs created by the company were mostly taken up by immigrants who came from the highland parts of the country, especially from Wolaita Soddo and Jimma areas. During peak season in 2013, Karuturi farm in Gambela created unskilled wage employment for 735 individuals. The daily wage rate was ETB35 ($US1.86) and the majority of the workers were from outside the villages. Expressing their dissatisfaction with the limited job opportunities they received from the farm, the local youth (part of the discussion held at Ilia village on 23 April 2013) said that they were engaged daily as unskilled labour, with low wages which are not life-changing. They compared themselves with immigrants whom they perceived to be preferred by the company and obtained better-paying skilled jobs. Their experiences ran contrary to their expectations of better paying skilled jobs.

Of the total general workforce, 14.9 per cent were from the villages in Gambela and the remaining 85.1 per cent were from regions outside Gambela. During the same period, skilled and semi-skilled employment was created for 226 individuals, 32.9 per cent of whom were from different districts within Gambela Regional State and the remainder from other regions. While labourers from the region were mostly engaged in security, weeding and harvesting activities, those from the highlands were mostly involved in machinery operations, surveying, supervision and time-keeping activities. Women at the Ilia maize farm have participated in maize harvesting activities.

Technology transfer, the other benefit envisaged from large-scale farming, has not materialised in Gambela. Karuturi is cultivating maize and sugarcane, but the major livelihood strategy in the region is extensive livestock production with very limited crop production. Inclusive business models (contract farming and outgrower schemes) that may increase the chance of technology transfer from big farms to small farms are not well developed in the region. Participation of Karuturi in community development activities in Gambela Regional State was another unrealised outcome. The local governments of Makuey and Itang Districts expected Karuturi to contribute to the construction of social and physical infrastructure. One view expressed was that the farm is a business enterprise governed by the profit motive, meaning that it cannot invest its resources in infrastructure development for the community while it is in the initial stages of its operation. (Interview with the manager of Karuturi farm at the Ilia site on 22 April 2013.)

Karuturi is blamed for significant environmental damage as well. It bulldozed indigenous tree species at the Ilia site as well as pasture lands to make way for a maize and sugarcane farm at the Jikawo site. It diverted water from the Baro River to its sugarcane farm, aggravating flooding in the area. Elderly respondents (interviewed in Bildak and Ilia villages) raised these negative environmental impacts of Karuturi's operations, saying that the indigenous Anuak at Ilia village used to collect different non-timber forest products as sources of food and income, but had now lost these to the land development by Karuturi. Flooding is aggravated in Bildak village due to the construction of diversion canals, and the local people are afraid of more flooding that will pose serious environmental problems and shortage of pasture in the future.

Another environmental concern is the likely conflict of large-scale farming with wildlife resources. Gambela National Park, which has not been officially gazetted, partly overlaps with the lease concession of Karuturi farm. The park is known to be home to the endangered shoebill stork, the Nile lechwe antelope and the white-eared kob antelope. The world's second largest mammal migration is found here with hundreds of thousands of animals crossing the South Sudanese border through the Boma-Jonglei landscape and returning to Gambela when the weather is right (HoAREC 2013). Three scouts working for the Gambela National Park (interviewed on 27 March 2013) said that 'wild animals are seen in the Karuturi farm and we expect conflict between the farm and the wildlife resources'.

The politics of land investments in Ethiopia

What then can we learn from these cases, and the wider Ethiopian context? Emerging from these two cases, as well as the wider context, are two themes: first, the role of the state, and second, the importance of contest and resistance. Both feed into a new politics around land investment in areas being targeted for land-based investment.

The Ethiopian government played a key role in attracting foreign large-scale farming with its open-door policy of land transfers since it considered the rush for farmland as more of an opportunity than a threat. It provided various incentives such as tax holidays, duty-free import of machinery and loans from the Ethiopian Development Bank. For example, an ETB1.3 billion (US$71 million) loan was provided to a total of eleven companies that acquired 212,715ha of land to establish their large-scale commercial farming operations. Karuturi Global alone received an ETB127.3 million (US$6.64 million) loan from Ethiopian banks, of which ETB65 million was provided by the overdraft facility of the state-owned Commercial Bank of Ethiopia (Table 4.2).

Table 4.2 Loans provided to large-scale farms by banks in Ethiopia (2008–2013)

Company	Land Size (ha)	Origin of Company Founder	Loan Size (in millions)	
			ETB	US$ equivalent
Karuturi Agro Products plc	111,700	Indian	127.27	6.64
Basen Agric. & Industrial plc	10,000	Ethiopian	122.00	6.36
Lucci Farm plc	4,003	Ethiopian	106.49	5.55
CLC (Spentex)	25,000	Indian	124.39	6.49
White field	10,000	Indian	90.15	4.70
Verdanta Harvest	3,012	Indian	89.49	4.67
BHO	27,000	Indian	45.48	2.37
Tracon Trading	5,000	Ethiopian	46.47	2.42
Ruchi	25,000	Indian	410.07	21.38
Green Valley Agro plc	5,000	Indian	99.90	5.21
Agro Peace Bio Ethiopia plc	2,000	Israel	109.24	5.69
Total	227,715		1,370.97	71.48

Source: authors' compilation of records at the AISD. Base data derived from company records.

Based on these data, Ethiopian banks provided ETB6,020 (US$314) for each hectare of land acquired by the investors, far more than the rent payable. This means that the state is subsidising large-scale commercial investors with both cheap land and credit. A key question here is whether, if smallholder farmers and pastoralists were to receive similar support, it would be possible to transform and commercialise the agricultural sector as envisaged by the government.

In 2014, Karuturi was reported to be bankrupted and a foreclosure statement was issued by the state-owned Commercial Bank of Ethiopia after the company failed to repay the loans (*The Reporter* 2014; 2015). Although it is too soon to speculate about the long-term consequences of the failure of this particular case for the transfer of large tracts of land in Ethiopia, the government has decided at least for now, not to lease out more than 5,000ha in any single deal, and the availability of additional plots is to be decided based on performance. Further, the case proved that the process of land identification by the AISD did not examine the suitability of the land for farming, nor did the land deal process consider the capacity and farming experience of the investor in conditions subject to water-logging as in the case of Bako Tibe and Makuey districts. The collapse of the investment also occurred after the company had cleared indigenous trees in its Ilia site that are important sources of food and livelihood for the Anuak, and such environmental damages are irreversible.

Emerging agrarian struggles
The second theme is the emergence of conflict and resistance. Sporadic conflicts between the local people and commercial farmers are common in Bako Tibe District in Oromia in response to the loss of land to the investment. Two unsuccessfully organised efforts have been made by the community to date, including when members of eleven mutual aid groups in the community contributed ETB200 (US$10.43) each and sent a five-member delegation to His Excellency Abadula Gemeda, former President of Oromia Regional State, to communicate their dissatisfaction with the project. The representatives were not allowed to meet the President, but were sent back to their villages, with the government labelling them as 'community agitators'. Secondly, more than 400 farmers in the district signed a petition and submitted it to the district administration asking for compensation for the lost land. Expressing their efforts and the responses they received from the district administration, the five members of the discussion conducted at Goromitti village on 3 April 2012 said that the local people elected representatives to speak for their request for their land rights. However, this was ignored by the local government. Those who resisted the land transfer to the company were detained, labelled as anti-development activists and released after they received serious warnings about taking any similar action in the future.

The district government argues that the farmers in Bako Tibe District who claim to have lost their land to Karuturi have no statutory land rights and cannot claim compensation. A woman who has a land certificate at Goromitti village (Interview conducted on 7 April 2012) said that 'Karuturi has constructed an airplane runway partly on my plot of land to which I have a certificate but I didn't receive any compensation for it'. Similarly, 'the company has dug boreholes on the plots of farmers with land certificates but no compensation is given to these farmers'. Discussions with the manager of Karuturi farm in Bako Tibe also confirmed that the company faced severe resistance from the local people in different forms including theft and abduction of Indian staff. The district Justice Office confirmed that there had been theft and abduction cases filed by the company against the local people, with security guards working at the farm being called as witnesses. However, the suspected detainees were released on bail because the security guards were not willing to testify. Further, a letter of complaint was also filed, addressed directly to His Excellency, the then Prime Minister Meles Zenawi, on 30 March 2010 about the life-threatening warnings that the Indian employees were receiving from the local community.

The local community in Gambela Regional State did not welcome the Karuturi company as they believed that its arrival signalled a threat of dispossession from their ancestral lands and livelihood sources. The company was in conflict with villagers in Palbol *kebele* (neighbourhood) due to the construction of diversion canals to take water from the Baro River, which led to the community members losing their farmlands. Similarly, community members in Lar village elected a four-member committee to present their dissatisfaction with Karaturi to the district authorities, but got no response. The members contributed money and sent their representatives to the regional government to present their concern to the Head of the State. But again, they did not get any response to their complaints.

Conclusion

Agricultural investment can be an important source of economic growth when tapped properly. Land transfer for large-scale agricultural invest-ment in Ethiopia, however, has been done hastily without adequate and careful mapping of the land resources available. The land identification process ignored previous land uses and the suitability of the land for the proposed type of farming. The fact that the local community does not have statutory land rights does not necessarily mean that the land is vacant. Since land belongs to the state under Ethiopian law, the local people are easily dispossessed of their livelihood resources. This is especially problematic where land is owned customarily by the local people, as in the lowlands of Gambela and the highlands of Oromia.

Land is a key resource for peasants and agro-pastoralists in both sites. The land acquired by the Karuturi company had been used previously by the local people as a source of food and livelihood. Livestock, which is a key livelihood source, is negatively affected and land for the production of crops that are important for food security has been transferred. Little attention has been given to consulting the community before the decision to transfer the land. Competing claims over land and the land transfer processes have brought conflict between investors and the local people. Sporadic conflicts occur because different levels of government back investors while the local people have no recourse in law. While protests of various sorts have occurred in response to the land transfers, they have not brought significant changes so far.

Large-scale farming was expected to contribute to transformation of the economy and to the commercialisation of smallholder farming. This was to be achieved through technology spill-over and inclusion of smallholder farmers in the value chain from production to consumption. But, as this chapter has shown, with the current business model of mechanised, plantation-based large-scale farming adopted by Karuturi, there is very little contribution to the agricultural transformation of the country. The employment generated was very small and technology spill-over to smallholder farmers and agro-pastoralists effectively absent.

5

Land Deals & Pastoralist Livelihoods in Laikipia County, Kenya

JOHN LETAI

Introduction

Laikipia County in Kenya's central drylands has had a long and complex history of land appropriation and reorganisation, from the colonial era to the present. Even so, the scale of recent and proposed land deals is unprecedented. These involve a range of foreign and domestic investors and different interest groups. Former commercial ranch managers are setting up as brokers and identifying absentee title holders in order to persuade them to consolidate their holdings and sell. The latter are responding to the new rush, which is fuelled by foreign entrepreneurs, diplomats, aid workers and some white Zimbabwean farmers. The buyers of these consolidated plots are now fencing their ranches, which has created tensions with the Maasai pastoralists and other herders who have been using this land for generations.

Thus, over recent years, there have been significant changes in the pattern of land ownership in Laikipia. These changes are set against a background of profound inequalities in land ownership and control: 40.3 per cent of land in Laikipia is controlled by just 48 individuals (as shown in the Ministry of Lands registry for Laikipia County in 2010). As this chapter demonstrates, contemporary changes in land ownership are not leading to better livelihood outcomes, particularly for Maasai pastoralists.

This chapter starts with a brief overview of the changes in land control in Laikipia from the colonial era to the present. It discusses the geography of land use and the patterns of inequality evident in land ownership and access. It then addresses the emerging rural livelihoods, food security and patterns of social differentiation that are compounding an already precarious situation related to access, use and management of resources. The chapter further explores the conflicts and resistance that have arisen as a result of land appropriation, and concludes by urging the government to address land issues in the county.

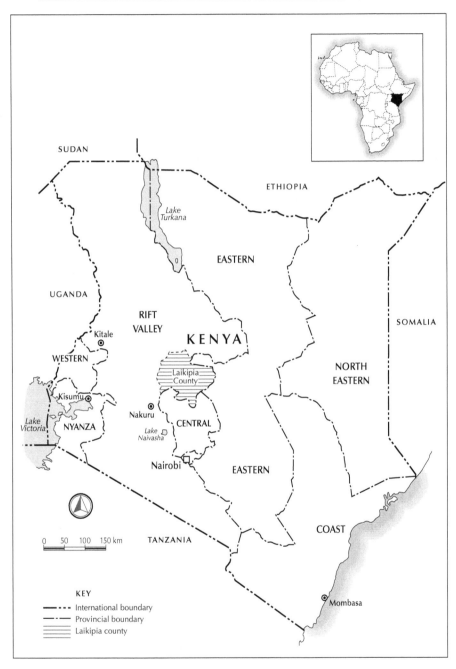

Map 5.1 Kenya, showing the location of Laikipia County

The chapter is based on many years working with pastoralists in the Laikipia area (Map 5.1), complemented by a detailed field study carried out between 2011 and 2013, which involved interviews with different stakeholders in the study area and beyond.

A short history of changes in land control in Laikipia

The history of land expropriation in Laikipia can be traced back to colonial times when the British forcibly moved sections of the Maasai population from their grazing grounds around Nakuru and Naivasha in the Rift Valley (Letai and Lind 2012). The first of these waves of land appropriation occurred in 1904 when the Maasai chief Oloibon was manipulated into signing a treaty with the colonial government, leasing the community's most fertile land to the British (Lindsay 1987).

This led to the creation of two Maasai reservations: the northern reserve in Laikipia and the southern reserve along and even straddling the border with Tanzania (Rutten 1992). The northern reserve to which the Maasai were confined was later found to be disease-free and suitable for dairy and beef ranching. This led to another negotiation in which almost all the Maasai were moved to the southern reserve. In exchange for the loss of the northern reserve, the southern reserve was slightly extended to accommodate the new group of Maasai (Hughes 2006), while the entire northern reserve was given to the Europeans for settlement.

By 1906, the Maasai had lost two-thirds of their best and richest upland drought refuges and prime seasonal grazing lands that were later dubbed the Kenyan White Highlands. However, with European demands for more land, a Second Maasai Treaty was negotiated in 1911. With some minor changes and extensions, this Treaty demarcated the southern reserve (now Kajiado and Narok districts) as the area legally under Maasai jurisdiction. These treaties were to endure so long as the Maasai as a group existed, and prohibited Europeans or other settlers from acquiring land in the Maasai settlements (Rutten 1992).

Some Maasai did not make the move to the southern reserve and remained in Laikipia. Those who stayed behind were predominantly from Mukogodo, the north-eastern frontier of Laikipia bordering Samburu (Herren 1987). Because they were in conflict with other sections of the Maasai they feared moving to the southern reserve. Instead they affiliated themselves to the Yaaku who resided in the Mukogodo forest. The British settlers were initially sympathetic to this group and they were able to move widely across the plateau, even though later the entire area was registered for settler occupation as the White Highlands, with most of the land granted to British ex-service men from the First World War (Hughes 2006)

In the 1930s, colonial officials made their first moves to control the movement of the Maasai in Laikipia Plateau. In 1934, a Native Reserve was demarcated on the north-eastern edge of the plateau to cater for the Maasai who remained behind. This was followed by the Native Trust Lands Ordinance of 1938 that excised native lands from crown land and vested these lands in a Native Lands Trust Board. This enactment initiated the expropriation through law of pastoral lands, even though in practice most pastoral lands continued to be utilised for customary livestock-keeping systems and were administered under customary institutions.

At independence in 1963, the Maasai land that was appropriated by the British did not revert back to them, but instead was taken over by the independent state. President Jomo Kenyatta took steps to resettle landless Kikuyu people in these territories rather than returning them to the Maasai. The process of transferring British-owned land to Kenyan peasants through the British- and World Bank-sponsored Settlement Transfer Fund Schemes (STFS) was riddled with corruption. Kenyatta saw to it that most of those who benefited were his close Kikuyu cronies, a few non-Kikuyu senior civil servants and other politicians (Kenya Land Alliance 2004b). Using the political and economic leverage available to them during the Kenyatta regime, the Kikuyu took advantage of the situation and formed many land-buying companies. Throughout the 1960s and 1970s, these companies facilitated the settlement of hundreds of thousands of Kikuyu in the Rift Valley. Those who did not settle in their lands used their title-holdings as collateral to acquire loans from the Agricultural Development Corporation and other institutions, leading to cases of absentee landlords with vast areas of land remaining open and unoccupied in the Laikipia plateau.

However, as a result of land pressure in the group ranches and inward migration from neighbouring districts (now counties), Maasai, Samburu and Pokot herders began settling as squatters and grazing on this land in the 1970s. The absentee landlords are at the centre of the current land rush in Laikipia and form part of the wider push to appropriate land, while reducing the space available for pastoralist herders to graze their livestock and support their livelihoods.

The geography of land tenure arrangements in Laikipia

After independence, white-owned large commercial ranches were retained as part of the agreement between the colonial government and the new government under Kenyatta. However, there were settlers who opted to leave or sell their land to the Kenyatta administration, and this land was either settled by Kikuyu under land purchase company arrangements or registered as state land. Pastoralists were later settled in group ranches within the area that was demarcated in 1934 by the colonial government as a Native Reserve on the northern edge of the plateau to cater for Maasai that remained behind. The creation of group ranches was carried out under

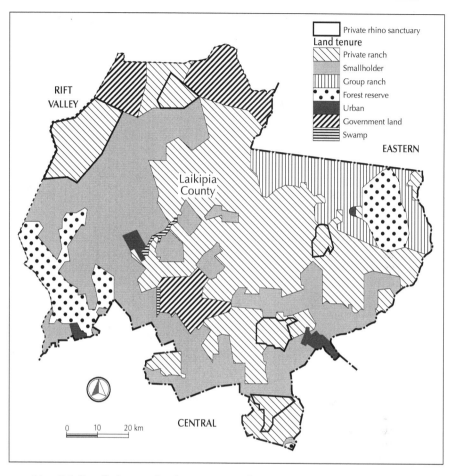

Map 5.2 Detailed map of Laikipia County, showing land tenure and uses

the World Bank Livestock Development and Rangeland Management Project that was meant to provide development interventions and social services to group ranches and other drylands, including the northern grazing blocks within the trust lands.

This land-use arrangement was maintained up until the late 1990s when agitation for reforms under a new Constitution began. By then, much of the government land reserves had already been grabbed by senior government officials, politicians and military officers. At the same time, Maasai elites had also acquired large land holdings. However, most Maasai continued to live on group ranches in the north-eastern region of Mukogodo. A few pastoralists had, however, moved out due to population pressure or increasing aridity in the group ranches, to buy land or settle as squatters on the smallholder farms that were divided by the Kenyatta regime among the Kikuyu community. Map 5.2 shows a land-use map of Laikipia County.

The area is unique and represents a multiplicity of diverse land-use types, linked to different tenure regimes, which can be differentiated as follows:

Large-scale ranches. There are 48 large-scale ranches which occupy huge tracts of land totalling 531,581ha, representing 40.3 per cent of the total land area (according to the Ministry of Lands registry in Laikipia County in 2010). Most of these ranches were acquired during colonial times and legislation governing their ownership was carried over into Kenya's Independence Constitution under the land transfer agreement between the colonial government and the Kenyatta regime.

Large-scale farms. Somewhat smaller than the ranches are 23 large-scale farms that occupy 1.5 per cent of Laikipia. These are farms held mostly by individuals from Central Province who acquired them during sub-division after independence, or by land-buying companies that opted not to sub-divide them but use the land collectively as collateral to access bank loans. The farms belonging to land-buying companies include Suguroi (2,572ha) and Murera (787ha). Some of the farms held by individuals are still in the hands of descendants of colonial ancestry such as Jenning (1206ha), George (1,119ha) and John C. Cardoville (612ha). Other individually-owned farms reflect the political family dynasties of independent Kenya, and include Rware (17,664ha), held by former President Kibaki's family; Mathenge (1817ha), held by a former provincial commissioner in the Kenyatta and Moi regimes, and Mohammed (620ha), held by a former Chief of General Staff of the armed forces of Kenya.

Group ranches. There are 13 group ranches representing 7.5 per cent of the total land area. All are found in the northern dry part of the district and are occupied by pastoralists who use them for communal grazing. However, some of the group ranches such as Il-ngwesi, Kijabe, Lekurruki and Koija also have wildlife conservancies and tourist lodges situated on them. In terms of tenure arrangements all group ranches remain intact and have not been sub-divided, but are faced by growing population pressure that is putting a strain on natural resources.

Smallholder farms. There are 122 smallholder farms that were initially large-scale farms bought by people who later sub-divided them into small holdings of 2–5 acres. They account for 27.2 per cent of the land area. These farms represent three categories of farmers: those who bought and settled as a result of land pressure on their ancestral land; those who bought for speculative purposes in the hope of rising land prices and those who bought and used them as collateral to access bank loans. It is mainly the first group who live on these farms and practise subsistence agriculture, while most of the other two groups are absentee landlords with their land remaining idle and unoccupied. However, over time, pastoralists have moved on to these lands, settling there either as squatters or, in a few cases, even formally buying them.

Government land. Much less significant than the private categories of land mentioned above are 36 pieces of land owned by the government, which represent only 6.58 per cent of the land area. These are used for purposes ranging from military training grounds to holding grounds for disease quarantine of livestock and rangeland research by state institutions.

Forest reserves. There are two categories of forest reserves, comprising four disturbed forest reserves and eight intact forest reserves, representing 2.8 per cent and 4.8 per cent of the total land area respectively. Disturbed forests are those which have been exploited for firewood or timber production, and where the government now allows cultivation on condition that farmers plant trees and integrate crops in between. Intact forests are those that are earmarked for conservation where limited human activity is allowed; they are managed by communities or privately.

The influence of land tenure arrangements

All these different land-use and tenure arrangements described above sit uneasily alongside each other. In recent years there has been an intensified pattern of land transfer and consolidation, resulting in a shift in the overall agrarian structure. Much of this is happening under the radar, unrecorded by official statistics, while on the ground, key tensions are emerging.

Large-scale ranches, for example, are each consolidated and fenced as one unit. However, data from the Ministry of Local Government, where these ranches pay land rates, show that 16 of the 48 ranches are internally sub-divided into small units of varying acreage, with each unit having to pay land rates of varying amounts depending on their sizes. For example, Oljogi farm has ten units, Olpajeta has nine and Mpala farm has seven. According to discussions with local government officials, there are two main reasons for such parcelling of the land. One is that the parcels were each previously owned by individuals but have been amalgamated and consolidated in practice, if not on the cadastre. Many of these transactions are carried out at an individual level without necessarily involving the Ministry of Lands. The other is that ranches have been intentionally sub-divided in order to fall within a lower tax threshold and so pay lower property rates.

There are claims that some of the parcels within the bigger ranches have been sold to people of European origin, some coming from Zimbabwe while others are retiring people from Europe who want to settle in Kenya and find their way into property ownership in Laikipia through their social networks. There has been a sudden emergence of palatial private residences on portions of these ranches, pointing to the growth in population of settler elites in the area. Some of these new buildings are high-class tourist destinations built without government knowledge. It is alleged that tourists pay their fees in Europe and come to occupy the premises as private residents, thus avoiding taxation. This process of creating smaller units within big consolidated farms points to a process of land redistribution, but in a manner that deepens inequality, as these sub-divided portions are acquired by a social class of wealthy and well-connected individuals who live in enclaves with little relation to the surrounding economy and operate in isolation from the rest of the communities of Laikipia.

The large-scale farms meanwhile are rapidly being acquired by big multinationals for horticultural purposes, particularly near permanent water sources. Here, they have started to grow crops for export to the European market. Examples of such farms include Marania and Kisima Farm along the slopes of Mount Kenya, Olpajeta in the Eastern part of the Aberdares and Borana in lower Ngarendare. This conversion of land use has denied local communities access to these lands, which they previously accessed for grazing, and reduced the total acreage available to support their daily livelihoods. The large multinational companies are mainly carrying out wheat farming and high-quality beef cattle ranching, and include Homegrown, Batian, Vita Cress, Agri-Fresh Kenya Horticulture Exporters (KHE) and Agricultural Auto-growers Association of Kenya (AAAK). These farms are managed and run by a well-established class of business-oriented individuals who exploit both internal and external markets. They also engage local communities to grow horticultural crops to increase their market share by providing seeds, equipment and external services in the form of loans that are deducted at the end of the harvesting season, leaving the farmers with a net income. They also provide employment to peasant farmers who work as farm labourers alongside their own production, and pastoralists who are mostly employed as security guards.

In addition to commercial agriculture, land deals are being driven in particular by investment in the tourism and wildlife conservation sector. This is exemplified by the marketing discourses of the Laikipia tourism industry:

> Laikipia is widely accredited as Kenya's premier safari destination with ideals and practices that are at the forefront of conservation tourism. The combination of abundant wildlife and exceptional scenic beauty provides the basis for Laikipia's unique and high quality tourism. Here, wildlife is free to roam between ranches, conservancies and community lands into Kenya's northern rangelands (Laikipia Wildlife Forum, quoted from Letai 2011: 8)

Laikipia is the county with the highest number of wildlife in Kenya outside protected areas. Most of the ranches have been turned over time into wildlife sanctuaries. Group ranches have also been converted into community wildlife conservation trusts. Laikipia equally has more tourist facilities than any other county in the interior of the country. Some of the lodges are classified as world-class and are exceptionally luxurious, attracting British royalty among others, as the tourist promotion material emphasises:

Laikipia has some of Africa's most luxurious safari lodges and camps. The county also hosts the highest number of community-owned lodges in Kenya. Laikipia offers the freedom and space for visitors to walk, ride, cycle and camp amongst a great diversity of wildlife and wild landscapes, against the dramatic backdrop of Mount Kenya. A sense of belonging through engagement with Maasai guides, hosts and local people, is something that visitors take home with them. (Ibid.)

Some of the big ranches and large-scale farms have also developed research foundations or conservation trusts through which they receive funding from individuals or institutions with an interest in conserving wildlife species, particularly endangered species like the African black rhino, wild dogs, the African Grevy's Zebra and other species. Other ranches have created partnerships with neighbouring group ranches to initiate joint conservation projects and community eco-tourism lodges. Projects other than conservation include community-based healthcare outreach programmes, curio shops, tree nurseries and pasture bulking for sale to ranches with livestock during the dry season.

Large-scale ranches are also used for British army drills and training exercises. Initially only Lewa and Mpala farms were used for military exercises, but of late other farms like Oljogi, Oldaiga, Ole Naisho and Olpajeta have come to include British military activities on their farms. Of the large-scale farms, eleven are used for military activities by the British Training Unit in Kenya (BATUK). However, there is no information on this new form of land use, although interviews with employees of these ranches and casual labourers employed within the training camps confirmed this expansion of military activity.

Within the smallholder farming areas there has been a process of land consolidation. In recent years, a group of brokers has emerged who collude with the Ministry of Lands officials to consolidate these small parcels into large holdings and sell them to foreigners, mostly of European origin. The buyers may not be aware of the complexity of such dealings as they buy the land only to discover later that people are living there whom they then find difficult to move or evict. This scenario has provoked conflict. For example, in 2008 pastoralists invaded part of the Kimugandura ranch and pulled down the fence, protesting against the private enclosure and fencing of an important water source. They later went to court claiming ownership of the land as some of them had lived there since 1980, which is more than the 12-year period after which Kenyan law protects one's right to occupy and be able to claim the right of ownership. As of 2014, the case was still pending.

In contrast, group ranches have not been affected by the process of land changing hands. All of them are intact and occupied by pastoralists who practise communal grazing. However, most of them have limited ground cover due to intensive grazing and the increasing frequency of drought which does not allow them to regenerate to their full potential. Increases in population pressure and the reduction in the smallholder farm areas due to consolidation and sale have put pressure on pastoralists' access to resources, as they used to negotiate dry season access in these areas.

Government land was among the first to be grabbed in Laikipia. Only five of the 36 government outspans have not been privately enclosed and are managed by government parastatals, such as the Agricultural Development Corporation (ADC) or the National Youth Service (NYS). It is mostly senior government officials, politicians and military personnel who have grabbed these lands. Other government lands have been grabbed by managers of large-scale ranches in places where these areas neighbour large-scale ranches. Most of these lands have also changed hands since the individuals acquired them. Meanwhile, most of the forests are used for herding, with livestock driven into the forest during the day and out in the evening, except for Mukogodo forest where pastoralists live, and many of the intact forests are occupied either by pastoralists or conservation groups such as Lewa Wildlife Conservancy. The management of these forests is under communities or conservation groups with the Kenya Forest Service playing an oversight role.

Overall, the changing geography of land use and control, influenced by alliances of local and international elites, is having a major impact on pastoralists in particular. The consolidation of smallholder farms, the selling-off of land parcels within large ranches and the conversion of farms to horticulture are resulting in less access to grazing and water for pastoralists, particularly in dry seasons and during droughts. The next section explores the changing implications for livelihoods and food security, and the processes of social differentiation that are emerging as a result of the upsurge in land deals.

Rural livelihoods, food security and patterns of social differentiation

Land deals are compounding an already precarious situation related to access, use and management of resources. Declining grazing land undermines pastoral livelihoods. Large-scale farms and consolidated smallholder farms reduce pastoralists' access to common pool natural resources. Compared with neighbouring counties, Laikipia is a buffer zone that receives moderate rainfall and does not suffer severe droughts except in exceptional cases such as 2009. Over time, many pastoralists have moved from Baringo, Samburu and Isiolo counties to settle in

Laikipia in search of water and pasture for their livestock. At the same time, land pressure in Central Province is forcing subsistence farmers to move and settle in Laikipia, where they undertake rain-fed agriculture sometimes combined with small herds of sheep, goats and cattle. This has led to competition for space and resources. It has meant that, with slight changes in the weather pattern, these groups suffer heavy losses of livestock and crop failure, as they have limited options to adjust, leading to a general increase in vulnerability.

This scenario is exemplified by the following quote from one of the peasant farmers who migrated to Laikipia from Nyeri in 2007 due to land pressure and the need to explore new areas for expansion:

Since I moved to this area in 2007 there have been three seasons of rainfall failure. I have been tilling and planting the land in the hope that it will rain and crops grow to maturity so that I can harvest enough food to meet our household needs. However, our hopes have been dashed and we have limited options to survive. The few livestock I purchased with the last crop harvest in 2007 have not been spared either, I have lost four cows and eight sheep and I am now depending on my small farm back in Nyeri to provide for my household food needs as well as crop supplement for the two cows that I was left with. This continuous cycle of drought is neither good for me nor my neighbours, the pastoralists, who entirely depend on livestock keeping.[1]

Pressure on the land has consequences for the environment. In the areas people have moved into, there is a lot of degradation. Forests have been exploited for charcoal burning, firewood or timber production as people's different options to meet their household daily incomes. In the pastoral areas, sustained grazing of the rangelands due to constrained mobility has led to degradation and the invasion of unpalatable species. In some group ranches such as Makurian, Munipicha and Morupusi, land has been degraded due to sustained grazing over the years. *Opuntia* cactus has, as a result of intensive grazing, invaded the area. The species is unpalatable for livestock and leads to death when grazed.

In contrast to this scenario of scarcity, elsewhere in Laikipia there are areas that have plentiful resources but have been fenced, and people and their animals have been excluded. Some areas have been appropriated for wildlife and tourism and are stocked with animals at low rates. The availability of resources behind the fences results in conflicts, as those without land and resources encroach on wildlife areas and poach. This situation is compounded by the increasing frequency of drought.

In 2009 the worst drought in a generation gripped the drylands of Northern Kenya. On the Laikipia plateau stretching to the west of Mount Kenya, Maa-speaking herders were pushed to extraordinary lengths to support their livestock and sustain their livelihoods, as their land became completely bare and degraded with nothing for livestock to salvage.

---

[1] Interview with Mary Gathoni, Lamuria; Laikipia County, September 2012.

Meanwhile, in the neighbouring commercial ranches there was plenty of standing hay for the livestock and wildlife roaming the open ranges. This forced pastoralists to resort to illegal night grazing and forceful invasion of the commercial ranches, leading to arrests and increase in conflict between ranchers and pastoralists. This situation persisted for several weeks, but after negotiations it was resolved that the ranchers should accommodate a few livestock from the pastoralists, while the rest were moved to the Mount Kenya forest, where they suffered.

However, the pressures arising from land deals have also seen the building of alliances between different user groups, including the formation of joint conservation initiatives and user associations. Their aim is to conserve and use sustainably available resources. Joint access is negotiated for groups, so reducing conflict. For example, there have been strong partnerships between Lewa Wildlife Conservancy and Il-ngwesi group ranch and Borana and Lekurruki Wildlife Conservancy in the running of community lodges and the management of biodiversity conservation and wildlife eco-tourism. Lewa and Borana conservancies provide managerial, technical and donor-sourcing support, while Il-ngwesi and Lekurruki provide community scouts, land and pasture/water resources for wildlife, as well as space for undertaking eco-tourism, photography and enjoyment of natural scenic features.

Without access to resources in their own areas, pastoralists and farmers are increasingly seeking alternative options to support their livelihoods elsewhere. This includes moving to the Mount Kenya forest in search of pasture and water for their livestock and farmers setting up irrigation plots or moving around undertaking trade. These new livelihood options provide opportunities for some, but they may also result in new conflicts in areas where people move to.

Land deals affect both women and men. Consolidation of smallholder farms into single units often denies women access to key resources such as water and firewood. Fencing off big commercial ranches with electric fences has compounded the problem further, leading to a decline in common resources. Women have to walk long distances and a lot of time is spent fetching these resources. This has a negative impact on women as time for other activities is reduced and they have to strain to complete their daily chores. During drought, women have to spend three to four hours fetching water from far-off areas. This limits the time available to attend to other family needs including cooking, cleaning and tending the homesteads.

Most of the land deals are done in secret and do not involve community members. The deals are too technical and legalistic to be understood by local communities. In most cases, community responses to the deals occur after the deals have been sealed and their reaction is to the physical actions being taken on the land, such as demarcation. The high level of illiteracy among pastoralists contributes to loss of land as they have no means of protecting it from changing hands.

The result is that land deals create winners and losers. Those who gain include big commercial ranchers (most of them from a white colonial ancestry), multinational agribusiness corporations, foreign elites in search of holiday/retirement destinations, Kenyan politicians – with all three independent Kenya presidents owning land in Laikipia for example – and senior government officials and military officers who have been allocated government land. Pastoralist elites who are part of the government are an emerging social group who own land and have isolated themselves from poorer herders. These elites have played a big role in appropriating land at the expense of their communities, and are investing in horticulture, beef ranching and conservation tourism themselves.

Influencing land transfers and access to resources is done via the District Land Board where key elites control processes of land acquisition, investment and general development. They determine the different investment opportunities and set benchmarks for developing these lands while also mapping out the different livelihood options existing in the county. The groups that control the District Land Boards thus also control the land transfer processes. Many of the deals are done through private arrangements by signing a Memorandum of Understanding between the different parties without having to go through the legal and procedural requirements, as most of the deals involve non-citizens in search of tourist and retirement investments who can only own land under leasehold and not freehold.

Conflict and resistance

As already noted, the land deals in Laikipia County have involved multiple conflicts. The acquisition of land that pastoralists have been settling on as squatters and the resulting evictions have been a major cause of conflict and struggle. These struggles take different shapes and forms ranging from court cases, demonstrations and illegal night grazing to open resistance, sometimes leading to bloodshed and loss of life and property.

Attempts at land consolidation on smallholder farms occupied by pastoralists have been challenged, and when trying to settle the new owners of the land have found themselves unable to occupy it. Cases of such deals include Lekiji farm, East Laikipia farmers and Kimugandura where pastoralists have refused to move and instead gone to court to challenge the legality of the move, arguing that they should have been given priority to purchase the land.

In 2009, similar struggles were witnessed as a result of the ravaging drought that decimated pastoralists' herds. Many moved their animals to the Mount Kenya forest where they had access to pasture and water. Here, they had to negotiate with farmers living on the edge of the forest to kraal their animals at night and drive them to the forest during the day as the law does not allow people to live in the forest. Those pastoralists who remained in the lowlands neighbouring the big commercial ranches, where there was plenty of pasture and water, engaged in illegal night grazing, which led to arrests of pastoralists and strained relations between them and the ranchers. It took interventions by local leaders (chiefs and councillors) to negotiate with the ranchers to accommodate some of the pastoralists' herds on the ranches so that they could survive the drought and sustain their herds, and to hedge against the risk that those animals driven to the Mount Kenya forest might die of the cold weather conditions there.

This arrangement, forged in the midst of crisis, therefore led to relationships being built and mechanisms designed to resolve conflicts among different categories of people within Laikipia: between commercial ranchers and pastoralists and between pastoralists and farmers. These more cooperative relations extended far beyond the drought period as these groups were able to visit each other after the drought and exchange gifts during festive seasons to cement their relationships.

In 2000, another drought year, pastoralists in Laikipia invaded private ranches, which attracted international attention, echoing events in Zimbabwe at the time (Mathenge 2000). The invasions were repeated in 2004, when Maasai activists argued that the 99-year leases granted under the 1904 Maasai-British Agreement had expired and that pastoralists were entitled to graze on the enclosed lands that had once belonged to them. In response to the invasions, the provincial administration ordered the General Service Unit (GSU), a paramilitary wing of the Kenyan security forces, forcibly to remove the Maasai herders who entered the ranches. Some Maasai leaders alleged to have incited the invasion were detained and arraigned in court, charged with invasion of private property. Similar invasions were witnessed in 2008 during the post-election violence and again during the 2009 drought, although on a smaller scale. Instead of outright invasion, pastoralists have also resorted to night grazing, often leading to clashes with security personnel, including those security guards employed by the ranches, and several arrests.

Other forms of political struggle involved the eviction of pastoralists from two ranches: Eland Down, owned by former President Moi and sold to a nature conservancy, and Lekiji, a ranch apportioned by Oljogi Limited and given to three pastoralist elders who were its former employees. In both cases, the owners have sought court orders and mobilised security personnel to evict pastoralists who had refused to move. In the process of eviction, four people, including two police officers, lost their lives at Eland Down, while one person lost his life in the case of Lekiji. Property of unknown value was also lost. Many women and children were displaced and a lot of time was spent reconnecting them with their families.

In response, pastoralists went to court to block the eviction and to seek orders permitting them to stay within the ranches. In September 2013, a Parliamentary committee on land and natural resources visited the people of Lekiji in the company of the National Land Commission to take stock of their claims to that land. The team also visited the National Land Registry to verify the ownership of the land in dispute. According to an interview with the local Member of Parliament, the Honourable Sarah Lekorere, this process confirmed that the Lekiji ranch belongs to the pastoralist community living there and that those claiming this land had acquired an illegal title deed that was not found within the registry of the National Land Commission. However, as of 2014, this case was still pending, and the pastoralist complainants were waiting for the court to authenticate the validity of the title deed before they move ahead to demarcate the land.

Conclusion

The evolving situation of land deals in Laikipia County is a result of long-term processes of expropriation stretching back over more than a hundred years. Given the rapid rate at which land is changing hands and the involvement of pastoralist elites in land appropriation processes, there has emerged a struggle between different groups within the pastoralist community, with some gaining, while the majority lose out.

The land deals are fundamentally reshaping pastoralist livelihoods, with the result that, for many, the future is uncertain with the entrenching of vulnerability amongst these groups. These processes have led to dispossession of pastoralists' land and its consolidation among domestic elites and international investors. This is leading to growing pressure on existing resources resulting in increases in vulnerability and poverty. Consolidation of land results in resource deprivation, scarcity and often competition among different rural user groups, particularly where resources are managed and utilised as common property resources under customary tenure systems.

The recent land deals are putting additional strain on local communities' production systems. For pastoralists, this process is constraining mobility and reducing the amount of resources available for their livestock. These land deals also lead to conflicts between the different user groups, as shown in instances of violence and evictions leading to loss of life and insecurity on the part of investors.

As a result of the disparities in land ownership between those in power and the ordinary people, and the recent spate of appropriations and acquisitions, there has been a big clamour within Kenya, including by pastoralists, for the government to address land issues in the country and at the national level. There have been calls to address historical injustices in land distribution and access, and efforts have been made to influence the government to implement provisions of the National Land Policy of 2009 and the Constitution of 2010.

There is arguably no more appropriate place to do this than in Laikipia County, where long-standing inequalities have been exacerbated by recent land deals, driven by local elites together with outside investors. Wildlife conservation, eco-tourism and livestock marketing by some of the big commercial ranches have been linked to community-based initiatives through partnerships and joint ventures. However, the degree to which these address fundamental structural inequalities is questionable. They may help to reduce agitation for implementation of provisions of the Constitution and National Land Policy temporarily, but the conflicts and associated struggles over land for pastoralists, in a context of heightened concentration and enclosure, continue with no signs of their being resolved in the near future.

6

Land Deals in the Tana Delta, Kenya

ABDIRIZAK ARALE NUNOW

Introduction

In recent years, large tracts of land within the Tana Delta and the adjacent districts have been set aside for industrial-scale farming, biofuel production and mining. This is threatening the livelihoods of both pastoralists and farmers. In addition, settlement schemes have taken up some of the most important dry season pastures within the Tana Delta and communities from outside the pastoral areas have been settled there to undertake crop farming. Individual/private ownership of land is increasingly replacing communal ownership. The consequences have included increasing levels of food insecurity in the area.

This chapter reviews the TARDA-Mumias partnership that is envisaged to alienate an additional 40,000ha of land within the delta, and is likely to displace more than 25,000 people in 30 villages from their traditional land. The chapter further provides some insights into other land acquisitions in the delta such as from Bedford Biofuels Inc., Tiomin Kenya Ltd, Galole Horticulture, Mat International and the Emirate of Qatar.

Ethnic conflict between the Pokomo farmers and the Orma and Wardei pastoralists that led to violence and destruction of lives and property in 2012 may have been the result of envisaged resource scarcity triggered by these proposed deals. While the local farmer and pastoral communities were united in their resistance to the deals, they were later set against each other politically, resulting in the loss of almost 200 lives during the conflict that ensued. The manipulation of local communities by government officials and national and local political elites is clearly discernible.

The data for this study were obtained between 2011 and 2013 through a mixture of approaches. Unfortunately, detailed information on land deals is lacking due to the unwillingness of both government and businesses with vested interests to fully disclose information. The research is therefore a picture pieced together from a variety of sources. These include a review

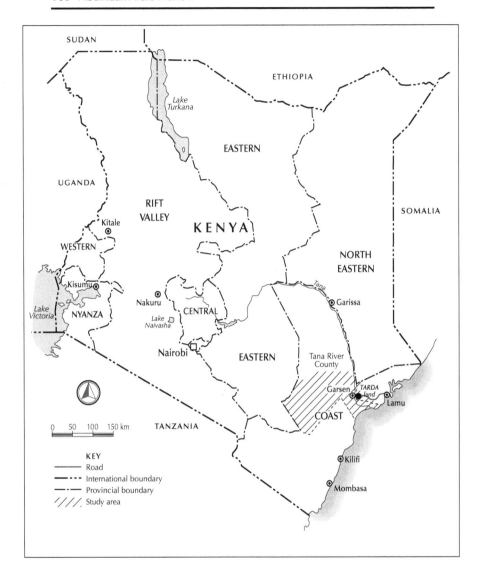

Map 6.1 Kenya, showing the location of Tana Delta and TARDA land

of the existing literature, focus group discussions and interviews with key informants including government officials, community leaders, and elders who were able to discuss their perceptions of the projects taking place in the delta and the alienation of their land.

Tana River County: background

Tana River County falls within the arid and semi-arid lands of Kenya. It is one of the six counties that make up the coast region and is extensive (38,694 km²) but sparsely populated, with an estimated population of 240,075 people, including the Pokomo farmers who are Bantus (44 per cent) and the Orma and Wardei pastoralists (52 per cent) who are Cushitic (KPHC 2009).

The Tana Delta forms a natural habitat for an enormously diverse collection of flora and fauna, providing a fallback grazing pasture for livestock during the dry season (for the pastoralists), while its waters are used for agriculture (by the Pokomo farmers and agro-pastoral Orma) and, to a limited extent, fishing (by both the farmers and the pastoralists), as well as by some communities including the Luo and the Luhyia around Lake Moa. The Tana Delta has a high prevalence of poverty at 76 per cent, compared with a national average of about 50 per cent (KPHC 2009).

Historically, land among pastoral communities could be acquired through a number of means including peaceful penetration and forceful military conquest. Whenever a particular community occupied an area that was not inhabited by any other community, it became that community's own territory. In such a situation, the community had a collective obligation to defend the newly acquired land from any rival group. In the event of such forceful conquest, the weaker group usually emigrated from its land and the conquerors became the new owners of the land by virtue of their conquest and subsequent occupation. However, in the case of peaceful penetration, the arriving community becomes a client of the original inhabitants (in a relationship known as *sheegat),* while waiting to gain numerical strength in order to lay its own claim on the land and gain it forcefully (Abdullahi 1997).

In the Tana Delta, the pastoral Orma and Wardei migrate according to the wet and dry season, with new grazing pastures becoming fertile while other lands are left to regenerate and provide necessary pastures in the future. However, when the integrity of the cycle is undermined or distorted by restriction of access to those most needed grazing and other land-based resources, the entire foundation and structure of the pastoral economy collapses.

The history of land deals in the Tana Delta dates back to the colonial period when many people were dispossessed of their ancestral lands and pushed into native reserves from where their labour could be extracted to create surplus capital for the colonial settlers. According to Kenya

Land Alliance (2004a) most of those who were displaced never got back their land after independence due to the limitations of the post-colonial land resettlement policy. After independence, the Kenyatta government opted for a land resettlement programme based on what was known as a 'willing-buyer willing-seller' system instead of land repossession and redistribution. However, there were two serious shortcomings that undermined the land resettlement programme as planned. Firstly, the market-based system required mobilisation of financial resources which many of the landless could not manage. Secondly, corruption in the land resettlement programme allowed the political and economic elites in the Kenyatta government to acquire land that was meant for the landless (Kenya Land Alliance 2004).

After Kenya attained independence, all land hitherto designated 'crown land' became 'government land', and the previous native reserves became 'trust land'. After independence, only a small portion of the trust land was adjudicated, with communities being given their tenure rights. However, throughout the Kenyan coast where the Tana Delta lies, indigenous communities' land rights were never adjudicated. More than 96,000 indigenous people living in the delta are still viewed as squatters in their own ancestral land. This makes them vulnerable to land grabs by powerful individuals or institutions that use the district administration and the Ministry of Lands officials to acquire title deeds for lands occupied and/or tilled by others. It is common to find an individual or a firm with a title deed for large tracts of land in the delta that they may never have seen at all.

The delta holds more than 50 per cent of the national potential for irrigable land (Temper [undated]). Seasonal flooding keeps the area fertile throughout the year and the local communities adapt their livelihood activities to such flooding patterns. The delta also provides critical pastures for hundreds of thousands of cattle for the Orma pastoralists and, to a lesser extent, the Wardei. During the dry season, the Orma and many other pastoralists from neighbouring districts rely entirely on the delta for pasture, sometimes reaching a peak of over 3 million head of livestock (as was the case during the 2009 drought), some of which remain within the delta throughout the year.

Besides pasture, the delta supports small-scale crop cultivation by Pokomo farmers and some Orma agro-pastoralists, growing crops such as maize, beans, peas, bananas, mangoes, cassava, melons and several vegetables, on small plots of less than 0.8ha each. In addition to the farmers and the pastoralists, the delta also supports minorities of hunter-gatherer communities, collectively known as the *Wasanya*.

The farming and pastoralist lifestyles are often in competition. This has created periodic conflicts between the two communities, particularly during the dry season. These conflicts occur whenever the Orma pastoralists try to access the river to water their livestock because the Pokomo farmers have occupied virtually all the river bank, leaving no space or access corridors for pastoralists to access the river water. The recent bloody conflicts in the area that claimed over 100 lives in 2012 have their genesis in competition for scarce resources, and have been exploited by political players.

It is in this context of resource competition and widespread poverty that land deals are emerging in Tana River County. It is no surprise therefore that these have become highly contested, generating varied narratives around them.

Land deals in the Tana Delta

The national development narrative often underpins the current land alienation in the Tana Delta. In Kenya, the national government advances such narratives as job creation, enhancement of food security and attraction of foreign direct investment to justify its support for the deals. In the development policies of the Kenya government, the Tana River catchment plays an important role in the national economy through provision of electricity – both for domestic use as well as for industry (Government of Kenya 2011).

The idea of converting much of the lower Tana Delta to large-scale irrigation projects has been in place since the 1980s when large-scale irrigation projects were established in Bura and Hola, but both were failures. In a project funded by the Japanese government from 1987, 16,800ha of land was irrigated, but was characterised by very low yields, and was finally abandoned after the destruction of its main embankment by the El-Niño rains of 1997. Although some 2,000ha of the project are now being rehabilitated, none of its structural deficiencies have been resolved (Mbonde 2012). Closer to the mouth of the River Tana at Kipini, a Greco-Kenyan company planned to put up a large-scale shrimp farm in the 1990s but the project was halted by the then President of Kenya, Daniel Moi, in 1992 (Duvail et al. 2010).

However, the recent wave of land acquisitions is unprecedented, both in scale and in nature. They are also unprecedented in the amount of the land acquired or sub-leased – more than 160,000ha for the production of *Jatropha curcas* and over 40,000ha for the irrigation of sugarcane. The origin of the investments is mainly from private international actors rather than bilateral or multilateral donors. The following sections examine different contemporary land deals in the delta. A number have been proposed, but, as with past projects, many have failed or are yet to be implemented, with only a few projects having reached the implementation stage.

TARDA-Mumias Project
This is the only large-scale project that has so far been implemented. The proponents of the project are a government owned company (parastatal), Tana-Athi River Development Authority (TARDA), and a private company

specialising in sugar production in western Kenya, Mumias. The land targeted for the project is located between the two main river branches and just upstream from the tidal freshwater wetland of the delta. The amount of land for this project is about 40,000ha, most of which is categorised as 'government land', while a relatively smaller portion is registered as 'trust land' (now 'community land' under the Constitution of Kenya, 2010). In 1995, TARDA received a 10-year lease in order to implement a development project on the floodplains of the delta. In 2007, TARDA sold it to the private company for the implementation of an 'integrated' project while retaining a 15 per cent stake. This sale occurred after the 10-year lease period had expired, and this irregularity was brought to the attention of the court in a subsequent court case. Consulting firms carried out an Environmental Impact Assessment (EIA).

TARDA was established in 1974 through an Act of Parliament as an integrated river basin development agency. Mumias, on the other hand, was started as a government agency in the late 1960s to produce and manage sugarcane production in western Kenya. However, it gradually changed shareholding and hence ownership through privatisation and withdrawal by the government of most of its shares in the stock exchange. Currently, it is a private company whose stocks are quoted and traded at the Nairobi Stock Exchange.

The initial proposal when the project first emerged in 2007 was for an estate of 16,000ha and an outgrower component of 4,000ha, making a total of 20,000ha. However, in the EIA and in a public notice issued in 2007 as part of the EIA, the proposed project was described as covering 33,000ha, including the outgrower land. It may be assumed that the additional 13,000ha cover additional land uses proposed as part of the project, including a sugar factory, an ethanol production plant and areas set aside for livestock. The amount of land owned by TARDA is somewhat shrouded in mystery since the government had allocated TARDA 28,680ha of mainly 'government land' in 1995 but TARDA was given a title deed for 40,000ha in 2009. The confusion is further compounded by the fact that TARDA already has several thousand hectares to the north of the C112 Garsen-Lamu road on which it grows rice, known as the Tana Delta Irrigation Project (TDIP). According to the EIA report, this land is not going to be converted to sugarcane production, but doubts were expressed by knowledgeable local informants during our study. The proposed sugar project is known as the Tana Integrated Sugar Project (TISP). It is believed that TARDA has a lease for the land until 2040, based on the 45-year lease granted in a letter of allotment in 1995. However, the local communities maintain that the initial lease granted in 1995 was for only ten years and the change to 45 years by TARDA was fraudulent and that they would contest it in the highest court in the country.[1] The EIA report on the TARDA-Mumias project refers to this

---

[1] Wario/Hashaqa, A. pers. comm. 2013.

land as a 'concession'. Although the terms of the lease are unknown to us so far, TARDA will be required to pay certain land rates or other fees for the land.

The legal status of the land after the deal raises more questions than answers. The role and contribution of each of the two partners (TARDA and Mumias) is quite unclear. According to information gathered from interviews and activist materials, TARDA was given an allotment letter in 1995 (ref. 106796/8), while it obtained a title deed fourteen years later, in April 2009 (ref. 28061). However, we could not find any official record of this. In Kenya, a letter of allotment is a necessary but not sufficient condition of proof of ownership of land – one must also obtain a title deed. As a fully government-owned corporate entity, the legality of TARDA's ownership of the land has been questioned on several grounds, namely: whether TARDA, as a regional development authority, should have been given the land (part of which was held in trust for the community) for commercial development; whether the lease is sound, given the long lapse of time between the award of the allotment letter in 1995[2] and the title deed in 2009; claims that TARDA did not pay the requisite fee of Ksh3 million (US$64,000) to the Commissioner of Lands for the land in 1995; and the change in the size of the land from the 28,860ha in the allotment letter of 1995 and the escalation of the same to 40,000ha in the title deed granted in 2009. Furthermore, the EIA report reveals that the 4,000ha that have been earmarked for outgrowers is government land that would need to be adjudicated by the government before plots for the contract farmers could be demarcated.

The proposed project will use land that was used by Pokomo farmers and the Orma and Wardei pastoralists for grazing their livestock. Traditionally, both the Pokomo and Orma do not have individual ownership of land but individuals only enjoy usufruct rights in cultivating the land or grazing their livestock. Both maintain that the land is 'theirs' and was used by previous generations of their respective communities.

The land consists of a large expanse of floodplain grassland. During the wet season, the southern part of the project area floods and the floods retreat during the dry season, leaving behind a vast rich grazing area that is used by livestock driven by pastoralists from drier areas. The main crops cultivated in the delta include maize, cowpeas, mango, green ram and bananas. Fishing is common in the river tributaries, ox-bow lakes and water pans – although our interviews reveal that these are drying up in recent times.

Water abstraction for the proposed project raises fundamental concerns of equity and sustainability. The meandering Tana River flows through the proposed project area. Large-scale efforts to redirect the river

---

[2] The fee payable to the Commissioner of Lands is computed and communicated in the letter of allotment – which usually contains conditions for expiry if the payment is not effected within the given period – usually within six months. Thus, no title deed can be given without payment of the land rates.

from where it forks into Matomba Brook have failed, and there are water pans that get filled during the wet season. The project would abstract water at Sailoni for the irrigation of sugarcane. Many of the impacts of the sugarcane project will be the result of a decrease in the water flow and water quality, and the exclusion of vast areas (beyond the project boundaries) from the beneficial biannual flooding.

Many of these impacts are expected to occur in the estuarine and coastal zones downstream of the project – an area not covered by the EIA for the project. The brackish water, the estuarine and coastal fisheries, and eventually the health of the mangrove systems are all intimately linked with the freshwater flows (Negelkerken et al. 2007). The nursery functions of the mangroves and the estuary may actually present one of the greatest economic values of the Tana Delta, values that will certainly be seriously affected by any substantial reduction of the flow and/ or damage to the mangrove stands. The floodplain forests will also be affected by the increased abstraction of water to meet the water demand of the project (Duvail et al. 2012).

The loss of the prime floodplain grazing land of the delta would likely constitute another major impact of the project. Spatially, the project covers the central part of the delta where the lushest pastures are found. On available maps, the boundaries of the irrigation project are defined by geographical elements such as the main Tana River branches, and the project is said to cover 22,000ha. However, reproduction of the spatial extent of the project using georeferenced satellite images reveals that the project area actually covers 38,000ha (ibid.). The EIA report proposes as a mitigation measure for the pastoralists the opening up the dryland grazing of the extensive Galana ranch. But that area, which has pasture only during the rainy season, cannot compensate for the loss of the dry season pastures that are confined to the central floodplain of the delta. In any case, the recently launched 480,000ha irrigation project of Galana ranch further takes away the terraces around the project. Both the nomadic pastoralists as well as the wildlife dependent on floodplain grazing (e.g. topi, buffalo and elephant) will suffer substantial reduction of their earlier pastures.

For many years during periods of drought, the Tana Delta has been the safety net for hundreds of thousand head of cattle ranging between the Somalia border and the Tsavo East National Park. Pasture will be lost in the actual land set to be converted by the project and in the form of the areas that will be excluded from flooding by the embankment and by the reduction of flooding frequency that results from the abstraction of a substantial proportion of the flow.

Our interviews as well as observations reveal that other activities including fishing and flood-recession agriculture will suffer damage due to the water abstraction by the proposed sugar project and the consequent change of water regime in the delta. While some of the areas will be affected directly because of inclusion in the project area, others

Box 6.1 Resistance to the TARDA-Mumias Project

- 1988: TDIP project starts, financed by the Japanese government.
- 1994: Residents of Wema village (Salama location) take TARDA to Mombasa court over grievances with the TDIP rice irrigation scheme.
- 1995: TARDA obtains an allotment letter for 28,860 ha of delta land, perhaps in response to the complaints raised in the court case.
- 1997: The TDIP project collapses following the El Niño flooding.
- 2006: TARDA sells mature sugarcane grown in the Mumias sugarcane experiment on Block A of the TDIP land at Kulesa.
- 2006: NEMA insists on EIA for the proposed sugar project.
- November 2007: EIA for a joint TARDA-Mumias proposal to grow sugarcane is published by HVA International and MA consulting.
- June 2008: NEMA provides a project approval letter, awarding a conditional licence for an initial rice-growing phase (5,000ha of the planned 28,860ha). NEMA clarifies that, following a public hearing, it has decided to split the project into phases I and II: neighbour pastoralists grazing areas to be developed later, in consultation with the local community, and based on the success of phase I.
- July 2008: Local communities and NGOs (including Tana River Pastoralist Development Organization, Tana Delta Conservation Organization, East African Wildlife Society, Centre for Environmental Legal Research and Education and George Mulama Wamukoya) take NEMA, Mumias Sugar Company, TARDA, Tana River County Council, the Commissioner of Lands and the Water Resources Management Authority to court. They obtain an injunction from Malindi High Court whose effect was to 'stop Mumias Sugar from making any further decisions regarding implementation of the sugar project' and halt the Tana River County Council from taking action in respect of the land that was the subject of the suit, the Commissioner of Lands from issuing a title deed for the land and the Water Resources Management Authority from issuing water abstraction permits to the Tana Integrated Sugar Project (TISP).
- July 2008: The Minister for Regional Development Authorities visits Tana Delta and states that the project will start in six months.
- April 2009: TARDA obtains a title deed for 40,000ha of land in the Delta.
- June 2009: Kenyan High Court rules in favour of the developers on a technicality.
- September 2009: TDIP project is rehabilitated by the government as part of the Emergency Food Program under the National Economic Stimulus Program.
- August 2010: A new court case against TARDA, NEMA, Commissioner of Lands, Tana River County Council, the Attorney General and the Water Management Authority is filed by a group of farmers, fisher folks and pastoralists, plus the Lower Tana Conservation Trust, at the High Court in Nairobi.
- May 2011: Kenya's Prime Minister, Raila Odinga, tells Parliament that the proposal is being discussed with Mumias Sugar Company, but that there is some resistance among the local communities.
- May 2011: Mumias Sugar Company joins TARDA to defend the suit, while Kituo Cha Sheria, an NGO that provides legal aid to marginalized communities, joins as a party for the petitioners.
- February 2013: High Court in Nairobi rules largely in favour of the community petition that there is a need to have one agency to oversee the development of the Tana Delta, that TARDA (one of the respondents in the suit) should develop, with full participation of the local community as well as the agencies and other stakeholders who have interests in Tana Delta, short-term, medium-term and long-term land use development plans for the Tana Delta where the projects are to be carried out within 45 days of the ruling date. The Court further orders periodic reviews of land-use development plans for the delta.

will be affected indirectly due to the loss of pasture, fishing zones and farming opportunities. The EIA report forecasts the displacement of only fourteen families from Milimani village, which has been selected as the site for the sugar factory. However, our study paints a completely different picture, with populations in more than 20 villages being earmarked for displacement by the project. At the time of our research, residents of Gamba village had already been evicted in December 2010, while the villages of Onkolde and Galili were reported to have been served with eviction notices. Lebrun et al. (2010) point out that entire villages have been omitted from the EIA maps (such as Kikomo, Kipao and Onkolde), although they are all included in the project area. The EIA report describes these villages as 'squatter villages' who need not be consulted, hence the public hearings were held far away from these villages. Furthermore, the participants in the mandatory public hearings in the name of community representatives ended up coming from non-impacted areas. In some cases, it was actually reported that unemployed youth were paid and transported to the venue of the hearings so as to endorse the project (Lebrun et al. 2010).

The sugar project advances the dual narratives of creating employment and producing cheap sugar for local consumption. However, it remains unclear whether these jobs will be created and taken up by the local communities or not as had been experienced earlier in the case of the TDIP on which model the sugarcane project is said to be based. This is a huge investment, estimated at about US$332.2 million or approximately Ksh 24 billion as widely reported in the national media. Given the high indebtedness of TARDA, Mumias has been reported as looking for a strategic investor for this project, and only a small section of the land is being used for maize and rice cultivation.

There have been various forms of resistance by local communities and conservation organisations to this project. These initiatives and various milestones in the life of the TARDA-Mumias project are summarised in Box 6.1.

Bedford Biofuel Jatropha Project
The proponent of this project is a Canadian private company aiming at growing *Jatropha curcas* on 64,000ha of the terraces surrounding the floodplain of the Tana Delta. In May 2011, NEMA granted a licence for the *Jatropha* project for an initial pilot phase of 10,000ha.

The company negotiated directly for a 45-year lease agreement covering a total of 64,000ha of land and dealing with six separate ranch-owner committees (including Ida-sa Godana, Giritu, Hganda, Kibusu, Kitangale and Kon-Dertu). Within the 64,000ha, 40 per cent of the area was earmarked for planting *Jatropha*. The contracts corresponded to sub-leases – meaning that the ranch owners retained the original leases in their own names. Bedford Biofuel agreed to make all the payments necessary to regularise the leases and sub-leases; the arrears in land rents were paid to the County Council and the ranches' debts were taken over by the investor in order to get official clearance for the project.

The investor established a large nursery for the *Jatropha* in 2012 on 16ha of the land, but we found this abandoned by 2013, in what looked to us to be the closure of the company's activities. We were also informed that the company might have suspended its activities, but was planning to come back when some of the other investors in the delta started their operations.

Similar to the defects noted in the EIA for the sugar project, the Environmental and Social Impact Assessment (ESIA) of the *Jatropha* project was not only poorly executed but it also failed to factor in the costs of water and of the biodiversity of the delta. The report further maintains that the growth of *Jatropha* trees qualifies for carbon mitigation support, as the trees sequester carbon and also produce oil that will be used as replacement for diesel. However, this disregards the fact that 64,000ha of bushland and woodland forest will have been cleared to pave the way for the plantations. Furthermore, the delta was declared to be Kenya's newest protected wetland Ramsar site in October 2012, a development that should be taken into account by any development.

During the collection of views from the local communities on the project, it had the support of the Pokomo farmers who expressed high expectations. However, the leaders of the Orma pastoralists intimated that they were suspicious of the project, and indeed some of them refused to sub-lease one of the ranches to the company. Thus, by creating an imbalance between the Pokomo agriculturalists and the Orma pastoralists in support for the project, there is the risk of worsening the conflict between the two communities.

The proponents of the *Jatropha* project tend to see their initiative as 'a major change in land use from subsistence pastoralism and dormant wasteland to intensively managed plantation and pasture' (Duvail et al. 2012). The project aims to solve the so-called 'livestock problem' by introducing modern livestock husbandry skills among the pastoralists in the area. Yet this ignores the traditional pastoral practices. The *balo* terraces are an essential grazing area at the start of the dry season when the herds return from the hinterland pastures and are waiting for the flood to recede. Over the years, the Orma and Wardei pastoralists keep their cattle in these intermediary dryland pastures as long as possible, so as to save on the richer floodplain pastures as the dry season advances. Removal of such areas for *Jatropha* cultivation could have disastrous consequences (ibid.).

However, by the end of 2012, the project had only established a nursery, and by 2013, its activities had been suspended. This project met the fate of many biofuels projects negotiated at the peak of the biofuels boom. Agronomic, economic and social challenges have plagued such projects across Africa. However, even if no production is happening, uncertainties about land use and access remain, and many local informants are concerned that the company will return.

Other Land Deals in the Tana Delta
The post 2008 'land rush' saw many other companies strike deals in the delta. However, most of these companies have either withdrawn completely or put their activities on hold.

For instance, G4 Industries is a UK-based company that authorised an impact assessment for a project to grow oil crops on Wachu ranch, but the company was said to have pulled out in July 2011, citing technical issues with the soil type in the area, long-term effects of climate change on their potential production and the Government of Kenya's mismanagement of the delta's resources. Nonetheless, the company is said to be still holding the more than 28,000ha of land that it leased from the local community.

Mat International is a locally owned company targeting sugar production, and planned to take up more than 30,000ha of land in the delta and another 90,000ha in the adjacent Lamu County. However, the recent controversies over land allocations in Lamu and the cancellation of titles for more than 200,000ha of land in that area affected the proposed project in Lamu. In addition, the company has been silent about its proposal for more than two years and may have abandoned the idea altogether.

A Kenyan-owned firm, Galole Horticulture, claims to have been allocated 5,000ha of delta land by the Tana River County Council. However, the Council denies allocating any land to this firm and there is no official record of the land being transferred, but the grabbed land is already under use by the project developer who has cleared about 10 per cent of it so far and planted maize. When he clears the rest of the land and fences it off, more delta land will be lost and the grazing needs of the Orma and Wardei pastoralists will come under additional pressure.

Media reports in 2010 suggested that the Kenya government was in negotiation with the Emirate of Qatar to lease 40,000ha of land for a period of 80 years in exchange for a US$$3.5 billion loan to be used for the construction of Lamu Port. Although the exact location of the proposed project was never defined, the local communities point out that the only possible location would be somewhere in the central part of the delta.

Another company, Coastal Aquaculture Ltd, owns more than 13,000ha in the Lower Tana Delta. The ownership of this land came to public attention in the early 1990s when the company unsuccessfully tried to farm prawns. Chara and Ozi locations fall within the land owned by Coastal Aquaculture. It therefore came as a shock to the local communities when, in May 2011, auctioneers put notices in the national press to auction the land on which the communities have lived for hundreds of years.

Besides deals for land for agriculture, there are also deals linked to mineral exploitation. Tiomin Kenya Ltd, a company that was originally incorporated in Canada but the local subsidiary has now been bought by the Chinese, proposes to extract titanium from the sand dunes of the Tana Delta in an area of more than 20,000ha. Flow Energy, an Australian company, is currently proposing to explore for gas and oil in the delta.

FAR Ltd's takeover of Flow Energy (formerly Gippsland Offshore Petroleum Ltd) was completed in October 2011.

In addition to the large-scale land deals intended for capital investment, there are several private ranches in the area, the most prominent of which is a 32,000ha ranch, the Nyangoro ranch. This was appropriated by certain Orma elites so that they could keep their animals there and protect the pastures from encroachment. They are yet to be given documents of ownership but everyone knows the land as their ranch. There are also several other private ranches – each ranging between 12,000ha and 16,000ha. Most of these are owned by members of the Orma community who live in the urban areas of Nairobi, Mombasa and (some) outside the country, while others are owned by Pokomo elites. A feature of almost all the private ranches is that they are not fenced and access by the pastoralists for grazing their livestock is usually less controlled.

A recent government project on the terrace land of the Tana Delta, the Galana-Kulalu Food Project, is intended to bring more than 500,000ha of land under irrigation and aims at integrating crop farming, livestock husbandry and fish production for local consumption and export. The project is planned to bring 200,000ha under maize production, 80,000ha under sugarcane, 60,000ha in beef and game animals, 20,000ha in horticulture, 20,000ha in dairy animals and a further 20,000ha for growing fruits such as mangoes and guavas.[3] The land proposed for this project falls within the area where the Orma and Wardei take their livestock for grazing during the dry season and periods when they would be waiting for the delta floodplains to recede.

Land deals, livelihoods and local politics

The intensifying interest in land in the Tana Delta points to a multi-faceted 'rush' for land. A whole array of deals exists – some happening, some proposed, some speculative. All have impacts on local resource access and livelihoods, and have resulted in various forms of resistance.

Although the communities were initially united in organising resistance and in seeking legal redress for the expropriation of their most valued land, they turned against each other in 2012 with unprecedented violence and wanton destruction of lives and properties. The reluctance of the state in containing the spiral of violence between the farmers and the pastoralists suggests that the violence was possibly being used as a diversionary tactic by powerful people in government to distract the local

---

[3] Felix Koskei, Cabinet Secretary for Agriculture, *Coast Week*, March 10, 2014. This is a large project that is converting land formerly owned by a government agency, Agricultural Development Corporation (ADC), and to which the pastoralists from the Tana Delta had access during the dry seasons. The land making up Galana-Kulalu measures more than 700,000ha. Once developed, this dry season fallback pasture will not be accessible to the pastoralists.

communities from their united resistance to the land deals. The ethnic political competition resulted in the Pokomo farmers being dislodged from the entire political landscape of Tana River County where they have lost all the elective positions to a combined onslaught of the pastoralist Orma and Wardei.

While the elites of both sides had security for their land in the form of titles, the poor peasants and the pastoralists who had only customary tenure rights and who were dependent on the commons became those most affected by the loss of land and land resources. The chiefs and the politicians are usually the loudest in public but are often involved in the negotiations and cutting of deals with investors, thus weakening community bargaining and resistance. The resistance by the communities seems to have been largely successful since only two of the cases – the TARDA rice project and, to a lesser extent, the Bedford Biofuel – have so far started some operations.

Land deals are thus very much wrapped up in elite interests and local politics in the Tana Delta. Those who are educated and those in positions of power at the national and county levels who tend to represent their own interests and welfare rather than those of their communities often capture deals. Some of these elites have been accused of colluding with the external investors, or doing little in campaigning against them.

Conclusion

The Tana Delta has experienced various large-scale land investments by both foreign-based investors as well as government-owned agencies, with the resultant disruption of livelihood activities. Women and children are most affected, as traditional means of ensuring food security are undermined. However, most deals so far have not resulted in production on the ground. Many appear to be abandoned or put on hold. The political and economic uncertainties in the area have had a major influence, as have wider trends in commodity prices and demand for goods, notably biofuel. Yet, despite the land deals having resulted in few tangible results, they have still had an impact through changes in access to land and water.

Wider impacts have yet to be felt, but could be huge. In particular, the consequences of water abstraction in the delta will be far-reaching, with impacts on the biodiversity of the delta and the livelihoods of the local communities who are dependent on the delta for farming, fishing and livestock grazing. Due to their influence on wider ecological and economic factors, the projects have effects over an area much wider than the actual land appropriated.

There have been many efforts at resisting the alienation of land, including by the local communities and the conservation organisations, spearheaded by bird conservation organisations such as Nature Kenya and Birdlife International. It has been largely through their initiative that the delta was declared a Ramsar Site in 2012. Applauding the resistance to the land deals in the Tana Delta, Smalley and Corbera (2012) point out that many of the deals were not sealed as such and could be open to challenges in law. They further maintain that opposition from pastoralists and the formation of what they refer to as 'resistance coalitions' could be one of the primary reasons why many of the land deals in the Tana Delta have stalled. The designation as a Ramsar site obliges the government to prepare a management plan for the Tana Delta, in consultation with all stakeholders, and the sustainable management of the delta.

Although intense campaigns and advocacy by local communities and conservationist organisations, combined with shifts in the political and economic conditions for investment, have so far spared the delta any massive land alienation, numerous challenges still remain and until an agreed land-use framework for the delta is put in place, the future remains precarious and uncertain.

7

The State & Foreign Capital in Agricultural Commercialisation

The Case of Tanzania's Kilombero Sugar Company

EMMANUEL SULLE
& REBECCA SMALLEY

Introduction

As we walk from the village through the cane fields, several exhausted cane-cutters, carrying their *pangas*, trudge past in rubber boots. In an outgrower's field, the owner stands with a man holding a clipboard and two field workers, while a small yellow loader picks up bundles of burnt sugarcane and piles them on to a truck. A second truck, already half filled, sits stranded by a broken drive shaft. The owner says he is relieved to have harvested 35 tonnes in dry weather, but must still harvest the rest of his cane and then prepare his fields for the next season.

This is the sugar business in Kilombero in south-eastern Tanzania, where industrial agriculture has squeezed itself into a strip of fertile land between high mountains and protected parks and bushland. Once, villagers cleared that bushland to grow rice paddy; now it is contracted cane that dominates the landscape. Since the first sugar mill was established here 50 years ago, there has been constant development and change in outgrower operations. Now, at a time of renewed interest in Tanzanian agriculture as an investment destination, we looked to Kilombero for useful lessons and, as we show in this chapter, found dynamics of differentiation, accumulation and grievance that signal the likelihood of further contestation and change in the future.

Sugar has emerged as one of Southern Africa's most significant commodities, with profound economic, environmental, political and social effects. The region is undergoing a sugar boom, and Tanzania intends to become an important player. In 2012, the Tanzanian government announced plans to develop three to five new large sugar projects and earmarked a number of potential sites for their development (SAGCOT 2012). In 2013, plans were released for a further fifteen commercial deals in sugarcane farming (URT 2013: 18). According to our calculations, the sugarcane estates from those fifteen deals would, if implemented as planned, cover a total area of 329,900ha.

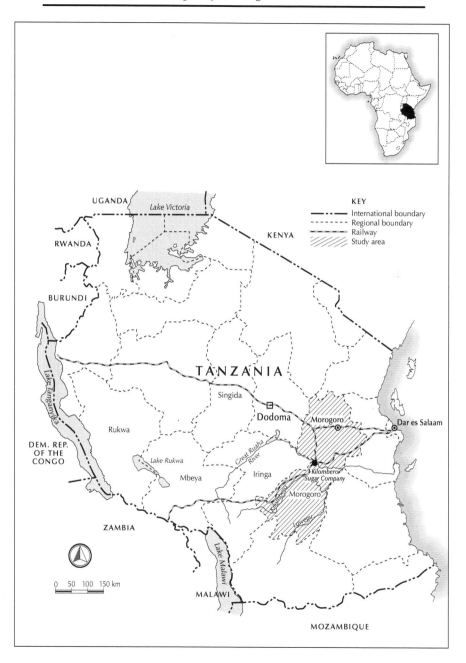

Map 7.1 Tanzania, showing the location of Kilombero Sugar Company in Morogoro District

These ambitious sugar plans form part of several initiatives by the government of Tanzania to encourage foreign direct investment in agriculture. Under the 'Kilimo Kwanza' (meaning 'agriculture first') strategy, it intends to establish large-scale plantations, ranging between 20,000 and 50,000ha, alongside smallholder schemes with irrigation and supporting transportation and marketing infrastructure. The focus is on the development of a Southern Agricultural Growth Corridor of Tanzania (SAGCOT) through public–private partnerships. As one of five pilots that ministries are implementing as part of a programme called 'Big Results Now', inspired by Malaysia's 'Big Fast Results' initiative, the Ministry of Agriculture will seek investors for a further range of agricultural developments in paddy and sugarcane.

Most past initiatives in Tanzanian agriculture have been focused on smallholder farmers. But the latest government efforts have widened to incorporate medium- and large-scale farming, as well as private-sector involvement. Already, over 20 agribusiness corporations have teamed up with the government and donor agencies (Cooksey 2013). Supported by the consultancy firm McKinsey and Malaysian experts, the Big Results Now programme is oriented towards commercial agriculture, with roles for the private sector envisaged throughout the value chains.

One way to combine smallholders with large-scale agriculture and agri-business is the nucleus–outgrower model, which links estate production with on-site processing facilities to small- and medium-scale contract farming. In 2012, the Ministry of Lands announced plans to prioritise investments that are based on the nucleus–outgrower model (Nshala et al. 2013), and it is central to the SAGCOT and Big Results Now visions of more connected, professional smallholder systems (SAGCOT 2011, 2012; URT 2013).

This chapter asks: can new land and agricultural commercialisation initiatives be used as opportunities to promote growth and reduce poverty and inequality in developing countries? And if so, how? Which institutional arrangements between investors and smallholders provide the best opportunities for benefit-sharing and for synergies between large and small farms? The chapter uses as a case study the nucleus–outgrower sugarcane operation in Kilombero, which is run by Kilombero Sugar Company Ltd (KSCL).

One of four sugar-producing companies in the country, KSCL was privatised in 1998 and is now majority-owned by the South Africa-based corporation Illovo Sugar. KSCL is located in the Kilombero valley in Morogoro Region, which is the site of a planned development 'cluster' within the SAGCOT corridor and has also been identified for development in the Big Results Now programme (see Map 7.2). The cluster would include a new sugarcane mill and estate alongside irrigated rice schemes and several citrus, banana and mixed farms. Government and SAGCOT-supporting organisations have been establishing village land-use plans in the Kilombero cluster area in order to identify potential farmland

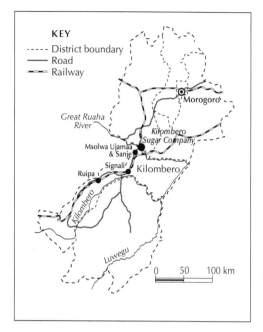

Map 7.2 Detailed map of Morogoro, showing Kilombero and outgrower villages

and facilitate its acquisition. As well as providing useful lessons for Tanzania's current plans for sugarcane development, studying the KSCL case can contribute to discussions about the value of contract farming as an appropriate investment model (Vermeulen and Cotula 2010a; FAO 2013; World Bank 2013).

Fieldwork took place in Dar es Salaam, Morogoro town and Kilombero and Kilosa Districts during 2013 and 2014. It involved 47 individual and group interviews with farmers (mostly but not exclusively sugarcane outgrowers) based in three villages – Msolwa Ujamaa, Sanje and Signali – and 40 interviews with national and local stakeholders, among them researchers, representatives of sugarcane grower associations and representatives of KSCL.

The sugar industry in Tanzania

Sugarcane is produced commercially in Tanzania by four companies in three regions: KSCL and Mtibwa Sugar in Morogoro; Tanganyika Planting Company (TPC) in Kilimanjaro; and Kagera Sugar in Kagera. Before Tanzania's independence in 1961, the sugar industry was run by private investors. Following the Arusha Declaration in 1967, the state nationalised privately-owned industries and estates. In the late 1990s, following the adoption of economic liberalisation policies, the sugar industry underwent major reforms. All four sugar companies were privatised between 1998 and 2001. In two cases – KSCL and TPC – the state retained 25 per cent of the shares; the majority of the remaining shares were sold to South African and Mauritian companies. With the other two companies – Mtibwa Sugar and Kagera Sugar – the state divested all ownership and sold them to Tanzanian investors with 100 per cent shareholdings. While TPC relies wholly on its own estate, the other three companies use outgrowers to complement production on their estates. As of 2010, they contracted a combined total of over 20,000 smallholder farmers cultivating sugar on an area of 23,300ha (Mlingwa 2009; Sulle 2010).

According to the Tanzania Sugar Producers Association, since privatisations between 1998 and 2001, over TZS813.5 billion (US$500 million)[1] has been invested in sugar production in the country (TSPA 2013: 2). The industry supports 18,000 people in direct jobs and over 300,000 family members and people employed in related businesses. Since privatisation, the sector has contributed TZS100 billion (US$ 61.5 million) in tax revenue and a further TZS4 billion (US$ 2.5 million) was invested in social services, mostly in sugar-producing areas (TSPA 2013: 2). KSCL alone is reported to have generated about TZS34.4 billion (US$ 21 million) for small-scale outgrowers in the financial year 2011/2012 (Kiishweko 2012: 1). Nevertheless, despite steps taken following privatisation to improve productivity and efficiency, domestic sugar production falls short of demand within Tanzania. In 2010, the four companies met only 60 per cent of the domestic non-industrial demand for sugar (Sulle 2010: 78).

The Kilombero Sugar Company

Kilombero Sugar Company began operating with foreign donor backing in 1962. Having gone through nationalisation in 1967 and subsequent privatisation in 1998, KSCL is now owned 55 per cent by Illovo, which is itself a subsidiary of Associated British Foods (since 2006); 20 per cent by ED&F Man, a commodity trader; and 25 per cent by the Tanzanian government. The company runs two irrigated estates and two mills, with one plant (K1) south of the Great Ruaha River in Kilombero District, and the smaller (K2) estate and mill north of the river in Kilosa District (see Map 7.3). In total, KSCL has 8,022ha of its own land under cane cultivation. It also receives cane for crushing from approximately 8,000 registered outgrowers, whose non-irrigated cane fields cover around 12,000ha within a radius of at least 60km (interview, KSCL staff, 28 September 2014). It generates its own electricity from bagasse (the fibre remaining after juice is extracted from sugarcane), and an ethanol distillery became operational in mid-2014.

[1]   Exchange rate: US$1 = TZS1,627 (Bank of Tanzania, February 2013).

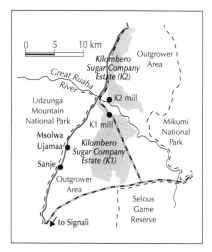

Map 7.3 Detailed map showing villages and the estates and mills of Kilombero Sugar Company

While Illovo has increased production over the past fifteen or so years since acquiring majority ownership, it is yet to meet the annual target for sugar production agreed with the government of 200,000 tonnes. It currently produces around 130,000 tonnes of sugar per year. Company officials say they would like to increase crushing capacity, but face a prohibitive business environment in which prices in the domestic market have been depressed by the importation of cheap foreign sugar (see Kiishweko 2012). In addition, KSCL is somewhat hemmed in by surrounding geographical features: Mikumi National Park to the north, the Udzungwa Mountains to the west and Selous Game Reserve to the east. Given the difficulties in accessing land for further expansion of its estates and processing facilities, the company's strategy so far has been to increase contributions from its outgrowers by persuading local people to cultivate more sugarcane on contract.

During the years of state ownership of Kilombero Sugar Company, the contribution made by outgrowers to overall production peaked at 42 per cent in 1978 but the provision of services to farmers fluctuated and the outgrowers' share never recovered after falling to 15 per cent by 1986 (Sprenger 1989, Mbilinyi and Semakafu 1995). When it took over, Illovo faced a situation of under-productive factories and disillusioned producers. 'The company was almost dead – no cane in the field, no salaries,' recalled one elderly respondent who is now an association official. 'Farmers had given up growing cane' (interview, 3 December 2013). As well as rehabilitating the mills, the company encouraged villagers to increase sugarcane production and convert fields from other crops. It offered incentives including cheap loans, road improvements and funding for clinics and primary schools (Kamuzora 2011). Previous campaigns to increase smallholder production were led by the state-owned company in the late 1970s and early 1990s, but the expansion since privatisation has been on a much larger scale (Sprenger 1989, Mbilinyi and Semakafu 1995).

Outgrowers

Today, outgrowers supply 43 per cent of the cane crushed by the two mills. They range from smallholders cultivating less than 0.4ha to a handful of large private estates. KSCL pays outgrowers for the weight and sucrose content of their delivered cane, minus the costs of harvesting, transport, processing, marketing and distribution. The price per tonne paid to farmers is estimated at the start of each season and adjusted if necessary at season's end in light of actual sale prices achieved for sugar and molasses. Outgrowers are paid a cut of profits through a division of proceeds system, with 57 per cent of KSCL's net proceeds going to the outgrowers and the company retaining 43 per cent. For the 2013/2014 season, the provisional price paid for farmers' cane, before adjustment for the sucrose level and actual sales, was TZS 58,000/tonne (US$35.6/tonne), down from TZS62,889 (US$38.45) in 2012/2013 – an 8 per cent decrease in one year. From this, farmers must pay around TZS20,000 (US$12.3) per tonne in deductions and at least TZS23,000 (US$14.3) per tonne in farming costs, assuming a yield of 28 tonnes per acre (69.2t/ha) as reported by some outgrowers,[2] leaving a net TZS15,000 (US$9.2) per tonne.

To sell their cane to KSCL, farmers need to join a local cane growers' association and register as outgrowers with the national Sugar Board, but do not have individual contracts with the company. Instead, a contract is signed between the company and the farmers' associations, which have proliferated from two in 1998 to fifteen by 2014. There are no additional conditions for participation as an outgrower other than to have a plot of land available for growing sugar. Under the contract, association farmers cannot grow sugarcane for any buyer other than KSCL, placing KSCL in a monopsony position.

A feature of the KSCL scheme which sets it apart from some other sugar outgrowing arrangements in Southern Africa is that the company offers very few services to its outgrowers. The farmers manage some of the tasks of producing sugarcane, either doing the work themselves or hiring labourers, and other tasks are done by private contractors engaged by the associations. When it took over in 1998, Illovo provided many of the services at cost to outgrowers, but between 2004 and 2006 the company transferred the provision of harvesting services to local private contractors, and built the capacity of associations to manage the contractors.[3] There are now around 26 private contractors serving the K1

---

[2] KSCL's average yield across outgrowers and estates was 78t/ha in 2012/13, against a Tanzanian average of 68t/ha (Rabobank 2013).

[3] This process was undertaken with World Bank financing as the Kilombero Business Linkages Project (see KBLP 2005).

and K2 areas. KSCL uses its own firm, the South African supply-chain company Unitrans, for operations on its estates. Outgrowers are concerned about the lack of sufficient technical and infrastructure support, but who should provide this remains unclear. The company is not prepared to finance irrigation for its farmers: 'Irrigation infrastructure for outgrowers is in the company's interest but we can't be a banker,' explained one of the company's staff (interview, 19 July 2013). KSCL also transferred some of its extension, lending, community development and infrastructure costs to a charitable trust, and some outgrower support measures are now being funded by foreign donors.

A negative consequence of the devolution of services is a lack of central oversight, exacerbated by ineffective third-party monitoring. There is widespread suspicion among farmers that sucrose is not measured fairly. A male outgrower said: 'Previously, we could achieve 10–11 per cent sucrose. Now it is 7–9 per cent. To get a higher level, you need to have a network and be able to bribe people at the factory.' He said he had done this himself several times. Small farmers would find it difficult to bribe, he explained, but if you're a large farmer you can make an 'arrangement' (interview, 3 December 2013).

Bribery is also reported in the system of harvesting. Probably owing to a combination of outgrower overproduction, transport-related problems and inconsistent crushing capacity at the mills, each year some farmers' cane is not harvested. The company estimates that in the 2012/2013 season, 65,000 tonnes of outgrowers' cane could not be crushed, alongside 100,000 tonnes of estate cane (interview, KSCL staff, 11 December 2013). The largest outgrowers have disproportionate representation and influence in the associations, and may be able to get their cane harvested sooner than the smallest outgrowers. A young man in Sanje village whose family cultivates 1.2ha of sugarcane described common challenges:

> There is a lack of trucks to transport sugar, and rains can also cause delays. If cane has been harvested but is rained on for two days, it can start to ferment. If the contractor delays transport, you get no compensation and have to do it yourself. (Interview, 4 December 2013)

Although the company depends on outgrowers, it does not seem convinced by the long-term viability of its very smallest producers. One official said that some are being bought out by bigger growers, and predicted that more will be squeezed out. 'We would not like to see that happen,' he said, 'but the economics will determine it' (interview, 11 December 2013). To address this, KSCL and its Trust introduced the concept of block farming, whereby individual cane fields are conglomerated and farmed as a block of an average 27ha. The idea is to provide small farmers with economies of scale and other benefits of group farming, including title deeds for the block and access to loans. The block farm system is a work in progress, with some leadership problems and low returns reported.

Labour

As of 2012/2013, KSCL employed 870 permanent staff and 2,073 seasonal workers (Illovo Sugar Ltd 2014). Nombo (2010) reports that during the peak cane-harvesting season (May to December), 5–6,000 casual labourers are recruited from other regions. For all workers, the company offers accommodation according to their status; some in staff houses, and most of them in labourers' camps. The seasonal workers are usually employed for seven months and most of them work as cane-cutters on the estates. Other workers are employed by Unitrans, KSCL's haulage contractor. According to respondents from the villages, few local people are hired for professional positions with the company, and it is easier to find manual work on local farms than on the estates.

The private firms that are contracted by associations to cut, load and transport outgrowers' cane also generate jobs. The work is seasonal and attracts migrants. They work four men to one acre (0.4ha), moving from farm to farm a few hours after the cane is burned, and are typically paid fortnightly or monthly, around TZS7,500 (US$ 4.60) per day. The national minimum wage for the agricultural services sector is TZS3,846.50 (US$2.36) per day.

Outgrowers themselves manage other tasks prior to harvesting. The wealthier the farmers, the more they outsource these tasks, although households constantly adjust their labour patterns in accordance with how much time and cash they have available. Outgrowers hire both local villagers and migrants who stay on after working on the KSCL estates. Labour supply is not an apparent problem.

Land ownership and livelihoods

The company owns the land of the estates and the mills. Before and after privatisation, there were some instances of eviction and disruption to local people's access to land. As it stands, the company has almost completely utilised its allocated estate land. As a means to increase production, KSCL is looking for more land in different villages, including some far from the current locations (interview, KSCL staff, 19 July 2013). Illovo is a key supporter of SAGCOT, and it is therefore possible that the company could expand within the planned corridor region.

Regarding the status of outgrowers' land, the farmers own or rent their sugarcane fields. Most of the land is under customary ownership, having come into farmers' possession through clearance, inheritance, village grant or unofficial private sale. While a farmer does not need a title deed to become a registered sugarcane outgrower, the demand for title is increasing.

Even without official deeds, there is an active market in the leasing of small sugarcane plots. This could be for a period of three years, but there is also a practice of renting for one harvest, which means that if the cane is not harvested, the land remains with the lessee for the next season. We met a man in Msolwa Ujamaa village who had rented out his 0.6ha field to raise money for school fees, which his sugar payment would not cover. He said outgrowers usually rent their plots to people from outside the village. 'Most small growers are poor,' he explained. 'They might get TZS1.5 million [US$922] for their sugarcane and spend that money on expenses, but then perhaps an emergency arises, so the obvious solution is to rent out their land to raise money. The problem is, you wait the whole year for a big payment, and it can't sustain the family' (interview, 12 December 2013).

KSCL's efforts at encouraging farmers to grow sugarcane have been remarkably successful. The current outgrower area of 12,000ha, which includes a handful of large private estates of 100ha or more, has grown from 4,450ha in 1997/1998. By 2005, the company became overloaded with cane produced in the expanded outgrowing areas, and had to introduce schedules and quotas for harvesting. Land was already becoming scarce in the 1990s and has become more so with the cane-farming boom and influx of people since privatisation. Historically, this part of the valley produced mainly millet, which by the 1960s had been largely overtaken by rice and maize (Baum 1968). But the current dominance of sugarcane in the outgrower villages means that there is little room for food crops. Farmers want to grow as much cane as possible because of the potential profits, but there are consequences for livelihoods and food security. 'If you depend too much on sugar you will die of hunger,' said one young woman in Sanje (interview, 6 December 2013). Consequently, most people cultivate other crops in addition to sugarcane and perhaps keep one or two cattle or small stock, even if this means buying or leasing farmland several kilometres away.

Agrarian change and large-scale agricultural investments

The Kilombero investment has wrought many changes on land, livelihoods and local economies. There are many tensions and challenges. In this section we look at the processes of agrarian change unfolding, exploring insights on the diverse and differentiated impacts of agricultural investments.

Impacts of commercialisation

Sugarcane has transformed the economy of the upper Kilombero valley since the 1960s. The area has witnessed the arrival of industrial agriculture, shown by the presence of trucks, tractors and other machinery; a landscape marked by factories and plantations; and the outsourcing and mechanisation of farm labour. Several farmers differentiated sugarcane from rice by describing cane as a 'commercial' crop. As one woman in Signali village, outside the sugarcane-growing zone, noted, 'with sugarcane, you just wait for the one big payment to come, but with rice, you bring it home and sell it every so often' (interview, 9 December 2013). An agricultural service sector has grown up alongside KSCL, particularly since privatisation. In the town of Ruaha and along the main north–south trunk road can be found many input suppliers, spare-part stores, construction firms, and bicycle and motorbike dealers. Once a small village, Ruaha is now a busy trading centre and township with several financial institutions. An elderly man observed, 'Look how busy the people of Ruaha are – it's because of Illovo!' (Interview, 3 December 2013). This change accelerated when KSCL devolved outgrower services to local businesses and associations. Local leaders are increasingly acquiring equipment for farming, transportation and loading cane into lorries, pointing to elite capture of these new business opportunities, which they finance with capital accumulated from their own sugarcane farming or other business interests. Some salaried workers settled in the area after working on the nearby TAZARA railway, and a few other local enterprises – a hydropower station, mechanical plant and sawmill – have created further opportunities for migrants and traders.

Although places such as Ruaha are suggestive of multiplier effects from the sugarcane operation, there is less evidence for another widely cited benefit of nucleus–outgrower schemes: technology transfer. Sugarcane does not lend itself to technological innovation among small-scale farmers or to the transfer of technology to other crops, especially when no irrigation is used. Sugarcane is capital-intensive but not particularly labour-intensive, except at harvest time. Many outgrowers have little specialist knowledge of sugarcane cultivation, perhaps because they receive so little training, few visits from extension officers and minimal instruction from the company (Siyao 2012). Farmers may be advised to use fertiliser, herbicide and insecticide but as one respondent from Sanje village said, this is not particularly helpful for the poorer outgrowers who cannot afford them; alternative low-input, traditional ways of cultivating have been forgotten (interview, 7 December 2013).

Commuter farmers
The most significant change that the company has brought about over the past decades is the increase in the number and size of outgrower farms. Over time, the upper Kilombero valley has experienced population growth and the emergence of sugarcane as the dominant crop. But the story is not complete without also considering the cultivation of rice here and elsewhere. One dramatic consequence of food crops being marginalised in the sugarcane areas is the common practice for farmers to commute between cane fields near their homes and rice and maize fields at locations farther down the valley.

The effect of commuting on people's living patterns and farming calendars depends in large part on their available income: the poorest farmers simply cannot afford to hire workers or to commute frequently, and so tend to stay in the rice location for weeks or even months at a time. For all commuter households, but particularly the poorest whose members stay away for long periods of time, there are potentially negative consequences when it comes to children. They may be left alone while their parents farm on the other *shamba* (cultivated plot), with respondents reporting problems such as truancy from school, illness and vulnerability to theft by those who know the adults are away. Other studies suggest that girls in self-care arrangements are prone to sexual abuse or engaging in sexual activity for money (Nombo 2010; Makungu 2011).

The phenomenon of commuter farmers raises questions about future agricultural investment in the area: should investors increase the capacity for crushing cane, so that all outgrowers' cane can be harvested? Or should the government and development partners support farmers to convert some of their land under cane back to food crops through irrigation schemes such as the one in Msolwa Ujamaa village?

Social differentiation
Sugarcane contract farming has brought in money. In the villages, mud houses with thatch have been replaced by square houses built with kiln-fired bricks and metal roofs. In Msolwa Ujamaa, proceeds from the 400ha village farm have paid for a village office, dispensary and classrooms. 'Each and every thing you see in this village is because of sugar,' said a resident (interview, 1 December 2013). Incomes from outgrowing and auxiliary businesses have raised the living standards of many villagers in Kilombero, but the distribution of wealth is uneven and some people have not been included, leading to social differentiation.

The requirements of land and capital to become a KSCL outgrower are relatively small, but they still pose a barrier to entry. Some villagers would like to begin farming sugarcane but cannot afford to do so. They continue to farm rice, maize and other crops, or run small businesses or work as farm labourers. At present, sugarcane outgrowers are likely to be better-off than those farmers who only grow rice. Indeed, sugarcane provides cash which they can use to subsidise their rice farms, for example by hiring tractors and workers or buying inputs.

A local teacher explained that it is only the 'pure' rice farmers and very small sugarcane farmers who send their children to the local ward[4] public secondary schools. Sugarcane outgrowers aim for good-quality private education and make school fees the top priority for their cane payments. One respondent in Sanje told us, 'It is better to starve and send your children to good schools' (interview, 6 December 2013). With 1.6ha of sugarcane and 1.2ha of paddy, he could only afford to send his daughter to a good private school, while his sons go to the local school.

There is also differentiation among the outgrowers. Medium- and large-scale sugarcane farmers receive substantial payments at harvest,

---

[4] Administrative level below division and above village.

and make heavy use of wage labour. Owners of contracting firms often also own large sugarcane farms, and a large holding (20–40ha) can be a requirement for election as an association leader. This creates clear opportunities for elites to control the harvesting process and push for their own interests and those of other larger outgrowers.

With the proceeds from their sugar production, many outgrowers have reinvested their incomes in houses, education and farming. Some have been able to acquire extra land. However, the poorest outgrowers cannot afford to invest in capital accumulation. In addition to school fees, their priorities are food, household expenses and unexpected health costs. Members of small-farm households are likely to do more of the farm work themselves and may also sell their labour to wealthier farmers. They have the least capacity to buffer payment shocks, and are the most vulnerable to harvesting delays.

In both sugarcane and rice, the poorest farmers are losing, or failing to increase, their land endowments. Land scarcity and high prices for plots in the upper part of the valley, set against a backdrop of falling returns from sugar and rice, mean that newcomers and the smallest farmers may struggle to expand their farming operations. Some lack the capital to enter the sugarcane business, while existing outgrowers with few assets or who suffer a financial crisis may decide to rent out their holdings to others.

During 2013, many farmers could not afford to cultivate all of their land. Nevertheless, they preferred not to sell their land outright, and continued cultivating food crops on small parcels. While some large-scale outgrowers have acquired land from others, we did not find a wholesale process of proletarianisation whereby the smallest farmers are relinquishing their land and replacing it with waged work. Rather, some of the small-scale farmers are spending less on hiring wage workers and doing more of the farm work themselves. Conversely, however, they may also be selling a larger proportion of their food crop than previously, because the price of rice has fallen so drastically. This could create a challenge to food security.

There is also a generational aspect to this differentiation. The older generation often acquired land for free or at a low price through *Ujamaa*[5] land reform initiatives during the time of Julius Nyerere, when land was more freely available. As this elderly woman from Sanje village narrates: 'All you needed to acquire land was the power of your labour [to clear it]' (interview, 3 December 2013). The younger generation faces land scarcity and sub-division of family plots, but also has the opportunity of education and a life outside farming. This is where class or wealth differences may determine how people will fare. For example, the children of better-off farmers might receive better education than the children of poor smallholders, and therefore be less negatively affected by the unavailability of cheap land for farming.

[5] Nyerere's ideology of African brotherhood and equal opportunities.

Livelihoods and vulnerability
A consequence of the proliferation in outgrowing in Kilombero valley is the increased dependence of local people on income from sugarcane. Many farmers have benefited from incomes from sugar. But the flipside of this is greater vulnerability to indebtedness and exposure to market risk through their contractual relationship with KSCL. KSCL's sugar business is vulnerable to variable international prices and poor governance of cheap sugar imports, with these risks being passed on to the outgrowers through lower prices and late payments. In 2013, KSCL began delaying the payments due to outgrowers for their cane deliveries, claiming that arbitrary importation of foreign sugar had affected its ability to sell sugar in the Tanzanian market and hence the company could not pay its suppliers. Payments to contractors were also suspended, and firms were forced to pay cane-cutters a fraction of their full wages. Outgrowers were informed of the news by text message.

Farmers are vulnerable to indebtedness when payment is delayed or cane is not harvested. Also, if their final end-of-season payments are revised downwards to reflect actual market prices, farmers' debts can accumulate from one season to the next. Villagers with large debts have been forced to withdraw from sugarcane. In addition to the payment delays, people complain that deductions have increased to the point that sugarcane farming is no longer financially viable. Over time the cost of services deducted has generally risen in line with the price paid to farmers but that price has fallen since 2011 and if farmers are achieving – or being stated as achieving – lower levels of sucrose than previously, this further reduces payments. Because of these financial challenges and recurring grievances about corruption, some outgrowers have either pulled out of the scheme or are considering doing so. In March 2013, farmers from six villages in the K2 area were threatening to withdraw from sugarcane in response to a fall in the cane price (Balaigwa 2013).

But the decision to leave sugarcane is not easy, and focusing instead on rice or maize is problematic: both crops are more labour-intensive and vulnerable to flooding and drought than sugarcane, and they sell at low prices. Furthermore, some small farmers are unable to shift out of sugarcane because they lack the capital needed to uproot the cane, replant the land and apply inputs. One woman in Msolwa Ujamaa village told us that she was waiting to harvest her sugarcane and could not afford to buy meat. She would like to quit sugar farming but said 'We continue [with sugarcane] – there's no way out. We just hope that one day things will improve' (interview, 1 December 2013). Given the fluctuating markets and prices of sugar, rice and maize, the relationship between sugarcane outgrowers and other farmers is not necessarily a fixed hierarchy. This makes the pattern of differentiation discussed above all the more complex.

Business model, institutions and development outcomes

In this section we consider how the KSCL business model and its institutional context have affected agricultural development in the valley, including outcomes for small-scale farmers, setting this within an historical context. Given the profile given to similar models in new national initiatives in Tanzania, and elsewhere, the lessons have wider importance.

The legacy of Ujamaa and earlier agricultural development

Although Illovo introduced many changes after acquiring KSCL in 1998, the business has also been shaped by the local context. There is already a long history in the area of small- and large-scale farmers supplying sugarcane to jaggery plants or factories through relatively informal arrangements mostly overseen by an intermediary. During the 1960s, smallholders at a resettlement scheme supplied the new Kilombero Sugar Company in a quasi-outgrower relationship that was overseen by the scheme's management (Baum 1968). A network of farmers' groups, producer associations, farming blocks and collective *Ujamaa* village farms had developed before Illovo took over and streamlined the supply chain. Today's legacy associations are a key component of the KSCL outgrowing model, and continue to keep most farmers in indirect relationships with the company. In addition, the history of collectivism and land reform has partly determined farmers' access to land for cultivating sugarcane. For example, residents of Msolwa Ujamaa village benefited from a successful village sugarcane farm and the redistribution of private farmland, which many have used for cultivating cane as outgrowers. Multiple attempts were made, not only by the socialist government, to involve small-scale farmers in the sugar business at Kilombero and the high participation of outgrowers with very small holdings of less than 1ha makes KSCL unusual among Illovo's operations and many other sugarcane businesses in Southern Africa.

Withdrawal and devolution of services

As we have seen, since 2004, several of KSCL's outgrower services and benefits have been withdrawn or transferred to private service providers. In contrast to more tightly controlled contract farming schemes, outgrowing at Kilombero has always been a loosely regulated arrangement and Illovo's changes have in some ways reduced control still further. Yet the main tasks of cane cutting, loading and transport remain out of farmers' hands, being arranged on their behalf by their associations.

This business model has stimulated the growth of independent contractors in the area and changed the role of associations from farmer representatives to overseers of production and contractors of services.

However, the situation appears detrimental to farmers in two ways. Firstly, KSCL outgrowers are somewhat passive recipients of services, and interviews revealed that farmers feel powerless in the face of low-quality or unfair treatment by contractors. The transferral of contracting power to the associations, combined with their role in scheduling harvests, seems to have created opportunities for bribery and favouritism. Secondly, farmers feel the absence of centralised monitoring and extension: they receive little advice about pests, disease or growing practices, which contributes to their suspicions that the low sucrose levels recorded for their cane are due to corruption and incompetence. The harvesting system lacks oversight, and there is no strict control over the numbers of farmers that can join the scheme or the acreage that can be cultivated, which has allowed regular over-production of cane by outgrowers.

Low barriers to entry
Part of what makes KSCL a loose arrangement is its minimal conditions of participation. Farmers do not need title deeds for the land that they intend to cultivate, and most associations do not require a minimum plot size. This has allowed small farmers with as little as 0.4ha of rented land to participate. It is also easy to leave the scheme by subleasing the plot or withdrawing in writing – although there are some exit costs – and for a woman to register her husband's or male relative's plot in her name. The KSCL outgrower scheme is therefore relatively inclusive. But the smallest and poorest farmers are not well protected within it. Farmers were encouraged to convert small paddy farms to sugarcane and are now told that their fields are inaccessible at harvest time. Small farmers are disproportionately affected by payment delays and low sucrose levels, and lack the alleged capital and influence needed for bribes. It remains to be seen whether block farms will offer a solution to these problems or simply present more opportunities for elite capture.

Policies and regulation
The current regulatory framework in Tanzania does not address the sugar value chain, its contributions to rural livelihoods in sugar-growing regions, or contentious issues related to processing capacity, distribution, oligopolies and monopolies, marketing and distribution. As Massimba et al. (2013: 17) observe, these elements 'cannot simply be undermined in the view of regulatory framework since they are the key drivers that determine and safeguard interest of all chain actors within the sugar value chain'. There have been efforts by the company and outgrowers' representatives to get the government to stop the arbitrary importation of sugar, but sustained policy responses have been lacking. As a member of the Association of Mang'ula Cane Outgrowers put it: 'The whole system is rotten... Even after we battled with the Prime Minster, another consignment [of sugar] came in [to the country]' (interview, November 2013). In September 2014 the government convened a meeting of key stakeholders in the sugar industry to find a lasting solution – particularly the strict regulation of sugar imports through tariff and non-tariff barriers (interview, KSCL official, 29 September 2014).

Conclusion

The injection of foreign capital into the Kilombero Sugar Company since 1998 has revitalised sugar production in the area, increasing the area under cane and the number of outgrowers; creating more associations of cane growers and more products from cane; and generating opportunities for (mostly migrant) workers and local businesses. Capital has been poured in not only by KSCL itself, but also by foreign donors and lending agencies that have sponsored infrastructure and capacity-building projects.

The changes since privatisation have contributed to land scarcity, both in absolute terms and in terms of the land available for food crops. This scarcity has been created not by (re)acquisition of land for estate production, but mostly by expansion of outgrower areas and the rising demand for land from migrants. As land is becoming scarce and sugarcane profitability is declining, and influential or wealthy actors in the system are increasingly alleged to be resorting to bribery, poor and newcomer households are finding it difficult to participate in the industry. The changes have encouraged the phenomenon of commuter farming, with attendant challenges particularly for the children of poor families. Local elites and wealthy migrants have been able to accumulate land and take control of business opportunities brought about by the sugar boom.

This wave of elite capture of land and other resources is linked to their financial, economic and even political connections. This puts them in a better position to negotiate business deals with national and international corporations (ILC 2012). In particular, KSCL's devolved harvesting system, and the company's inability to process all of the outgrowers' cane, is fostering nepotism and corruption. The benefits of commercial sugarcane and donor-sponsored social projects are not being felt by everyone in this society. The current outgrower scheme at Kilombero needs redesigning if it is to contribute better to reducing poverty and inequality, and improving social welfare.

Despite the invested capital and associated increase in production, Tanzania remains a sugar-deficit country. This leads the government to allow importation of sugar to fill the gap but poor coordination and abuse of the system by corrupt and illegal traders badly hurts poor farmers when their payments are delayed and, as in some years, their cane remains unharvested and unprocessed.

Large-scale farming has significant consequences for smallholder farmers as these sectors compete for the same land. The recent ambitious 'Big Results Now' and SAGCOT initiatives aim to open up agriculture for more foreign private investments in sugarcane and rice through large nucleus–outgrower schemes. While the incorporation of smallholder farmers sounds encouraging, it is unclear how this new initiative will differ from the existing KSCL model, and whether it will address the problems that KSCL outgrowers and the company currently face. Unless these challenges are fully addressed, poor outgrowers are unlikely to benefit much from these kinds of commercialisation initiatives.

8

Trapped between the Farm Input Subsidy Programme & the Green Belt Initiative

BLESSINGS CHINSINGA
& MICHAEL CHASUKWA

Malawi's Contemporary Agrarian Political Economy

Introduction

Malawi's agrarian story is a complex and intriguing one. The unequal and skewed land distribution was one of the major rallying points of the independence struggle, although it remains unresolved to date (Kanyongolo 2005). With the transition from a one-party dictatorship to a multiparty democracy in 1994, many expected change, yet a new legislative framework for land has still not been endorsed.

The agrarian future of Malawi is therefore quite precarious, and land remains a central concern for politics, economics and livelihoods. Land ownership per capita is as low as 0.4ha (Government of Malawi 2002) and the productive capacity of households has declined following the Structural Adjustment Programmes (SAPs) of the 1990s that made inputs such as hybrid maize seed and fertiliser unaffordable for the majority of households. Chronic food insecurity became more or less routine (Devereux 2002). The country was basically unable to feed itself without either food aid or commercial food imports, even during years of favourable weather. The head count of poverty is estimated at 50.3 per cent, while the proportion of ultra-poor Malawians is 25 per cent. Moreover, smallholder farmers are caught up in a low productivity maize trap due to inter-year maize price instability (Chirwa and Dorward 2013).

While numerous government initiatives have been launched to deal with the problems of poverty and chronic hunger, Malawi hit international headlines for pioneering the implementation of a 'smart subsidy' as a catalyst for a long-overdue African 'Green Revolution' (Chinsinga 2012). Following two severe hunger crises in quick succession in 2001 and 2004 that affected about 3-4 million people, the government resolved to implement a Farm Input Subsidy Programme (FISP) through which it provided improved seed and fertiliser to about 3 million smallholder farming families as a strategy to address chronic hunger and food insecurity (Government of Malawi 2010). Introduced in the 2005/06 growing season, against the fierce resistance of donors and domestic fiscal conservatives, the FISP turned out to be a reasonable success for at least seven consecutive growing seasons, transforming the country from a food importer to a food exporter, and even a food donor (Chinsinga 2012). Although the success story of the FISP has somewhat unravelled since (Chirwa and Dorward 2013), it has nonetheless had a tremendous impact on the configuration of Malawi's contemporary agrarian economy with apparently long-run ramifications.

The Green Belt Initiative (GBI) launched in 2009 has been promoted as a complement, and a high-profile successor, to the FISP. While the GBI has a wide range of objectives, its core aim is to consolidate the food security gains of the FISP (Government of Malawi 2010) and to facilitate the progressive expansion of land under irrigation in order to ensure that the country's food security is not entirely reliant on rain-fed agriculture. This was influenced to a great extent by donors' incessant criticism that the apparent success of the FISP was contingent on good rainfall, and not necessarily on the incremental impact of fertiliser use (Dorward and Chirwa 2013). Through the GBI, the government is courting both local and international investors to acquire land for the development of irrigated agriculture to the tune of one million hectares (Chinsinga and Chasukwa 2012a). The GBI is further justified as a strategy to commercialise the country's agricultural sector to boost farmers' earnings so that they can become self-reliant, while at the same time increasing the country's foreign-exchange reserves through improved export earnings.

Despite the claims of complementarity between the GBI and the FISP, there are important tensions and contradictions between the two, situated at the heart of Malawi's political economy of land. The GBI is focused on high-value irrigated production, and requires the appropriation of land from the very smallholders who were at the centre of the 'Green Revolution' transition envisaged under the FISP. The switch from domestic food production by smallholders on rainfed land to corporate-led agriculture with outgrower arrangements, changes relationships of land-holding, labour and economic control in fundamental ways.

The case study

This chapter focuses on Dwangwa in Nkhotakota District (see Map 8.1). Nkhotakota District is situated in the central region of Malawi, about 200km from Lilongwe. It is one of the least-densely populated districts in the country with 71 persons per square kilometre compared with the central region's population density estimated at 154 persons per square kilometre. Nkhotakota District covers 7,500 square kilometres (Government of Malawi 2009b).

Just like the rest of the country, Nkhotakota has three categories of landholding system, namely: customary, private leasehold/freehold and

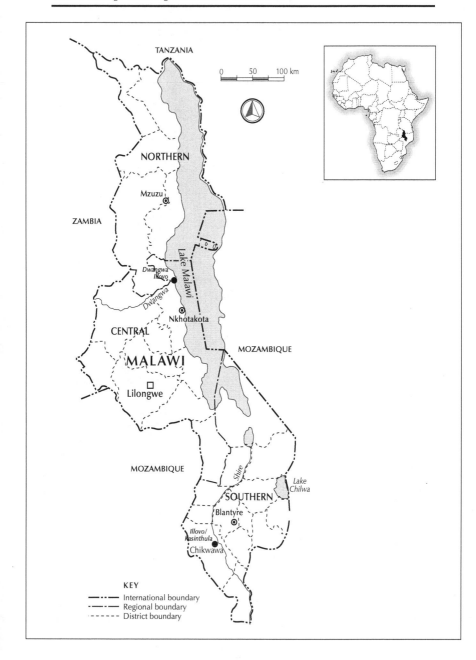

Map 8.1 Malawi, showing the location of Illovo Dwangwa estates

public. The customary land constitutes about 55 per cent of the total land in the district, which, according to the existing legislative framework, is held in trust by traditional leaders on behalf of their respective communities. This accords traditional leaders a prominent role in the transactions pertaining to customary land. Private leasehold/freehold land takes up as much as 22.2 per cent of the total land. Most of this land is devoted to commercial farming.

There are about 71,090 farming families in Nkhotakota, organised into 76 sections and 608 blocks. The main crops grown in the district are maize, cassava, sugarcane, rice, cotton, and burley tobacco. These crops are planted on about 55 per cent of the total cultivable land. Sugarcane is grown almost entirely for Dwangwa Illovo Sugar Estate and Dwangwa Cane Growers Limited (Government of Malawi 2009b).

The chapter is based on a three-year study examining the experiences of farmers involved in growing sugarcane either as independent outgrowers or affiliated with companies under the auspices of the GBI. Qualitative research involving semi-structured interviews and focus group discussions with a range of actors was undertaken, examining how the change of cropping system – from grain crops to sugarcane – had affected social and economic relations in the area.

From agricultural subsidies to commercial land deals: FISP and GBI

Since its launch in the 2005-06 growing season, the FISP has become a flagship programme for the government for dealing with the twin challenges of chronic hunger and food insecurity in Malawi. Under the FISP, eligible smallholder farmers, who are mostly resource-constrained and identified as beneficiaries in open village meetings, are given two 50kg bags of fertiliser, one for basal dressing and the other one for top dressing, 5kg of hybrid or open-pollinated variety maize and 1kg of legume seed such as soya or groundnuts. Farmers access these inputs through vouchers which are redeemed at designated state marketing outlets (particularly for fertiliser) and various agro-dealers (particularly for seed) (Chinsinga 2007, 2012).

The FISP has tremendous potential to facilitate farmers' escape from the low-productivity maize trap, since they are able to access productivity-enhancing inputs that they would not otherwise have been able to afford. For seven consecutive growing seasons since its launch in 2005/06, Malawi was able to produce enough to feed itself over and above the annual food requirements now estimated at 2.8 million metric tonnes. However, this changed in 2012/13, and by the end of 2013 more than 1.63 million people, or 11 per cent of the population, were facing severe food shortages. Doubts have therefore begun to spread about the long-term efficacy and sustainability of the programme. Indeed, from its launch there has been scepticism. Donors and domestic fiscal conservatives who objected to subsidies felt that the FISP would jeopardise Malawi's qualification for debt relief under the Malawi Poverty Reduction Strategy (Rakner et al. 2004). Yet, in the face of such criticism, Malawi was able to produce in the first year of FISP's operation about 500,000 metric tonnes of surplus maize above its annual food requirements after almost two decades of persistent failure to produce adequate food to meet domestic demand (Chinsinga 2007).

Although the dramatic success of the FISP in its maiden year of implementation altered the hard-line position of donors, this development did not completely eliminate debates about the future of FISP, particularly with regard to its long-term sustainability. Concerns that were raised included the high cost of the programme, with 75 per cent of the Ministry of Agriculture and Food Security's budget being spent on it; that other initiatives to improve efficient use of inputs, like extension and research services, were side-lined; that it displaced commercial input purchases by farmers; that the distribution of inputs favours households which are more food secure; and that there was an unclear exit and graduation plan (Chinsinga 2012). A particular question raised by the donor community was whether the successes of the FISP could be attributed to fertiliser inputs or favourable weather. Studies in Zambia, for example, had shown that it was rainfall rather than fertilisers which had the greatest effect on yields (Burke et al. 2010). The government thus reacted to this debate by announcing the implementation of an irrigation-focused initiative, the GBI, to counter the donors' criticism.

The Green Belt Initiative was conceived by the late President Mutharika in 2010 as an integral part of the Malawi Growth and Development Strategy (MGDS) that was flagged as the country's overarching development planning framework (Government of Malawi 2010). The overriding aim of the GBI is to reduce poverty, improve livelihoods and ensure sustainable food security at both household and national levels through increased production and productivity of agricultural crops, livestock and fisheries.

The GBI is thus seen as a mechanism to protect the gains in food security, reduce vulnerability to drought, and diversify crop production by increasing the irrigated area from 78,000ha to one million hectares lying within 20km of the country's three lakes and thirteen perennial rivers (Chinsinga and Chasukwa 2012b). These are all laudable aims. Yet in a land-constrained country, gaining access to irrigable land for large-scale commercial production is not without its challenges. In Malawi about 25 per cent of smallholder farmers cultivate less than 0.5ha; 55 per cent less than 1ha; 31 per cent between 1 and 2ha and only 14 per cent more than 2ha (Chirwa 2008). However, despite being resource-constrained, these smallholder farmers produce about 80 per cent of Malawi's food and 20 per cent of total agricultural exports (Chinsinga et al. 2013). The GBI envisages a new pattern of land use and ownership, requiring displacement of some existing farmers, and a fundamental shift in the pattern and relations of production. In its plans, the government explains:

> The large growers need vast acres for large-scale production...land has to be identified for them along the [GBI] and these have to be linked to banking institutions for inputs such as machinery, fertilizers, seeds, pesticides, labour, and cash. Large growers will have to engage in discussions with local assemblies to relocate villages for intensified farming by use of heavy machinery. Irrigation schemes [will] be owned by large-scale commercial farmers and corporate companies [who]... will be responsible for developing and operating them (Government of Malawi 2009a: 3-4).

The idea of a transformation of agriculture to a large-scale, commercially-oriented system is inspired by the 2002 land policy (Breytenbach 2003). According to this policy, Malawi has a total of 9.4 million hectares of land, of which 7.7 million hectares are available for both smallholder and estate agriculture. Of this land, smallholder farmers have up to 6.5 million hectares, while estate farming takes up about 1.2 million hectares, but according to FAO (2012a), smallholder farmers cultivate about 2.4 million hectares only. The land balance sheet therefore shows that as much as 4.1 million hectares, or 28 per cent of arable land, is not utilised. This paints a picture of plentiful available land and wastefulness in its utilisation. This narrative of underutilisation, in the context of extreme land constraints within the smallholder sector, is contradictory and relates to the dramatic decline of estate agriculture that expanded quite rapidly in the 1970s and 1980s (Chirwa 1998, Chinsinga 2007). During this period, it is estimated that the number of estates increased from 1,200 in 1979 to 14,671 in 1989, covering one million hectares of fertile arable land. The majority of these estates are no longer viable mainly as a result of changes in the economic environment precipitated by SAPs that made it impossible for the estate farmers to enjoy preferential access to credit guaranteed by the state.

While the government is reliant on – and heavily investing in – smallholder agriculture, it is not promoting it through redistributive land reform. The collapse of estate agriculture, coupled with the evidence that smallholder agriculture has always been the leading driver of agricultural growth and development even at the peak of estate farming presents a strong case for agrarian reform. This has, however, not happened. Due to elite interests, the country is still stuck with a dualistic model of agriculture in which a few large estates sit side by side with a majority of smallholders. The beneficiaries of the 1967 land reforms, which paved the way for the rapid expansion of the estate sector in the 1970s and 1980s, comprising chiefs, politicians, senior civil servants and high-ranking parastatal and industrial employees, have an interest in the existing patterns of land tenure. They are not prepared to give up, without compensation, the vast tracts of land they accumulated. Malawi's political economy thus explains the apparent shift away from smallholder productivity towards the revival of the estate sector, now buoyed up by external investment as reflected by the GBI. The current direction provides space for continued smallholder participation while maintaining the unequal land distribution and dualistic agrarian structure.

While the GBI is, at least officially, justified as a mechanism for protecting the food security gains achieved under the FISP, the reality is totally different on the ground. At Dwangwa in Nkhotakota District, the GBI has been almost entirely hijacked by sugarcane cultivation (Chinsinga et al. 2013). Three models of sugarcane cultivation were discerned on the ground: estate farming, outgrower schemes and private or individual farming. What distinguishes these models from one another is that they use different techniques and strategies to acquire land for sugarcane cultivation and distribute risk and value in diverse ways.

The estate model is the most dominant. Under this model, land is accessed either through lease arrangements or outright purchases. The main player is the South Africa-based company, Illovo Sugar Ltd, now part-owned by Associated British Foods plc, which plans to expand its current hectarage in Malawi by 6,000ha by 2015. The outgrower model is presented primarily as a strategy to promote the cultivation of sugarcane by smallholder farmers on a sustainable commercial basis (Phillips 2009, World Bank et al. 2011). The outgrower model is operationalised through trusts which in turn constitute limited companies. The main player in this regard is the Dwangwa Cane Growers Trust (DCGT), managed by Dwangwa Cane Growers Ltd (DCGL), a Malawian organisation which operates about 2,670ha of sugarcane fields. Private or individual farming is largely the preserve of the privileged few who are able to muster economic, social and political capital to navigate processes of buying and leasing land as well as selling to Illovo (Chasukwa 2013). There are only two private farmers in Dwangwa, one being a former Member of Parliament and Cabinet Minister, and the other a senior manager at Illovo.

Land deal politics

The expansion of the sugar industry in Malawi has been propelled by a loose coalition of politicians, bureaucrats, and some donor agencies. Politicians are predominantly inspired by the image of the existence of plentiful land that can be converted to sugarcane production without any significant opportunity cost. Consequently, the majority of politicians interpret the statistics from the land balance-sheet studies as implying that the unfarmed lands are not owned, and are vacant, idle and therefore available to accelerate the development agenda, especially in rural areas. Politicians project the GBI as an opportunity to solve the country's development challenges, since they anticipate that the expansion of sugar plantations will promote job creation, bolster infrastructural development such as roads, schools, health centres and water services, and promote the availability of improved agricultural technologies to farmers through outgrower arrangements.

These optimistic projections of the benefits of corporate-led commercialisation echo justifications for large-scale agricultural investments at the global level. Such investments, which import commercial enterprises, are seen as a faster way of developing local agriculture than engaging in slower processes of supporting smallholder farmers to accumulate and expand their operations (Beekman and Veldwisch 2012). For politicians in Malawi, commercialisation can be achieved through the establishment of outgrower schemes and estates under either private or public-private partnership arrangements. Such narratives also echo earlier positions: indeed, as early as 1977 the government established the Smallholder Sugar Authority whose main objective was to reduce poverty among the smallholder farmers through similar arrangements (Chasukwa 2013).

Malawian bureaucrats support the GBI, but with a great deal of caution. For most, prioritising the cultivation of cash crops such as sugarcane under the auspices of the GBI is a potential panacea to the country's deepening foreign-exchange crisis. Tobacco, which earns 70 per cent of the country's foreign exchange, is under siege in the wake of the fierce international anti-smoking lobby. Sugar is seen as part of a diversification strategy to prepare for the eventual collapse of tobacco as a leading foreign-exchange earner. Sugar is a significant potential alternative since it already contributes about 8 per cent to GDP and 9 per cent to export earnings.

This sense of optimism on the part of bureaucrats is, of course, tempered by concerns that the forceful drive to expand sugar cultivation could have a negative impact on food security. Most smallholder farmers commit their land to sugarcane cultivation without really fully understanding the implications of their contractual obligations. Most bureaucrats interviewed pointed to the conflict between DCGL and smallholder farmers at Kazilira who agreed to cultivate sugarcane, hoping that they would still be able to use part of their land to grow food crops. However, DCGL is pushing its suppliers to turn all of their land over to sugarcane cultivation. One of the bureaucrats commented: 'I sympathise with the communities because if their land is used to grow sugarcane, they will struggle a lot getting foodstuffs'.[1]

Not only bureaucrats, but also influential actors from outside the country have promoted the shift to sugar. International donor agencies, mainly the European Union (EU) and the African Development Bank (AfDB), have taken advantage of the apparent foreign-exchange crisis in the country to promote sugarcane cultivation as a potential alternative to tobacco. 30 per cent of the sugar is exported, generating considerable

---

[1] Interview with a bureaucrat at Nkhotakota District Council, 3 September 2012.

foreign exchange. This, however, masks the EU's self-interest, since 50 per cent of the sugar that is exported from Malawi is sold in EU countries. The EU is keen to promote sugar cultivation in Malawi following reforms that it implemented in the sugar trade which phased out sugar subsidies for its farmers and sugar import quotas. Malawi has been specifically targeted to benefit from such reforms because 'its comparative advantage in the sector is low cost production, excellent cane growing conditions, and the presence of adequate water and land resources'.[2] The EU's interest in Malawi's sugar is underpinned by the support it has extended to the Malawi government to develop the sugar industry. With respect to sugarcane cultivation in Dwangwa, the EU provided the Malawi government with a grant of 6 million Euros to develop 670ha of irrigated sugarcane involving 200 smallholder farmers at Kasitu. The AfDB also extended a grant to the Malawi government of US$7 million for an Agriculture Infrastructure Support Project (2010-2014) to promote sugarcane cultivation. This is to develop 1,200ha of irrigated sugarcane targeting 500ha at Liwaladzi and 700ha at Kazilira, involving 219 and 230 farmers, respectively in the same district of Nkhotakota. The EU has engaged an international organisation, Concern Universal International, to provide technical support to smallholder farmers to improve the governance and management of sugarcane cultivation enterprises to ensure that they produce high quality export sugar (European Union 2011).

Opposition to the GBI is focused on local civil society organisations which have seized on the GBI as an opportunity to advance counter-narratives on human rights, democracy and social justice. They condemn the GBI as facilitating the dispossession of land, thereby removing the main productive asset for the majority of the rural poor in Malawi (Chinsinga and Chasukwa 2012). Some CSOs have developed specific projects to work with communities fighting against dispossession of their land. For instance, the Church and Society Programme of the Livingstonia Synod played a key role in mediating a conflict between DCGL and smallholder farmers at Kazilira in Dwangwa, providing legal advice to smallholder farmers who were challenging the decisions of the government authorities in the courts. It intervened by equipping smallholder farmers for negotiation and mediation processes so that they were able to make persuasive and plausible arguments. When the dispute escalated, the Church and Society Programme summoned the Nkhunga police to present their side of the story on allegations that they had damaged farmers' crops at Kazilira.

---

[2]   See European Commission: 'Malawi-2011 Annual Action Programme for the Accompanying Measures for Sugar Protocol Countries' DCI-SUCRE/MW023-135. Available at www.ec.europa.eu/europeaid/documents/aap/2011/af_aap_2011_sugar_mwi.pdf. Accessed 25 May 2013.

Gaining access to land

Land-related conflicts have been sparked by the process through which DCGL has gained access to land, resulting in extremely strained relationships between the company and outgrowers, whom DCGL has been recruiting in an attempt to expand its land holdings. Negotiations are not held directly with the would-be outgrower but rather with traditional leaders, 'on the understanding that they do represent the interests of their subjects'.[3] Under the 2002 land policy, however, customary land is considered to be vacant and unallocated land, and to be vested in traditional leaders. This means that the customary claims of landholders who occupy or use the land are not recognised in law or in practice – the main basis for continued land conflicts.

In Dwangwa, most communities felt betrayed by their traditional leaders, arguing that they did not consult them and that, where such consultations were carried out, they 'were not provided with adequate information in order to make informed decisions and choices'.[4] This has contributed to feelings of widespread resentment among outgrowers as it has dawned upon them that they have almost completely ceded control of their land to the sugarcane companies. As one outgrower explained:

> I feel dumped by the company because there are many restrictions in the outgrower arrangement. I have to seek consent to this and that on my own piece of land for they claim that I have no expertise in sugarcane growing and they might end up making losses.[5]

The feeling of powerlessness is aggravated by the fact that out-growers are not allowed to opt out of their contract with DCGL until it has recovered its land development costs, estimated to take between five and ten years. Such costs are not made clear to would-be outgrowers when the deals are negotiated on their behalf by traditional leaders. For most farmers, the contractual obligation not to opt out for a period of five to ten years is tantamount to DCGL leasing their land. In a discussion at Mkangadzinja in Dwangwa, one smallholder farmer observed that:

> The contractual arrangements with DCGL are as good as saying that they have leased our land, only that they cannot come out in the open on this; we have to live on their terms because penalties for non-observance of the terms and conditions of the contract are even worse than what we have now.[6]

---

[3] Interview with an official of DCGL on 22 September 2011, Dwangwa, Nkhotakota District.
[4] A participant in a discussion with male outgrowers, Dwangwa, Nkhotakota District, 20 August 2012.
[5] Interview with an outgrower, Dwangwa, Nkhotakota District, 17 January 2012.
[6] Discussion with outgrowers at Mkangadzinja, Dwangwa, Nkhotakota District, 22 January 2012.

The role of traditional leaders in brokering land deals suggests that local-level politics is critical in understanding the underlying dynamics of land deals which hardly ever work out in favour of smallholder farmers. The inequality in bargaining power is particularly exacerbated when such smallholders whose land is being acquired for investment projects have no formal title to the land, but have been using it under customary tenure arrangements.

Traditional leaders themselves have not been immune to internal disagreements and divisions. Some chiefs, for instance, protested against the inclusion of Senior Chief Kanyenda as a board member of DCGL, arguing that his appointment created a conflict of interest and was a strategic ploy to suppress views from village headmen and their communities. As one observed, 'as the authorities would simply say...your Senior Chief has already endorsed the proposals that you are protesting against'.[7] Such concessions by the traditional leaders paved the way for local elite capture of sugarcane cultivation under the auspices of the GBI.

A clear case of elite capture in Dwangwa was Chief Kanyenda's decree to establish the Kazilira Development Committee to operate in parallel with the Area Development Committee (ADC), which is within the local governance framework sanctioned as a legitimate body to oversee development projects at the sub-district level. The Kazilira Development Committee was charged with overseeing the development of land designated for sugarcane cultivation. Traditional leaders falling within the jurisdiction of the ADC protested fiercely against the establishment of a separate committee because they feared it could circumvent the criteria for identifying eligible smallholder farmers as beneficiaries of the sugarcane project, which would undermine their authority. The protests notwithstanding, Senior Chief Kanyenda proceeded to establish the Kazilira Development Committee, which was aimed to facilitate the cultivation of sugarcane.

Following the assignment of plots to complete strangers, contrary to prior arrangements that the plots of land would revert back to the owners after being developed, smallholder farmers 'started demanding their land back from DCGT which created enormous tension in the area'.[8] This forced the DCGT to hire police to fight off the resistance, and in the process several houses and crop fields were destroyed. Senior Chief Kanyenda used this incident to justify his actions as being in the interests of development of the area, 'contending that the people of his area led by their village headmen were simply resisting development just as was the case with Kayerekera Uranium Project'.[9]

[7] Interview with an outgrower, Kazilira Village, Dwangwa, Nkhotakota District, 28 December 2012.

[8] See 'Disgruntled Farmers Turn Violent': www.zodiakmalawi.com/a%/20m/index.phpphp?iption=com_content&view=articleid=1648%t3disgrunted-farmers-turn-violent&Item=81.

[9] See 'Sugar Company Chases Villagers from their Land': www.gondwe.blogspot.com/2009/01/sugar-company-chases-villages-from.html.

The expansion of sugarcane cultivation under the auspices of DCGL has also created divisions among community members themselves. Combined with the underhand tactics and manoeuvres of the Senior Chief, divisions at community level have created a persistently tense atmosphere that has led to struggles turning violent at times. The communities have either engaged in confrontation amongst one another or against the sugar companies or the police. The conflicts within communities reflect patterns of socio-economic differentiation, since those with larger landholdings, multiple plots of land or alternative means of livelihood have tended to be supportive of the sugarcane cultivation expansion project, while the rest are fiercely opposed to surrendering their land for the development of sugarcane cultivation. The large landholders find the outgrower modality profitable because they benefit from economies of scale, while those with more than one piece of land can use the others for cultivation of food crops, and equally those with alternative means of livelihood such as wage employment can commit their land to sugarcane cultivation even when they only have a single plot of land.

Resistance to land deals

Both violent and non-violent strategies have been used in the agrarian struggles that have unfolded in Dwangwa. In these struggles, the DCGL and the communities have lost property, police officers and community members have sustained serious injuries, and some people have even lost their lives. In November 2010, for instance, a 21-year-old man was shot dead by the police following disagreements over sugarcane outgrowing in the traditional authority of Kazilira in Dwangwa,[10] two government agricultural officials were severely wounded while conducting land assessments in Mphikapika in the area of Senior Chief Kanyenda in October 2011,[11] 25 people were injured following a fracas between pro- and anti-sugarcane cultivation expansion camps in November 2011 in the area of Kafuzira,[12] and outgrowers burnt four tractors valued at MK 12 million (US$72,950) and wounded 26 DCGL employees following unresolved disputes over deductions from their sales sheets at the end of the growing season in May 2012.[13]

Civil case No. 2127 illustrates how the contestation over land has played out in the legal arena. In this case, Senior Chief Kanyenda and the Kazilira Development Committee sought the court's determination,

[10] See 'Sugar Plantation Wrangles Rage On'. www.zodiakmalawi.com/index.php?option=c om_content&view=articleid=3125:sugar-plantation-wrangeles-rage-on.

[11] Ibid.

[12] See 'KK Sugarcane Fracas: 25 Injured': www.zodiakmalawi.com/zbs%/20malawi/index. php?option_content&view=article&id=3509:kk-sugarcane-fracas-25-injured-&catid=41:top-headlines&Itemid=97.

[13] See 'Irate Farmers Razes Four Tractors, Injure 26'. www.nyasatimes.com/malawi/2012/ 05/29/irate-farmers-razes-four-tractors-injure.

declaration and order on: '(a) a permanent order of mandatory injunction requiring the defendants (thus 15 people from Kazilira community), their servants, agents and/or employees howsoever acting to allow the Plaintiffs, howsoever acting to carry out the smallholder sugarcane project; (b) a declaration that the Defendants' efforts and acts in blocking or otherwise obstructing the implementation of Smallholder Outgrowers Sugarcane Production Project were wrongful and in violation of the Plaintiff's right to development as enshrined in S. 30 of the constitution...'. The community members defended the cases and the court ruled in their favour.

...when one is allocated customary land, one has the right [of use to] the surface only, in respect of what one can grow or build on the land. One does not have the right of [use] to the sub-soil and whatever lies under....if the canals are dug for the purpose of laying irrigation pipes 2 metres in the ground, the government and the developer have a right to dig the land. The government and the developer, however, should refill the trenches and render the land useable by the citizens who do not wish to join the scheme. Should there be open canals or crops or trees destroyed then the citizens are entitled to compensation for the land and crops.[14]

However, DCGL did not act quickly to compensate the community members it had sued for obstructing development in their area as stipulated by the court order. Using the court order, community members petitioned their District Commissioner who ordered DCGL 'to compensate the people whose crops you damaged at Kazilira and that the land on which you have grown sugarcane without the consent of the land owners should be given back to the owners immediately'.[15] The community members were politically savvy in handling the matter as they drew in their Member of Parliament to reinforce the petition to the District Commissioner by raising the matter with DCGL as well as the Ministry of Agriculture and Food Security (MoAFS). CSOs, notably those linked to the church, have also entered the fray, supporting the rights of local villagers. A strongly worded letter from the churches states:

... [as] Church and Society Programme, a desk advocacy of the CCAP Synod of Livingstonia....we received claims from 262 people from Kazilira that the state using the Nkhunga Police chased people from their gardens, destroyed their crops, pulled down many houses and finally have illegally appropriated land belonging to them. These displaced people sought refuge in the Dwangwa CCAP church. Our visit to the scene revealed that the situation is indeed unbearable and unbelievable to have been [created] by a government institution which has a duty to

---

[14] See court order under Civil Case No. 2127 in the High Court of Malawi between DCGL, Senior Chief Kanyenda and Kazilira Development Committee and Henry Chisangwala and 14 others.

[15] See letter from Nkhotakota District Commissioner to the Executive Director, DCGL dated 20 May 2010.

protect lives and property of the people. To support their claims, there is a court judgment in favour of our clients ordering compensation to be paid to the land owners and restraining the assailant to the use of surface land. In view of all the allegations levelled above, we humbly invite you to give the side of your story probably within a fortnight lest we recommend for legal action to mandated institutions.[16]

Livelihood impacts: winners and losers

While resistance to the land deals has been mounted on a number of fronts, the debate about who wins and loses continues to rage. In the context of a highly differentiated local setting, there are some who stand to gain while others may lose out. The evidence from Dwangwa, as elsewhere where land deals are being implemented, suggests that such kinds of investments are a double-edged sword.

Involvement in sugarcane cultivation through outgrower contracts has the potential to catalyse robust rural livelihoods because it creates opportunities for smallholder farmers to access financial resources that they can use to promote a wide range of alternative means of livelihood. This is possible because working under DCGL makes it easier for them to get loans from financial institutions and banks since it acts as a guarantor. This offers a very rare 'opportunity for enterprising smallholder farmers to diversify their livelihood portfolios by venturing into small to medium-scale businesses'.[17] The main challenge is that not many smallholder farmers are eligible to access loans on the basis of their expected earnings from sugarcane sales. It is therefore mostly those smallholder farmers with larger landholdings that benefit from the loan facilities, provoking tensions at community level.

However, the decision by DCGL to act as a guarantor of loans for outgrowers is quite strategic on its part. It helped diffuse tensions by shifting the blame in cases of problems to a third party. This was illustrated when one of the outgrowers said, 'we are paid three times a year. The company [DCGL] tries its best to pay us well but we are in a web of huge debts with banks. We cannot blame the company but the banks for high interest rates. The company does not force people to get loans but it is us that request it to help us with letters of recommendation so that we fix ourselves on the cross'.[18]

For those outgrowers who own only a single plot of land, the expansion of sugarcane cultivation poses a huge threat to food security because DCGL allows only mono-cropping. The farmers in the area used

---

[16] Letter by the Church and Society Programme of Livingstonia Synod: Displacement of Several People, Land Grabbing and Malicious Damage to Property by the Nkhunga Police, 8 December 2010.

[17] Discussion with outgrowers in Dwangwa, Nkhotakota District, 6 February 2012.

[18] Key informant interview with an outgrower, Dwangwa, Nkhotakota District, 8 February 2012.

to grow crops such as maize, cassava, sweet potatoes and groundnuts.
If the farmers decide to plant other crops alongside sugarcane in their
fields, these crops are uprooted because 'DCGL extension workers
consider them as weeds'.[19] The expectation is that the farmers would
use the proceeds from sugar sales to buy food. While there is an
acknowledgment that farmers will get decent returns three times a
year, they argue that 'you will have to be a superstar to control your
expenditure...most of us, by the time we think of buying food, we will
have already spent more than three-quarters of the money. It becomes
too late to save enough money to sustain buying foodstuffs. The coping
strategy is to get a loan'.[20]

This is less of a problem for farmers who have multiple plots of land.
They find sugarcane cultivation ideal for those with larger landholdings
because, as one farmer put it, sugar 'somehow makes one free such that
I concentrate on farming in the other fields where I grow food crops'.[21]
These sentiments corroborate a 2004 study that observed that sugarcane
cultivation is less labour intensive but very profitable for farmers because
it can withstand bad weather conditions and requires less weeding.
This, in turn, frees labour for cultivation of maize and cassava which
are the main staples for the area. Among the outgrowers, 91.4 per cent
and 8.5 per cent report maize and cassava as their staples, respectively
(Concern Universal International 2012). Thus, sugarcane cultivation has
the potential to improve household food security by providing additional
income without undermining staple food production, but this is true only
for a very small number of households which own more than a single plot.
Meanwhile, the majority grapple with food insecurity when they commit
their land to sugarcane cultivation. A survey done by Concern Universal
among the outgrowers established that 21 per cent of the outgrowers ran
short of their harvested food stocks for 7-12 months and 17 per cent ran
out for 4-6 months in the year, respectively. The same survey established
that only 1 per cent of the outgrowers ran short of their harvested food
stocks for 1-3 months in a year. Thus, in total, 39 per cent of the outgrowers
experience deficits in their food stocks for extended periods of the year.
In cases of food shortage, outgrowers' coping strategies include food
purchased on credit (17 per cent), food purchased with own cash (45 per
cent) and casual labour (14 per cent) (Concern Universal 2012).

Gendered consequences

The expansion of the sugar industry has generated differential gender
impacts and effects for communities in Dwangwa. While there are claims

[19] Discussion with outgrowers, Dwangwa, Nkhotakota, 5 November 2012.
[20] Interview with an outgrower in Dwangwa, Nkhotakota District, 11 February 2012.
[21] A participant at a discussion with community members in Dwangwa, Nkhatabay District,
16 November 2012.

that sugarcane cultivation is beneficial for communities, empirical evidence shows that the benefits are unevenly distributed between men and women. Overall, sugarcane cultivation has promoted the feminisation of poverty through the marginalisation of women in benefits, employment, governance and resources. This is mainly attributed to the control and management of the proceeds from sugarcane cultivation at the household level. Outgrowers can provide paid labour on the estate sugarcane fields every Monday, allowing them to acquire expert knowledge in the cultivation of sugarcane, but also to earn income to take care of their day-to-day needs. Women and children mostly supply this labour. The modalities of payment for the work marginalise women because DCGL pays the contract holder and not necessarily the individuals who actually perform the work. In discussions, women consistently complained that 'when payment is finally made, we are often told by [our men] that they want to use the money to boost the capital base of their businesses so that they can make more profit for our future prosperity'.[22]

Women are further marginalised in the management and governance structures of sugarcane enterprises and associations. While membership of the upper-level governance structures is by invitation, there are no guidelines that stipulate the gender composition of membership. At the lower level of the governance structures, membership is through elections, which are very competitive, further excluding women. Furthermore, women are not interested in contesting such positions because of the history of conflicts and violence associated with the expansion of the sugar industry in Dwangwa. Even when women are successful, they often do not take these positions. In discussions, women described the sugarcane industry as a war, arguing that 'it makes sense that men should be commanders [meaning leaders] since it is them that want to be fighting'.[23]

The organisation of production

Sugar cultivation poses challenges to rural households mainly due to the way the projects are designed and managed. In managing the schemes, the priority is to serve commercial interests at the expense of 'addressing the problems of the owners of land'.[24] Farmers are subject to a wide range of taxes, management fees and operational fees, as well as extension fees, haulage charges and input (fertiliser and herbicides) costs. According to Church et al. (2008:120), DCGL takes a 15 per cent handling fee on all purchases such as fertiliser and chemicals, and 30 per cent of the sugarcane proceeds as a management fee to cover the costs of

[22] Discussion with women outgrowers at Mkangadzinja, Dwangwa, Nkhotakota District, 20 August 2012.
[23] Ibid.
[24] Interview with an outgrower, 11 February 2012.

administration, bank charges and input application. The sales statement of one outgrower is illustrative in this regard. In 2011, with 5.39ha of land devoted to sugarcane cultivation, he harvested 606.33 tonnes. His gross sales amounted to US$8,270[25] but he took home only US$2,529[26] with his costs representing 69.4 per cent of his gross income. Frustration with the exploitative tendencies of DCGL has resulted in the formation of community-led associations. These have been authorised by the Ministry of Agriculture and Food Security (MoAFS), describing the formations as 'an attempt to diffuse persistent tensions and the attendant political implications that protracted struggles between the farmers and DCGL may have on the government's image'.[27] The new associations are nonetheless modelled on the DCGL organisational structure but 'motivated to move away from an elitist and capitalist way of managing outgrowers to an inclusive, community based style...outgrowers in our scheme are our bosses and those of us in management are their servants'.[28] The underlying motivation is to limit overheads as much as possible, so as to leave outgrowers with decent amounts of disposable income earned as dividends. However, it remains to be seen whether these associations will be effective in the long run.

Conclusion

What is the future of smallholder farmers in Malawi? The FISP, which was considered as a potential lever for smallholder farmers to break free from the low-productivity maize trap, is unravelling. It is not as successful as was once claimed, and has been plagued by corruption and political capture. Delivery and distribution of inputs through the FISP have become a lucrative opportunity for political patronage, which determines who gains. This has sidelined other private-sector players, undermining the sustainability of the programme (Chinsinga 2011; Dorward and Chirwa 2011).

As a result, the prospect of the FISP catalysing substantial agrarian transformation remains remote. Moreover, without a redistributive land reform, which looks unlikely for political reasons, smallholders remain trapped in a low-productivity spiral, and any escape may be temporary and highly reliant on good rainfall, and dependent on state-based patronage relationships as a route to input subsidies. While the GBI was conceived and widely justified as the strategy to protect the gains achieved through the FISP, the experiences in Dwangwa suggest otherwise. The GBI is squeezing smallholders off their land, yet there is virtual impasse in wider land reform efforts (Peters and Kambewa 2007;

---

[25] MK3,266,650.01 in local currency.
[26] MK998,823.16 in local currency.
[27] Discussion with outgrowers at Mkangadzinja, Dwangwa, 20 August 2012.
[28] Ibid.

Chinsinga 2011). Instead of promoting the cultivation of food crops, the GBI in Nkhotakota focuses on the cultivation of sugarcane, which has precipitated a wave of land grabs resulting in running physical and judicial battles between smallholder farmers fighting to hold on to their small plots (usually their only productive assets) and investors intent on expanding sugar production. The situation for smallholder farmers is therefore highly precarious. While the government appears keen to promote smallholder farming through the FISP and GBI, the paradox is that it shows no sign of being willing to undertake the necessary reforms to enable smallholder farmers to realise their full potential. The existing political economy makes it difficult for the elites to push for progressive land reforms, at least in a decisive manner, not least because such elites are the main beneficiaries of the existing land tenure pattern. This situation has created a new configuration in the agrarian political economy, in which the smallholder farmer is caught between a rock and a hard place. This emerging agrarian political economy is manifested in a wide range of struggles, as exemplified in Nkhotakota District. These struggles have been precipitated by the land lease processes of estates; shifts in patterns of land use from food to cash crops; low returns accruing to smallholder farmers engaged in sugarcane cultivation under the auspices of management companies; and weakened livelihoods for local communities committing their land to sugarcane cultivation under estate management arrangements.

9

Agrarian Struggles in Mozambique

Insights from Sugarcane Plantations

GAYNOR PARADZA
& EMMANUEL SULLE

Introduction

Mozambique is one of several countries in Southern Africa where big sugar companies have acquired land to produce cane, combining a nucleus estate and a mill, with an outgrower arrangement (Richardson 2010; Buur et al. 2011). This chapter focuses on the ways in which large-scale land investments are influencing agrarian structure, tenure dynamics, livelihood outcomes and social and institutional relationships around resources and investments in Mozambique. It looks at two cases: one established estate, and one proposed.

Since the early 2000s, Mozambique has been one of the main targets of large-scale land-based investments (Cotula et al. 2009; Nhantumbo and Salomão 2010; Hanlon 2011; Deininger et al. 2011). The country is endowed with abundant natural resources, fertile land and attractive investment policies. The combination of 'abundant' land for large-scale agriculture and expanding energy production, through natural gas and coal reserves, is core to its development plans.

Mozambique's national land legislation recognises its citizens' customary tenure as constituting legal property rights and allows these land rights to be owned and transacted. The Constitution states that all land belongs to the state (Article no. 109) so, while the land is nationalised, the property rights of those who hold and use the land are protected in law. As elsewhere on the continent, investments in Mozambique have targeted land that is under customary tenure, land that is the least secure and easiest to negotiate (Alden Wily 2011b). In Mozambique, loopholes in the law combined with poor enforcement leave the commons vulnerable to appropriation (ibid.). This has led to growing concerns about on-going large-scale investments in agriculture and mining.

Government efforts to revive sugar estates and mills have attracted private investors to the sugar industry (Buur et al. 2011). Sugar production in Mozambique dates back to the mid-1960s when a private company,

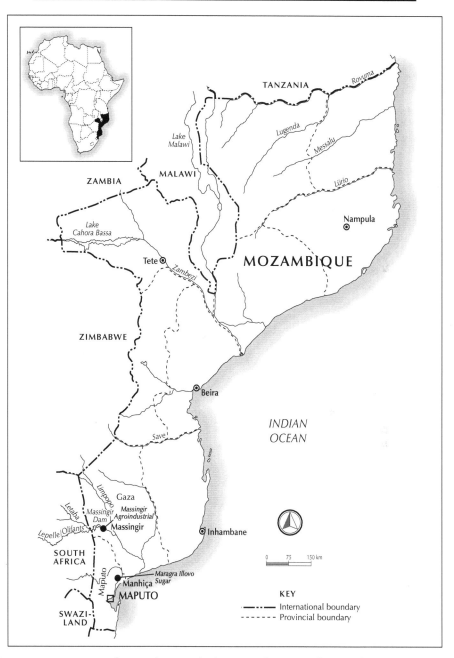

Map 9.1 Mozambique, showing the location of Maragra Illovo and Massingir Agroindustrial

Sena Sugar Estates Ltd, set up operations. By 1972, the sugar industry was the third largest export sector and the biggest formal employer (Buur et al. 2011). However, the sector experienced a setback during the civil war and all the sugar mills were abandoned. In the 1990s, the post-war government intervened to ensure stability in the supply of sugar for both local and international markets. More recently, the 'Everything But Arms' provisions of the European Union allowed tariff-free importation of sugar produced in low-income countries, effectively subsidising the cost of producing sugar in Mozambique and making it an attractive production base for South African sugar companies.

This chapter critically assesses the dynamics surrounding two sugar-cane investments. The following section describes the research sites of Maragra Sugar Ltd, an established estate in Maputo province run by the South African company, Illovo Sugar Ltd, and Massingir Agroindustrial, an upcoming estate in Gaza province, run by a conglomerate of South African and Mozambican business interests. In each case, new terrains of struggle are identified and alternatives to large-scale estate farming emerge. The chapter identifies the narratives about and struggles in response to large-scale land-based investments. It further illustrates how these shape and influence policy outcomes in the country.

The chapter draws on the findings of site visits and data collection in the two case-study sites during 2012 and 2013. We used qualitative and quantitative research methods, including desktop research and fieldwork, consisting of key informant interviews, combined with a quantitative survey carried out in both field sites. We surveyed 55 Maragra company workers and conducted a separate survey of 75 households, including sugarcane and non-sugarcane outgrowers. In addition, we surveyed local businesses and women who sell food at the local market.

The Maragra Sugar Ltd Sugarcane Estate

Maragra Sugar estate is in Manhiça District, about 100km from Maputo. The area is served by a tarred road and railway line to the port of Beira, on the banks of the Inkomati River. Maragra was established during the colonial era and abandoned during the civil war. After having fallen into disuse in 1996, the South African sugar company Illovo acquired and rehabilitated the Maragra estate. In 2006, Associated British Foods acquired a 51 per cent shareholding in Illovo. The estate produced 6,000 tonnes of sugar in 2000, rising to 75,000 tons of sugar in 2009, and in 2013 the mill produced 84,000 tons (Illovo Sugar 2013). As well as the estate, Maragra depends on outgrowers to augment the supply of sugarcane for its mill. It now aims to produce around 400,000 tons of cane per annum which, combined with further supplies from its contracted outgrowers, will provide enough cane for the Maragra factory to reach its sugar production targets.

According to the cane supply and development manager for Maragra Sugar, the company does not merely implement corporate social responsibility, but rather sees its partnership with small farmers on outgrower contracts as part of its philosophy of an inclusive business model. As he argued, 'The company doesn't want to own 15,000ha, but it only owns 6,000ha and we rely on outgrowers and middlemen.' Currently outgrowers contribute about 30 per cent of the company's total output, cultivating an area of 3,240ha. Among the outgrowers are 42 large-scale farmers, 40 medium- and 18 small-scale farmers.[1] The company pays M1300 (US$42.50) per tonne of cane brought to the mill, but farmers developed concerns about the payment because the documents they receive from the sugar company are written in English and they are unclear about how the quality of their cane (its sucrose level), which determines the level of payment, is determined.

As of 2013 the company had contracts with 371 (337 small, 29 medium and 5 large) farmers producing sugarcane (Corporate Citizenship 2014). During our interview the company official stressed that special consideration is needed to understand the economics of sugar production: 'Sugarcane is different from crops like tobacco; to make a profit there needs to be a secured supply and factory and then outgrowers' (interview, company official, Maragra, 12 April 2013). Because of the need to secure adequate supply, and concerns about the scale of outgrowers' production, many sugar-producing companies opt to establish a nucleus estate as well as a processing factory. When the cane is produced far from the sugar mill, transporting the cane has proved expensive. To maintain the required sucrose level, cane must be delivered to the factory within 24 hours of harvesting. For this reason, companies tend to have their plantations close to the miller, and to target farmers in the immediate vicinity to become outgrowers.

The company provides its own processing and marketing facilities and hires a transportation agency (Unitrans) to carry its cane from the fields, while the smallholder farmers have to make transport arrangements with approved subcontractors to deliver their cane to the factory. Maragra pays its farmers 40 per cent of the proceeds of the sugar from their cane on delivery, and retains 60 per cent of the revenue. The balance of the money is paid when the trading price of the sugar and the taxes have been determined, normally at the end of the season. The company pays three extension officers to provide services to its outgrowers; teaches association members about basic agronomy; builds the capacity of its outgrowers and establishes associations to enable the small-scale farmers to organise themselves; and connects the

---

[1] The classification of the large, medium and small-scale farmers is done on the following basis. Large-scale farmers have an area of 100ha and above, medium an area of between 20 and 100ha and the small-scale farmer is the one with less than 20ha.

outgrowers to global fair trade programmes through which they earn an extra premium for their produce.

A major challenge that both the company and farmers face is their dependence on unpredictable weather conditions. If there are floods, they affect both estate and outgrower. But during drought, small-scale farmers cannot irrigate as they do not have the irrigation infrastructure in place, while the estate is able to sustain its production as it has adequate water supply systems. For this reason, the company's supply of cane fluctuates substantially every season, and this affects the running of the mill and the company's competitiveness.

Maragra Sugar estate occupies an area of 6,500ha which has been fully planted since the early 2000s. The land is owned by Illovo Sugar Ltd on the basis of a 50-year renewable *Direto de Uso e Aproveitamento dos Terras* (DUAT), or registered land-use right. The rest of the land in the area is held by family farmers who have recognised rights to their land on the basis of their customary occupation. Among them, very few have obtained DUATs. The fortunes of Maragra have ebbed and flowed with the civil war and the subsequent signing of the peace accord (Buur et al. 2011). Since then, the government of Mozambique has supported the rehabilitation and expansion of the sugar sector in order to boost foreign investments in the country.

Indeed, the ownership of land for the majority of Mozambicans is still by occupation and not by registered DUATs. In our survey of 75 households located in the immediate vicinity of the sugar mill (including outgrowers, farmers growing other crops and non-farmer households) we found that only 7 per cent of the respondents had registered DUATs and a further 7 per cent had applied for DUATs, while the remaining respondents did not have DUATs at all. We also found that in Manhiça, there was no clear correlation between the level of education and the possession of land through registered DUATs.

Maragra Sugar estate employs both local residents and immigrants for various industrial and plantation tasks that include operating machinery and farm work. However, the company is not the only or the most significant employer in the area, as Manhiça is located in a strategic position, with a highway from Maputo passing through it, which makes it a temporary destination for truck and vehicle drivers. In addition, the presence of the sugar estate with its processing facility attracts people from elsewhere to seek employment in its factory and its fields. Given that the work of harvesting the cane is considered to be hard labour, most work is done by men; 61 per cent of the employees in our survey of randomly selected company workers in Maragra were men.

Maragra mill and nucleus sugar estate employ a total of 4,857, among them 1,043 permanent agricultural workers and 3,812 seasonal workers who are hired particularly during the peak harvesting season (Corporate Citizenship 2014). The majority of the workers are employed on a temporary basis. This means that the non-permanent workers have to find other means to complement their employment income.

In an attempt to organise themselves and improve their bargaining power, the workers have established a workers' union. However, key informant interviews revealed that the workers' unions were not effective, in part due to alleged victimisation of union members (Interview with outgrower, Manhiça, April 2013). We also heard workers explaining that, since Maragra is part-owned by the Frelimo government, they feel less able to challenge labour conditions than if it were a wholly private company.

The people we interviewed in the area around Maragra are engaged in semi-subsistence farming activities, with many sending their agricultural produce for sale in the capital city of Maputo. Manhiça town is currently growing fast and boasts hotels, bars, convenience and service industry facilities, four major banks, four churches, two markets, a maize grinding mill, a slaughterhouse, a public hospital and the sugar mill. Most of these businesses were established between 2010 and 2013 and are linked to servicing the agricultural sector which is the main economic driver in the area. This suggests the importance of incomes from sugarcane in driving economic development in the district.

Census data show that women outnumber men in the population, and more than half of the population are aged below fourteen or above 65 years old, indicating a high dependency ratio. Typically, while men either work at Maragra Sugar, produce charcoal for sale or undertake piece work, women grow food for subsistence and to sell at local markets. Women also work piece-jobs and are seasonally employed at Maragra Sugar. Many of the young men who cannot find work at Maragra Sugar migrate to South Africa in search of jobs.

Massingir Agroindustrial sugarcane plantation

Massingir is a rapidly-growing town in Gaza province, on the banks of the Olifants River. The Massingir Dam was built in the 1970s but construction was disrupted by the war. After the war, the African Development Bank assisted the Mozambican government to complete the dam, thereby providing a basis both for more irrigated agriculture and for hydroelectricity, which together were expected to provide a catalyst for development in the district (Manuel and Salomão 2009).

Between 2007 and 2009, the government allocated land adjacent to the Olifants River to a company called ProCana, a subsidiary of the London-based company Central African Mining and Exploration Company (CAMEC) to produce sugarcane and ethanol for export to the region and to Europe (Manuel and Salomão 2009, Borras et al. 2011a). According to its plans, the investment was expected to generate employment for

7,000 people (Manuel and Salomão 2009). In November 2010, when it had not yet commenced operations, the government took the unusual step of revoking ProCana's contract (Borras et al. 2011b). In October 2011, however, the government allocated 31,000ha of the land that had been allocated to ProCana to Massingir Agroindustrial (MAI) – a consortium made up of 51 per cent shareholding by the South African company Transvaal Suiker Beperk (TSB) Sugar and 49 per cent by a consortium of Mozambican businessmen known as SIAL (Sociedade de Investimentos Agro-Industrias do Limpopo), chaired by the former Minister of Industry (Allafrica 2012).

MAI planned to plant 37,000ha of sugarcane and to put a further 12,000ha under sugarcane through contracts with outgrowers. In addition, a further 2,500ha would be reserved as a 'community farm' where the local community would cultivate sugarcane also for sale to MAI on contract. To compensate for the loss of family plots, it made commitments to assist the community to develop food gardens on 1,000ha of land. The cane was to be processed into sugar, ethanol, molasses, animal feed and for the generation of electricity, with most (80 per cent) of the produce to be exported to Europe.

An official from MAI estimated that when operating at full capacity the company would offer employment to at least 4,500 people (MAI official 2012: pers. comm.). The official explained that the company was considering the adoption of outgrower schemes following the success stories of such models in Kilombero, Tanzania (see Chapter 7 in this volume). 'TSB is a leader in outgrower promotion...I think the value of outgrowers is now accepted – companies are understanding that you must see the outgrowers' cane as your own cane' (MAI official, interview in Massingir, April 2013). While MAI is a new company, residents and CSO representatives in Massingir do not see any difference between ProCana and MAI, as the land to be allocated by the district authorities is the same. A CSO representative we talked to in Massingir stated: 'What we see is a change of name, but not the programme. The programme is the same. We see the same people.'

Through our interviews with MAI's representatives and villagers in the district, we learned that MAI's Mozambican partners are the same who introduced ProCana to the villagers and district authorities. Government officials in Massingir consider MAI as a catalyst for development in the district. According to the district's Agriculture and Economic Director, the company is required to offer technical support to the communities, provide seed to them and develop community fields for both sugarcane (150ha) and cereals (150ha).

Competing views on land and property have been deployed by various camps around the contested meanings of 'marginal lands'. In Massingir, government officials justified the allocation of land to investors by arguing that it was 'idle', despite scattered settlements, small farms and use of the land by pastoralists for grazing. At Maragra, the struggle over land moved into the courts when a non-governmental organisation, ActionAid, assisted a community which took the investor to court for encroaching on the community's land without its consent.

This struggle over land has resulted in violent resistance by the claimants of the land seeking to assert their claims over those of the investors. In other cases, the struggles have precipitated efforts by peasants who hold unregistered DUATs to the land to secure their rights through registration and formalisation. This has attracted the attention of organisations that are working with the communities to delineate and secure land rights. In an effort to facilitate investor access to land, people have been moved from their sparse settlements into more 'efficient' and densely settled villages to pave the way for development of the sugar estate and national parks. Borras et al. (2011a) challenge the claim of vast and underutilised land in Massingir.

Massingir District has long been a labour-source area, with young people migrating elsewhere within the country or to South Africa to seek jobs. The arrival of MAI revived the youths' hopes, especially during the introductory meetings held between the company and villagers, as the company promised to create jobs, build water troughs for their cattle, install domestic water pipes and assist them with cultivating their farms. None of these promises were realised at the time of writing this chapter. MAI's projection of 4,500 jobs has also not been realised, as, despite the land being allocated to MAI in 2012, by 2014 production was not yet under way. After five years of investment deals at Massingir, then, the vision of job creation has not materialised.

Agrarian struggles: six themes from the cases

These two cases have offered examples of large-scale investments centred on sugar – an industry at the centre of Mozambique's agricultural commercialisation strategy. The state initially participated as a shareholder in the sugar companies but gradually reduced its shareholding. The result has been a significant expansion of sugar production, with major influences on agrarian structure and agrarian dynamics. The emergent agrarian structure is characterised by large nucleus estates, peasant farmers, associational land production systems and landless labourers.

What have been the consequences of these changes in these areas? The following sections outline some of the findings from interviews in the two sites. These highlight a number of struggles and conflicts. Divisions highlighted include sugarcane growers versus non-sugarcane growers; large versus small cane growers; associations versus individual cane growers; cane growers versus middle-men; and the company versus individual farmers. Within the associations, there are struggles between the various members about the system of sharing the benefits accruing to the association.

Displacement

At Maragra, while peasants had been displaced to make way for the colonial sugar estate, some reoccupied the land when the estate was abandoned. With the estate being revived as a state farm, there were further displacements and again a degree of reoccupation when the war took over. The pattern was reversed when the sugarcane plantation was re-established. Similar displacements occurred, or were threatened, in Massingir, where, in contrast, after ProCana's DUAT was revoked by the government, MAI has had to renegotiate for the land from the communities.

At Maragra, displaced people were relocated and provided with new plots, albeit smaller ones. Some also negotiated for land from other communities. In Massingir, displacement has yet to occur on any scale, as the estate is still to be established, but there has been extreme uncertainty now over many years.

Land distribution

A process of land concentration has occurred following investment. Resistance from local people, supported by civil society organisations, has limited this, however, and companies have often sought to develop outgrower arrangements, rather than large estates. In the case of Massingir, for example, the business model proposed includes a community block farm for sugar production as well as a community farm for food production.

For sugar production, the investors have encouraged 'grouping' of land rights through producer associations. Individuals with land below a certain threshold are obliged to work through an association if they want to grow sugarcane for sale to the investors, but in the process they cede control over their parcels of land to the association.

The high immigration of labour to Maragra to work on the sugar estate, in the mill and in related service industries, has produced a landless population of labourers alongside the local farming population. These labourers are either housed by their employers or must seek their own land, sparking rising demand for residential and subsistence farming land in the locality and heightening competition over land and fragmentation of land holdings. This has, as a result, fuelled the emergence of an informal land market in Maragra.

The processes to secure land in large holdings have in both sites resulted in the conversion of common resources of forest and grazing lands to privately-held land held under lease for exclusive use by the investor.

Land tenure

The local authority has facilitated the process of converting land from grazing and subsistence farming to the sugar estate by facilitating the DUAT system, spurred on by the requirement of Maragra Sugar that it will only buy sugarcane from farmers with a registered DUAT. This has resulted in the privatisation and exclusive use of land which has until now been managed and accessed as a common tenure resource.

The result has been the gradual loss of common property, aggravated by the increased fragmentation of land and the higher density of people occupying it. The local population has responded by sub-dividing and releasing some land on to the market, and there is a gradual reduction in the numbers of livestock keepers as the locals convert their land to more compatible uses. This struggle is manifest in Maragra where land tenure is converted from an unregistered DUAT to a registered one. The transfer of land from an unregistered to a registered DUAT under the middlemen who grow sugar means that the smallholders lose autonomy over their individual pieces of land. They cede this autonomy to the control of the middleman who assumes control of decision-making over the land.

Intergenerational conflicts
Intergenerational struggles are evident in both sites. In Maragra, elderly women who are too old to work on the sugar estate struggle to maintain their land as a subsistence asset. This is against pressure by the younger men and women who are more than willing to sub-divide and dispose of the land to the immigrants who are seeking to settle in Maragra. In Massingir, the same struggle pits the elderly who want to retain the land against the young who are willing to sub-divide land and dispose of it to accommodate the establishment of a sugar estate and mill.

Associations versus individual cane growers
Associations are farmer groups that come together for farming or for joint production purposes, in order to make the land use more contiguous and as a strategy to secure larger pieces of land. When farmers form an association, the decision-making is ceded to the larger group. There are different models among the outgrowers. This results in different costs and opportunities for members.

For example, farmers holding contiguous parcels of land will work together, register an association for the purpose of mobilising the contract, support and inputs from the company, and work together on the production and marketing process. Sometimes benefits are divided in proportion to the original land holding; at other times, the distributions are equal.

Tensions exist within associations over control of the distribution of costs and benefits, and some with larger land areas seek to establish additional individual plots in order to gain more individual control. Women association members are marginalised, since they are, on average, less educated than men. As a result, they lack the requisite documents such as national identity and a registered DUAT. The more educated men in the association control the strategic positions and negotiate with Illovo on behalf of the association. A woman sugarcane outgrower who belongs to an association voiced her frustration at the manner in which the association was run. She questioned how, although she controlled the most land in the association, she did not necessarily receive more returns than other association members. She also explained how she grew some of her own sugarcane outside the association land but had to sell it through a man as she did not have a contract with Illovo. She shared how the amount of sugarcane she loaded on the trucks was more than that which was reflected on the receipt that the man who represented her claimed was issued by Illovo. This woman was illiterate and relied on her teenage son to read the documents for her. These dynamics within associations and between association members and others result in conflicts between producers.

Conservation land use
While the struggles in Maragra can be simplified to sugarcane versus non-cane growers, the situation in Massingir is compounded by another claim to land and natural resources, namely the interest of the national parks and wildlife sector that has targeted the same land for conservation use. Wildlife and large-scale sugarcane production both claim to have the potential to reduce poverty and improve the situation in the district.

Unlike the other struggles between the sugarcane growers and peasants, that between the large-scale sugar growers and wildlife has been played out at the Ministerial level. This struggle has resulted in open confrontation over a specific piece of land which was earmarked for the sugar plantation and for the sugarcane growers, while also being earmarked by the Great Limpopo Transfrontier Park authorities for resettling people who have been moved to make way for the park.

Rural livelihood and food security impacts

Large-scale land investments result in a reorganisation of livelihood opportunities, which has an impact on food security. In both cases, sugarcane production undermines subsistence food production and deepens gender inequalities. In particular, women argued that a shift to cane increased the burden of securing subsistence food.

Impacts, of course, are differentiated. People hold varying amounts of land. Those people who have more land turn their unused and under-utilised land to sugarcane production, and this provides a complement to food production. However, for the majority with smaller plots, cane is taking up land which was previously used for growing food crops and for grazing.

The pressure on land is especially intense on the valuable floodplain plots in Maragra. Here, too, differences in water management practices cause disruption. Sugarcane growers' use of water is not consistent with the needs of subsistence food production. As a result, subsistence food is increasingly vulnerable to flooding when the sugarcane growers irrigate.

Sugarcane investments are also affecting livestock production. In part, this is because of the reduction of grazing due to the expansion of sugar plots, particularly on the floodplain – a key resource for grazing in the dry season. In addition, investors are seeking to acquire grazing land of their own for parallel businesses. At Massingir, for example, the company has come into conflict with local communities over the control of land for pasture, as part of its non-sugar operations. The proposed land-use plans mean that herders will have to move to new locations for grazing. The company had originally proposed to provide land for community food production, but this has yet to materialise and it is unclear how this land would be apportioned.

All of these factors have combined to affect food security and liveli-hoods for those in the vicinity of the sugar estates. While some have improved their livelihoods through increased income from outgrowing, such benefits are unevenly spread. Men control the sugarcane receipts, and women have lost their food plots. Livestock herders have lost out due to declining pasture areas or planned reallocations elsewhere, increasing herding costs. And those with small plots are now increasingly reliant on sugar income to supply food and sustain livelihoods. While many are keen to engage in sugar production, new vulnerabilities are emerging.

Conclusion

Experiences from the Maragra and Massingir cases illustrate the diverse and complex impacts of large-scale investments on livelihoods and agrar-ian dynamics. The outcomes are a product of globalising pressures that are mediated by the specific local contexts. The role of the state is also evident in shaping the outcomes in the two contexts which are articulated through the diverse interpretations of the law and exercise of state power. The influence of the state permeates the negotiations over land rights and influences their outcomes, even though the law stipulates that land-based investments must be negotiated between investors and local communities.

These dynamics also affect land-tenure relations between the com-munity and the private sector. The investors and local communities interact through negotiations over access to land resulting in compromises such as community farms, and concessions by investors to contribute to public infrastructure, extension support, and to assist local people with food production. These public benefits from private investments have been combined with the possibilities for accumulation for those with sufficient land to profit from sugarcane outgrowing arrangements. These benefits, however, are unevenly distributed, and the arrival of cane has generated a range of conflicts between different groups. Women, livestock owners, small plot holders and the poor have lost out. The result is a process of rural differentiation, with changing contours of vulnerability. Sugar may be sweet, but not for everyone.

10

South African Commercial Farmers in the Congo

RUTH HALL, WARD ANSEEUW
& GAYNOR PARADZA

Introduction

In the tropical southern belt of the Republic of Congo, a group of South African commercial farmers have cleared trees and long elephant grass on some parts of their 50,000ha to commence large-scale production of maize. As this case shows, alongside the former colonial powers and Northern economies in the rush for African farmland is a new generation of investors from the 'emerging economies'. Among these are the BRICS countries, including South Africa. Unlike China and Brazil which have launched bilateral partnerships with many African countries for technical assistance in agriculture, from India and South Africa the main actors are private companies that have secured deals with African governments, often in the form of long-term leases, to expand commercial farming operations in their countries. According to the Land Matrix (2014) database, South African companies have 28 large land deals either under negotiation or concluded in nine countries, with a total area of 679,262ha acquired in the deals concluded. Among these land deals involving South African investors is one brokered by the commercial farmers' association, Agri South Africa (AgriSA), for 80,000ha of prime farmland in Congo's Niari province, about 200km inland from the port city of Pointe-Noire.

As with many large land acquisitions that are reported in the media, contradictions have emerged in the information regarding this investment. There have been significant discrepancies between ambitious announcements and the area of land actually provided under a legal agreement, and again between the land acquired and the area cleared and cultivated. The deal was initially mooted to involve 10 million hectares, the total area the government claimed was available for investors, but the contract, which was ultimately signed in 2011 by the government of the Republic of Congo and the South African farmers, concerns 80,000ha. The South African farmers initially occupied 50,000ha, with the other 30,000ha to be released by the Minister of Agriculture upon a satisfactory record of harvest. By 2013, only 2,500ha were under cultivation (Land Matrix 2014). But by 2014, three years after taking occupation, with over 5,000ha (10 per cent) under production and finally achieving successful harvests, the farmers reported that the government had released the further 30,000ha to them, on which they would expand in the future (Dirk Hanekom, head of AgriSA's Africa Policy Committee, on the South African television channel Kyknet, 2 October 2014).

The parties to the deal have also given imprecise and inconsistent information with regard to the origins of the deal, its financial backers, its intended production, destination markets, the terms of the land allocation, the consultation with local people and the investors' sources of finance. Indeed, plans change. But these divergences also reflect actors' strategies – whether they are local activists defending local interests, or investors positioning themselves to access land, water and markets. So much is common across many land deals around the world. In this case of the South African farmers entering into the Congo, however, there is also a striking absence of coordination or consistent versions of events among state institutions, with different ministries and departments presenting competing versions of who did what to enable this investment and what its terms are. Overall, the contradictory information regarding this deal reflects a key feature it shares with many, if not most, transnational land deals in Africa: their non-transparent nature.

Our focus in this chapter is on the politics of this farmland investment: the complex processes through which this deal came to be, the competing versions advanced by actors with roles and interests in it, and how it and its significance for Congo as a whole and the people in its immediate vicinity changed over time. We therefore attend to interests at the national and local level. We aim to depict the dazzling array of people involved in different capacities in the deals: as intermediaries and facilitators, champions and opponents.

The empirical basis of the paper is from two separate fieldtrips to the Republic of Congo, to the capital Brazzaville and to the AgriSA project based at Malolo, in 2011 and again in 2012. It is mainly based on key informant interviews, with the Congolese authorities and South African representatives in Brazzaville, and with the South African farmers and local authorities in the Niari region where the farm is located. We conducted two pilot household surveys, later complemented by a full baseline study in the four villages of Malolo 1, Malolo 2, Dihesse and Mouindi, implemented by a research team from Marien Ngouabi University. Our survey data are reported in Pongui (2012).[1] In the future, we aim to return to conduct follow-up household surveys, and on this basis better determine the impacts of this deal on local people – to find out who is benefitting and who is losing out and what new dimensions of social differentiation are emerging as a result.

---

[1] This field report is available on request from the authors.

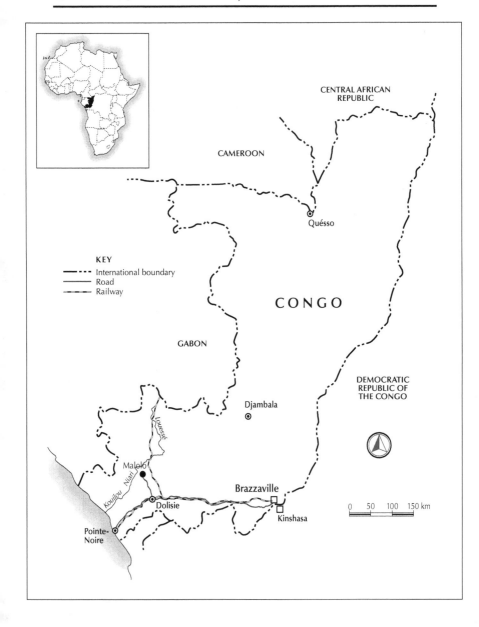

Map 10.1 Congo, showing the location of South African Agri-Congo at Malolo

South Africans trek north

In late 2011, a convoy of fifteen South African commercial farmers with their 4x4s, trucks loaded with implements, and tractors on trailers, set off on a 5,500km, six-week 'trek' from Pretoria through Namibia, Angola and the Democratic Republic of Congo (DRC), to the Republic of Congo. There they occupied the 'farms' allocated to them by the Congolese government. Like many land deals across Africa, this one is shrouded in mystery. Contradictory reports abound: from the farmers themselves, the Congolese and South African governments, Congolese NGOs and opposition parties, and local people and their leaders. Contradictions concern exactly what land was allocated, on what terms, for how long, and whether this land was already occupied and used by local villagers for their own production of food crops – or whether it was (as widely claimed) vacant and 'empty' land. This is not an isolated initiative; several initiatives are under way by South African commercial farmers, agribusinesses and related industries to secure rights to farmland, water and markets elsewhere in the continent (Hall 2012b; Hall 2011; Richardson 2010). AgriSA has indicated that as of 2014 it had land negotiations concluded or under way in 28 African countries. Even as the convoy to Congo was en route to their new land, while crossing through the DRC, the farmers were reportedly approached by an advisor to the President of DRC who made a further offer of land and wanted to know whether more South African farmers might be willing to move to the DRC (Bauer 2012).

On arrival at the Congolese border, they were met by the Minister of Agriculture and other dignitaries, with welcomes and speeches (Bauer 2012). Congo is, indeed, in dire need of improved food supply. The country has a population of 3.7 million people, and much of its 342,000 sq km (RAPDA 2010: 6) is defined by the World Bank as having some of the highest agricultural potential in the world (Arezki et al. 2011; Deininger et al. 2011). Yet, in this oil-dominated economy, agriculture currently accounts for only about 5 per cent of GDP, having declined from 27 per cent in the 1960s (RAPDA 2010: 3, 11). Without a significant commercial farming sector, and with a high urbanisation rate of 62 per cent (RAPDA 2010: 7), Congo imports as much as 95 per cent of its food needs, according to the Ministry of Agriculture (Fin24 2009). The Congolese government indicates that only 2 per cent of the 10 million hectares it deems appropriate for commercialisation is currently cultivated, and it aims to make available this land – most of which is in the fertile, high rain-fall south of the country – to investors (Dieudonne 2011: pers. comm.).[2]

---

[2] Dieudonne, Savour Simon. 2011. Director-General, Ministry of Agriculture, Brazzaville, Congo, 4 August 2011.

This recent South African venture into the Congo was a second attempt to revive some of the state farms which, after years of mismanagement, stopped being operated in the 1980s in the context of structural adjustment policies and policy advice from the World Bank and International Monetary Fund. The current deal to revive estate farms echoes a stalled South African farming venture in the area during 1995, under former Presidents Lissouba and Mandela, when a group of ten South African farmers were given former state farms in other parts of Niari province around Loudima, Madingou and Nkayi (P. T. Mabiala 2011: pers. comm.).[3] At the time, the Congo State Treasury provided them with funds to rehabilitate the state farms, growing maize, tomatoes, vegetables and establishing fruit orchards, but the deal was soon scuppered by the war that broke out in 1996 and all the farmers left (Dieudonne 2011: pers. comm). Ironically, at the time, the current Minister of Agriculture, Rigobert Maboundou, was in the political opposition: 'he had very harsh criticism of the first deal [with the South Africans], now it is he who is the godfather of this second deal. He is the firm defender of the project' (P. T. Mabiala 2011: pers. comm.).

The South African deal has been possible because of loan finance from South Africa's privatised agricultural grain co-operative, Afgri (formerly *Oos-Transvaal Koöperasie* or Eastern Transvaal Co-operative). Afgri's regional expansion is in partnership with John Deere tractors, for which it is an Africa-wide agent. Afgri was recently sold to a new consortium dominated by Joseph Investment Holdings (60 per cent), an offshore company majority-owned by Fairfax, a Canadian insurance and investment company without farming experience, and its local (South African) partners include Bafepi, a small black economic-empowerment group (20 per cent), the parastatal Public Investment Corporation (15 per cent) and Afgri's management (5 per cent) (Afgri 2014). The sell-off to foreign investors of one of the most successful creations of state subsidies through apartheid agricultural policies stirred up controversy at home, with black farmers objecting that the accumulated wealth and market power of Afgri, created through state subsidy, should be retained under South African control, for the benefit of South African black farmers as well as consumers (Sherry 2013).

With Afgri's backing, the South Africans now launching the second foray into the Congo represent their investment in terms of pan-African solidarity and an attempt to transfer skills:

> We have signed the agreement with the Government of the Republic of Congo to develop Agriculture in Congo and thereby making more affordable food available to the people of the Congo. Together with this initiative we will do skills transfer to the people of Congo to educate them to become successful farmers themselves. The humanitarian

---

[3] Mabiala, Pascal Tsati. 2011. Member of Parliament for Loudima (Bouenza) and General-Secretary, UDPS (opposition party), Brazzaville, Congo, 3 August 2011.

upliftment of the local people is high on the agenda and we will be involved in developing Schools and Clinics [sic] to let the people of Congo experience a better quality life.

(Congo Agriculture 2012)[4]

The South African embassy envisages the extension of South African commercial interests beyond farming into related processing and infrastructure projects, as confirmed by an embassy official:

> AgriSA is not just about agriculture, they [the South African farmers] will bring in the value chain. The aim is to add value to agricultural products. They will have to build infrastructure to store fresh produce, for instance. They will be well located between Brazzaville and Pointe-Noire, the two main cities. (Mohamed 2011: pers. comm.)[5]

South Africa's strategic business interests in Congo include transport, oil (mostly equipment and training aspects), telecoms and port authorities. In January 2012, South African Airways opened a direct route between Johannesburg and Pointe-Noire, and in September 2012 opened a second direct route, to Brazzaville. The South African government considered this farmland deal an initial foray of private enterprise into Congo, with the expectation that further investments up and down the value chain, and into other sectors, would follow. However, the difficulties, delays and non-transparent nature of this deal makes it difficult to conceive that it would automatically appeal to other investors. As the South African ambassador observed, 'Once they are producing, I suspect that South African business may come' (Genge 2011: pers. comm.).[6]

The Congolese government also envisages the South African investment as part of a package of development initiatives to generate economic growth and diversification. A Chinese-built highway from Pointe-Noire on the Atlantic coast (West Africa's busiest port)[7] to the provincial town of Dolisie provides the South African investors with ready access to a coastal port, a decisive element in the location of the land allocation. 'This four-lane highway, with a perfect camber in the corners meanders through the jungle', observed the documentary film-maker Win Bauer (2012), who accompanied the convoy. Access to

---

4 AgriSA has rebranded its new offshoots as national bodies that retain their South African roots. Its Congolese affiliate, initially called 'AgriSA Congo' was later called 'Agri-Congo' and then renamed 'Congo Agriculture', while forming part of a wider collection of subsidiaries of AgriSA entitled 'Agri-All-Africa' which includes AgriSAMoz, Congo Agriculture, 'AgriSA Kenia' (sic), AgriSA Malawi and AgriSA Zambia (Congo Agriculture 2012).

5 Mohamed, Shuaib. 2011. 1st Political Councillor, South African Embassy, Brazzaville, Congo, 3 August 2011.

6 Genge, Manelisi. 2011. South African ambassador to Congo, South African Embassy, Brazzaville, Congo, 3 August 2011.

7 In return for uplifting the country's infrastructure, the Chinese have apparently been given permission to saw down the ancient hardwood trees of the rainforest, on a 200m strip stretching out along both sides of the highway. 'Twenty four hours a day, seven days a week a stream of specially designed trucks is carting the precious timber to Pointe-Noire from where it is shipped to China' (Bauer 2012).

the national capital of Brazzaville is via a railway line which is being upgraded and which runs in proximity to the farm allocated to the South Africans. The port of Pointe-Noire, affected by degraded infrastructure and endemic administrative heaviness and corruption, is currently also being improved.

The contested features of the land deal

Among ministries, there was no agreement on whether the land was occupied or not, what the current land uses were, the intended land use by the South Africans, or the duration of the lease that the government had concluded with them. The Ministry of Agriculture spearheaded the project, inviting the South Africans through their association AgriSA, yet it is the Ministry of Lands that is authorised to allocate land to investors. They presented different information to us regarding the amount of land and the duration of the deal. The lack of precise information is linked to secrecy around the negotiations and project planning within the government, and probably also payments that are not recorded in the contract itself. Although such a deal engaging directly the Congolese government was supposed to be gazetted and publicised for public consultations, very little information was effectively released about it (P.T. Mabiala 2011: pers. comm.). Yet the Ministry of Lands claims to have consulted people in the area.

Area of land
The South African investment is for 53,000ha in Niari and 27,000ha in Bouenza (Ministère de l'économie, du plan, de l'aménagement du territoire et de l'intégration 2011). The area leased centres on the 'Dihesse ranch', a former state farm where the state asserts 'private state ownership'.[8] The area contains within it remnants of earlier colonial estates, and the crumbling farm houses of their French masters, but also living in the area are local Congolese people and refugees from regional conflicts, especially from Angola's Cabinda province. Their villages are adjacent to the allocated farms.

Duration and terms of the lease
The contract we obtained specifies a duration of 30 years, which is renewable, at a rent of 2,500FCFA[9] (US$4.75) per hectare per year, which is fixed for the first ten years (Ministère de l'économie, du plan, de

---

[8]   A tenure category, resulting from French law, referring to land owned by the state (i.e. the state has a private title deed) and which can be used for state interest (in opposition to public interest). Such land can be leased out, sold, exchanged, or undergo any transaction recognised by private law.

[9]   Calculated using exchange rate of 0.0019, the average US$ / FCFA exchange rate for 2011-2014.

l'aménagement du territoire et de l'intégration 2011). Not only is the rent set at a very low rate; it is payable only per *hectare under production*, rather than on the entire area allocated. The detail of the contract was far from agreed among many of the key people we interviewed who were involved in making the deal happen. The Minister of Lands himself claims that the contract provides the land to the investors for 99 years, while his own departmental director said it was for 20 years; the South African embassy which brokered the deal said it was for 35 years, and the Minister of Agriculture said it was for 50 years (Minister Mabiala, Matsoumba-Boungou, Mohamed, Maboundou 2011: pers. comm.).[10] When asked, local people were unable to say for how long the South Africans were expected to stay, and did not know the terms of the lease, let alone its duration. The Minister of Agriculture informed us that the investors would pay rent to the state, rather than compensation to the local population. He claimed that:

> They [the South African farmers] have signed the contract and the terms and conditions, and we agreed on the crops and the advantages that they will bring. These are documents between the investor and the state, so they are not available. If we release these documents to the world, we could compromise the confidentiality of our partners. When we sign [the terms and conditions], we put their name, the amount of money, and the duration, and so on (Maboundou 2011: pers. comm.).

Compensation

Contrary to the contract and to the expectations of the South African embassy (and the farmers themselves), according to the Regional Director of the Ministry of Lands, the South African farmers, through Congo Agriculture, would compensate the local people for the loss of their land (Badianga 2011: pers. comm.).[11] However, the chief of Malolo 2 village reported that the Minister himself told him that, aside from gifts, no money would be paid out, but that the people of the village would benefit in terms of employment and provision of seed and a ready market for their produce (Mazinga 2011: pers. comm.).[12]

The opposition Member of Parliament was also unaware of any rent to be paid to the government, or of any compensation paid to local landholders (P.T. Mabiala 2011: pers. comm.). The South African embassy insisted that the Congolese government had negotiated with local people to secure the land and would compensate them (Genge and

[10] HE Pierre Mabiala, Minister of Lands and Public Affairs, Brazzaville, 4 August 2011; Mohamed 2011, pers. comm.; Matsoumba-Boungou, Alphonse. 2011. Directeur de la Reglementation et du Contentieux, Ministère des Affaires Foncières et du Domaine Public, Brazzaville, 2 and 3 August 2011; Maboundou, Rigobert. 2011. Minister of Agriculture, Congo-Brazzaville, 5 August 2011.

[11] Alphonse Badianga. Regional Director of Ministry of Lands and Management, Dolisie, Congo, August 2011.

[12] Daniel Mazinga, Chief, Malolo II Village, Niari Province, Congo, 6 August 2011.

Mohamed 2011: pers. comm.), while the Congolese officials insisted that this was not the responsibility of the government, and that determining compensation was a matter to be settled between the local people and the investors themselves (Matsoumba-Boungou 2011: pers. comm.). Even the Chief Financial Officer of the Ministry of Lands was unclear whether any compensation would be paid by the investor to the local population, for loss of land. He suspected not:

> I'm not sure if they pay; I think down the road it is a win-win partnership, so there is no fee to be paid. If there is an amount to be paid at some point in the future, it will be just a symbolic amount (Makanga 2011: pers. comm.).[13]

Land uses
What would the farmers grow? The Congolese government initially preferred production of staple foods, notably rice and cassava, but the quality of the land is not conducive to production of rice and, as the South African ambassador, Manelisi Genge, observed:

> The [South African] farmers don't want to come and displace the local farmers – let them continue with cassava. Instead, they [the South Africans] plan to produce maize, soya, and do a combination of stock farming and cultivation. They are wanting to develop a local breed of cattle, and also get involved in forestry. (Genge 2011: pers. comm.)

The contract allows for a broad spectrum of commodities, from tropical fruits to vegetable production, cereals and livestock. By late 2011, 1,500ha of maize were planted, which was expanded by 2014 to 5,000ha of maize, as well as tropical fruits on a modest scale. The South African farmers chose to start production with maize, as a fast-growing seasonal crop, to enable them to start repaying their loan from Afgri, their main financial backer. By 2012, they had signed an off-take contract for the totality of their maize production with the Congolese Brewery *Brasserie du Congo*.

Local versus export markets
The contract states that export of produce by the South Africans is authorised once the domestic market is saturated. While the Minister of Agriculture insisted that the South Africans would produce exclusively for the domestic market in Congo, AgriSA's negotiator, Theo de Jager, intimated that they might target their tropical fruit at the European market (Sharife 2010). At present, incentives to export are minimal. As it has turned out, in their first three years of operation they have limited production to field crops, fetching good prices in the domestic market. With further expansion, they intend to take a more regional approach.

---

[13] Fred, Makanga, Chief Financial Officer, Ministère des Affaires Foncières, du Cadastre and du Topographie (Ministry of Lands, Cadastre and Topography), Brazzaville, 4 August 2011.

The South African ambassador, a key intermediary in the negotiations on the deal, pointed out that the Congolese market itself is quite limited, and the farmers would likely target other Central African countries, but he was clear that 'they are not going to export to South Africa' (Genge 2011: pers. comm.).

Contracting parties
AgriSA established a new affiliate for the purposes of concluding a legal agreement with the government of Congo, and, being registered in Congo, enabling its members to act as a legal entity in pursuit of common interests (Genge 2011: pers. comm.). In 2011, the awkwardly-named AgriSA Congo was established, with André Botha as its President and Wynand du Toit as Vice-President. Alongside this association, it also established an operational company, Congo Agriculture, to obtain finance capital and to manage its members' farming operations in the country. AgriSA Congo was later renamed the Congo Farmers' Union to emphasise its openness to including commercial farmers from within Congo, and in April 2014 renamed itself again as the Congo Farmers' Association, deftly referencing the regional currency, the CFA (Congo Farmers' Union 2014).

The farmers initially planned to establish separate farms and secure their own funding and inputs but, with limited finance through a collective agreement, they have adopted a cooperative structure which they refer to as a 'kibbutz'. This is managed through Congo Agriculture, which is the legal land concession holder and is responsible for the coordinated efforts of the farmers, their suppliers, the logistics, the marketing of products as well as servicing the initial loan (Congo Agriculture 2012). Later, smaller syndicates and individuals established their own operations, with the expectation that, once production stabilises, the land will be formally subdivided and transferred to the participating farmers.

State roles
The Ministry of Agriculture told us that it was the Ministry of Lands that identified the land (Dieudonne 2011: pers. comm.), while the Minister of Lands himself insisted that the Ministry of Agriculture identified the land and that he merely signed off the deal:

> We gave them [the South African farmers] 80,000ha and they will come to exploit it. It is me who gave the land to the investors. If I hadn't given them the land, there would be no deal... I am the facilitator between the state and the traditional chiefs. They were happy because this investment would create jobs and will also develop the area and it will bring new opportunities. We did not give them the land [ie. as private ownership], but we authorised them to use the land. At the end of the project, the land will become public land once more. It is not a cession [ie. not in perpetuity]. The duration is for 99 years. (Minister Mabiala 2011: pers. comm.)

Disputes about land rights and 'empty land'

On the one hand, government officials indicated that the land was unoccupied and unused. The South Africans, too, were insistent that, though there had been negotiations, there were no people there. As the South African ambassador declared: 'There are no people there; who would have to be displaced?' (Genge 2011: pers. comm.). One senior official explained, however, how negotiations were conducted with traditional leaders where it was agreed that 'the villages will remain, but they are compensated for their fields, and will have to go and work somewhere else' (Matsoumba-Boungou 2011: pers. comm.). But the Minister of Lands himself insisted that this public land was devoid of human habitation and use:

> This is public state reserve. No, there are no people living on that land – it is rural land that belongs to the state... We have lots of land available... We are creating state reserves, so that we can quite simply show new investors the land. (Minister Mabiala 2011: pers. comm.)

A local agricultural official in Niari tasked with escorting four South African farmers on their scoping trip took them to Malolo 2 to meet the Chief and, using a map from the Ministry of Agriculture, navigated their way from Mouindi, 50km to Macabana, then 25km to Dihesse and on to Malolo, taking soil samples every 5km. At the time, he recalled, they expressed some concern that there were people living on the land, growing cassava and other crops, including on the moribund Dihesse state farm, on which people were settled (Mboungou 2011: pers. comm.).[14] The opposition Member of Parliament for the area also claims that the current deal intrudes on 'peasant land', as well as covering the former state farms, and expects that, when it is fully implemented, it is likely to provoke substantial opposition.

> In the past, for the first deal, it was not really criticised. It had no impact; there was no contract. But this time it is different. The *size* [is bigger], and it involves *peasant land*, and a *contract* that we have not seen. These are the factors that make the current deal different... They [the government] only think of tractors, job opportunities, roads... What will happen to the people living on the land? They will lose their cultivable land. I am sure they will lose their land. There will be a negative effect in the long term. (P.T. Mabiala 2011: pers. comm.)

Local intermediaries

Who is actually responsible for negotiating the deal with the affected populations seems unclear in practice. The Ministry of Lands claimed that, while the central government is the go-between, it is actually the local authorities – the Prefect and Member of Parliament – who are

---

[14] Jean Claude Mboungou, Chief, Dihesse Village, Niari Province, Congo.

responsible for negotiating with local people. The national ministers themselves, however, suggested that they have this authority. What the officials agree on is that chiefs are important local interlocutors, and that, while they must provide written permission, they cannot get copies of the contracts they sign:

> The chief [*propriétaire foncière*] does not get the document, no! Yes, he must sign, to give the right for the land to be given, they give their approval, but some of them don't even know how to read, so no, they don't get to keep the document. (Matsoumba-Boungou 2011: pers. comm.)

Yet, in contrast to the views of officials in the Ministry of Lands, the opposition MP for the area claimed that the local chiefs are political appointees, rather than traditional leaders or custodians of custom, and have no powers of land allocation or administration:

> Tribal organisation doesn't exist anymore; each village has its own small organisation..... The chief of the village is no longer a traditional chief. He is not a civil servant either, but the governor appoints the person. He is not elected... If you need land, when you go to the chief, he has no power over land. Within each tribe there are families that have land, and you have to buy from them. (Mabiala 2011: pers. comm.)

The opposition MP was unaware of the deal until he heard about it on Radio France Internationale, following which the opposition party, UDPS, attempted to call the Minister of Agriculture to account for it, asking him to explain why it had not been tabled in Parliament for ratification. They were unable to get him to appear before the National Assembly to explain the deal:

> Unfortunately there is total opacity. I really can't tell you the terms of this deal. The Congo government through the Ministry of Agriculture has got these white farmers to come...We as parliamentarians were meant to ratify the contract [yet we were not informed of it]. There were no negotiations at all; it was the government that decided. Local MPs and the local parliament should be aware [of this deal] but they are not. When we got the news, we summoned the Minister of Agriculture [Rigobert Maboundou] to the National Assembly. He has never responded. (P.T. Mabiala 2011: pers. comm.)

The local councillor for Bouenza had also been unable to get information about the deal from the Ministry of Agriculture, and was not aware of any consultation having taken place (Yamba 2011: pers. comm.).[15] He, too, became aware of the deal through the media, after which the council tried to take action: 'we summoned the regional director of agriculture

---

[15] Yamba, Paul, Special councillor and member of local assembly, Department of Bouenza, Brazzaville, Congo, 3 August 2011.

who said he had no information, as it was a central state matter' (Yamba 2011: pers. comm.). While the central state may make the decisions, local officials carried out instructions. The regional director of the Ministry of Lands based in Dolisie indicated that:

> We [the Ministry] help investors identify and secure land. We negotiate land with the community as we did for the South African investors...The South Africans through the Ministry of Agriculture requested us to identify suitable land for them. We took instructions from the Ministry...When the South Africans came, we went to consult and inform the customary land owners. We informed them what was happening. We pegged the land and informed the Ministry of Agriculture that the land was ready. (Badianga 2011: pers. comm.)

Kickstarting commercial farming
Government officials, as cited above, insisted that this project will help to develop a commercial farming industry in Congo (Mazinga 2011: pers. comm.). At the same time, the farmers themselves and the South African embassy suggested that, as production gets under way, the government will need to take steps to support their venture: to enable access to inputs, to invest in infrastructure, and to embark on policy reforms that address the 'incomplete policy environment' (Mohamed 2011: pers. comm.). As the South African ambassador observed:

> For instance, at present they don't allow GMOs [genetically modified organisms] in this country. If the farmers will be of the view that they would need improved seed and technology, then that will have to be addressed...value chains will require them [the government] to adjust their laws, to allow the farmers to operate optimally. (Genge 2011: pers. comm.)

How such negotiations will proceed is difficult to foresee, but it appears that what will be at stake is constituting a policy framework on commercial agriculture.

Gearing up production

The South African convoy, having arrived in December 2011, took possession of (at least some of) the land allotted to them in their contract with the government. They moved into the 'dilapidated farm houses the French colonials left sixty-five years ago' and employed local people to start renovating them (Bauer 2012). By early 2012, land clearing commenced, and soon about 485ha of maize had been planted around Malolo 2. In the process, there has been one report of a family evicted from their cassava farm in the Dihesse area to make way for the South Africans, and additional reporting of a woman from Malolo 2 being displaced (Pongui 2012), but we have little detail on displacement or dispossession. Bauer (2012) presents a picture of the initial occupation:

> It took the Congo farmers only three months to clear 1800ha of land, plant maize and beans, put up masts for electrical cables not only lighting the area but also to keep the beers cold... But life is by no means easy though, the physical input needed to clear the land had been underestimated. Getting on top of the 2 meter high elephant grass and uprooting the ±100 trees per hectare, equalling 8 million trees on the 80,000 hectares provided is only a first step. Thousands of tons of uprooted trees need to be cut-up and removed.[16] Spare parts or tractor tires have to be shipped or air-freighted from South Africa at great costs and causing down-times. (Bauer 2012: 53)

The South Africans have begun to employ local people, though there are complaints both about too few jobs being created and about low wages. After an initial collective workforce of 52 people employed on a casual basis during January 2012, by April the number of workers had declined to 27. At one stage, total employment peaked at about 100 and since has stabilised at about 20 regular jobs that appear permanent, with further fluctuating seasonal and casual jobs. The jobs are only for men at this stage: 'No local woman has been identified at this stage of activities among the employees' (Pongui 2012), though every South African household hires at least one local woman for domestic work. Wages range from 14,500FCFA (US$27.55) to 58,000FCFA (US$110.20) per month, which while complying with minimum wages, is considered too low, particularly by young people who would prefer to work for themselves (doing farming or other activities) rather than work for low wages. One person complained that it was not worth it to 'work very hard for a pittance or for starvation wages in addition with bad working [conditions] and sun exposure every single day' (cited in Pongui 2012). In contrast, in fieldwork interviews several months later, all the workers interviewed wanted more jobs to expand salaried incomes.

Our research suggests relatively low levels of social differentiation within the host community, with most people living precarious livelihoods composed of farming for consumption, petty trade and remittances from family members in the cities. Within a year, some modest processes of accumulation were evident within the four villages: the baker from Malolo 2 had expanded operations by a factor of four, alcohol distilleries were mushrooming, there were several television sets (with generators) among the better-off households and one family had bought a motorbike. While these might appear marginal economic effects, they are significant relative to the limited pre-existing economy, and several people mentioned growing inequality in the villages, suggesting that there has been a process

---

[16] Much of the 50,000ha was cleared by the French colonial companies and later worked by the Congolese state, so the trees being removed now are not part of the established indigenous forest – like those the Chinese are felling elsewhere – but represent re-growth.

of accumulation for some of the population. Whether differentiation will continue to be accentuated through the commercialisation of agriculture remains to be seen; for now, its direct impact within the four villages is limited to low-waged employment, among few people, with some locals refusing to work for the wages offered.

Initial production mostly failed, putting pressure on the number of people employed and the salaries paid. The main reasons for the failure were technical. In opposition to claims that the soil is very fertile and the climate ideal, the farmers were quickly confronted by the logistical uncertainties of farming in an unknown environment. Besides abundant but irregular rains and unknown pests, the soils turned out to be shallow and highly acidic. The unavailability of technical support services and readily available inputs led to the failure of the first maize crop. This in turn forced many of the farmers to abandon their Congolese adventure. Three years and six seasons down the road, however, there seemed to be a stabilisation of production patterns and productivity has increased to four tonnes per hectare.

By late 2014, the farmers were able to secure a second convoy of equipment, spares and other supplies. With loan finance from the agribusiness giant Afgri, the convoy of twelve trucks packed with R35 million (US$3.21 million) in tractors and other equipment and supplies left Afgri's equipment hub at Grootvlei outside Johannesburg on 1 October 2014. Dirk Hanekom, head of AgriSA's Africa Policy Committee tasked with driving its regional expansion, explained that, after a successful previous season, Minister of Agriculture Rigobert Maboundou was pleased with the South Africans and had allocated them several more thousand hectares to cultivate. He described the most recent harvest as the largest harvest ever in the Congo, and argued that after a difficult initial few years, the colonist farmers were well placed to expand their operations.

> We understand the weather, the soil, the water and everything that influences the harvest better than we did three and a half years ago. And for this reason we can see our way clear to continuing to farm there (Hanekom, on the South African television channel Kyknet, 2 October 2014 – author's translation).

Responses from local people

Responses from local people were, unsurprisingly, varied, and have arguably changed over time as the investment materialised and then ran into crisis, with several of the South African farmers leaving and returning to South Africa and others regrouping and re-strategising. Even before operations started, however, local people were divided on the question of what the investment would mean for them. Our fieldwork found that the population had not given its free, prior and informed consent, which was confirmed by the survey we commissioned (Pongui 2012). No independent environmental and socio-economic studies were conducted (Ondoki 2011: pers. comm.),[17] nor were steps taken to mitigate the 'possible negative impacts of the project on affected populations' (Pongui 2012).

A fervent supporter of the deal, the chief of Malolo 2 was clear that there had been no consultation prior to the deal being concluded; rather, the residents had been 'informed' of the impending arrival of the South Africans as a *fait accompli*, and this apparently only several months after the final contract was signed.

> The Minister held a meeting to inform the community in June [2011]. He came with the prefect and sub-prefect. Everyone in the village attended. We are very happy. We are looking forward to the development. The community did not sign any paper. They are very happy. (Chief Mazinga, 2011: pers. comm.)

The chief reportedly spilled palm wine on the ground and 'the elders sipped palm wine and spat it on the ground – that is the customary sign of approval' (Badianga 2011: pers. comm.). He told us that there is an abundance of land, and that the South African deal would not seriously displace other land uses, also intimating that the new investors would assist the local farmers to farm better.

The experiences of and response by the chief of Dihesse village were quite different:

> A couple of months ago, some white farmers arrived and pegged some of the land in our village. I asked the sub-prefect [what was going on] and was informed that the land had been allocated to the South African farmers. 'Why was the land allocated yet it belongs to us?' [asked the village chief]. 'They will explain later' [responded the Prefect]. We saw them, they did not even come to inform us! We wondered how we would cope if they took away our land. We saw this [but] nobody talked to us. One of the pegs of the land is in the school area. If you go there you will see it. (Chief Mboungou 2011: pers. comm.)

Towards Mouindi village where the South African activities had not yet started, rumours were rife, with some villagers saying they had been told 'this is the last time you will plant on your land'. While some people were getting ready to contest the allocation of land they claimed, others were excited by the expectation that they might reap financial benefits. One young man observed, 'we did not get consultation...we do not expect any consultation as we are used to the government dictating what happens on the land,' but he still expected that there would be compensation for those whose land was allocated to the South Africans (interview, August

---

[17] Isidore, Ondoki, Advisor to the Minister of Finance. Congo-Brazzaville, 4 August 2011.

2011). Here, alongside the railway, communities had moved on to the abandoned state farm with their cattle, occupied old government housing there and planted cassava. The chief understood that the land would be expropriated, yet he explained that the villagers already used the fields for their own cultivation of maize, cassava, groundnuts, marrow, and used the surrounding forests. He also noted that the land allocated to the South Africans included the villages' water sources and lakes: 'We are not opposed to the project. It is a government project. [But] if they take our water, they have to provide us with wells as we will be cut off from our water sources' (Chief Mboungou 2011: pers. comm.).

Local people we interviewed acknowledged living on former state farms, which they believe they legitimately reclaimed after the war. Their opinions about the South Africans coming were varied. Some were concerned that some land must be left aside for their own farming – especially for those who may not secure alternative livelihoods through employment in the new investments. The chief of Dihesse village clarified that there are substantial differences among the residents of his and other villages; there are the *Kuni* (landowners), the *Pulu* (traders), the *Bemba* and the 'pygmies'. The *Kuni* control and allocate land (Chief Mboungou 2011: pers. comm.). In addition, many people in the region were in-migrants, including refugees from Gabon and Angola who had been living there for many years. The deal would have different implications for these different people. Indeed, a refugee from Angola said 'We will abide by whatever decision the government makes. If they say we must leave, we will leave. We can find somewhere else to stay and farm' (Kenge 2011: pers. comm.).[18] A 'pygmy' woman whom we interviewed while the South Africans were en route with their convoy is among about 50 pygmies who have been integrated into the village over the past few years, on the direction of the government, yet still described herself as being 'from the forest'. Unlike all of the other people we met, she was not aware of the deal at all.

Conclusion

The vision of exporting South African commercial agriculture to the Congo is, so far, being realised only on a very modest scale, confounding the ambitions of both the Congolese government and the farmers themselves. Practical impediments to production have become apparent, leading to a high attrition rate among the new settler farmers. Meanwhile, controversy surrounds the status of the land itself, amid overlapping and competing claims based on law, custom and practice. For now, these have not emerged as points of conflict, not least because the South Africans have been able to clear and cultivate only a small proportion of the land. Ironically, the commercial success of their enterprise which is now

---

[18] Therese Kenge, Angolan refugee, Malolo 2 village, Niari province, Congo, 2011.

becoming apparent, and which paves the way for them to expand their operations, may threaten their relations with surrounding communities, over land, forests and water.

This story shows that different parts of the Congolese government, even at central government level, had only partial understandings of what was going on, what the terms of the deal were (how long, how much land, current uses and claims to the land, whether any rent was payable) and the proposed future uses by the investors. All expected that the investors would grow food for the domestic market, while the South Africans – probably unrealistically – expected the government to invest in infrastructure to enable them to farm profitably and to adjust national policies in favour of commercial farming.

Congo illustrates the argument that 'Dependence on food imports emerges as a strong driver of demand for land acquisition which is more likely to be located in countries with ample supply of land that are far from the technology frontier' (Arezki et al. 2011: 20). Yet in this case it is not the investor country that is seeking to secure domestic food supply through the land deal, but the host country. Our study has implications for land governance. There is an absence of legislation or regulations governing the acquisition of agricultural land on a large scale – as envisaged in the African Union's Guiding Principles on Large-Scale Land-Based Investment and the FAO's Voluntary Guidelines on Responsible Tenure of Land, Fisheries and Forests in the Context of National Food Security. While Congo's forestry sector is bound by specific requirements for consultation and socio-economic and environmental impact studies, the deals for agriculture are unregulated and sit astride a lacuna in legal recognition of customary land rights. As Pongui (2012) observed: 'this contract has once again revealed the diversity of land systems in force in Congo and awakened the old battles between state (holders of formal land rights) and landowners (owners of customary land rights).'

This case has important historical resonance and political significance. Liberalisation policies in both South Africa and Congo have established the conditions for this land deal. Liberalisation policies adopted in the context of structural adjustment programmes and loan conditionalities in Congo saw the retreat of the state from direct involvement in production and food supply. State farms, themselves in some instances the descendants of colonial estates, were dismantled and gave way to small-scale peasant farming, and in turn to this most recent return to large-scale agriculture, this time in a way that connects local production to regional and global financial circuits. The case confirms the arguments that large-scale investments are not entirely new but represent intensified efforts in activities that have been going on since colonisation, under new conditions of globalised finance (White et al. 2012).

This story about the South African investment, and its many precursors since colonial times, illustrates the ways in which authorities have attempted to solve their land problems and to transform agriculture through a sequence of top-down, state-led land reform processes: nationalisation, decentralisation, recentralisation and now attempts through large-scale land transfers to re-assert private property rights as an incentive for foreign investment. On the other hand, the attempts by the state to secure and clarify property rights for South African investors in the Congo have been carried out in a manner that marginalises customary land rights and other unrecognised claims to these same lands. As a result international capital (represented by a Canadian insurance and investment company, alongside South African private and state capital) enjoys formally-recognised land rights on land while host communities' customary land rights are in flux and undermined by state authorities that have prioritised concessions to investors over customary land rights.

The South African case in the Congo shows the mismatch between the real complexities of establishing large-scale commercial farming and the grand plans that justify such land deals – and how investors change course in response. It also illustrates the long and circuitous routes through which African countries have returned to large-scale agriculture. Starting from colonial occupation and conquest, and the carving out of colonial estates, followed by wars of national liberation, Marxist-Leninist rule saw the establishment of state farms. Following the dismantling of these state farms as part of structural adjustment in the 1980s and 1990s and various attempts to initiate smallholder commercialisation, state control of unregistered land already occupied by citizens, whether through custom or not, is now being put to use to enable international capital to construct nodes of accumulation linked to global markets in some of the poorest and least developed states in Africa.

REFERENCES

Abbass, I.M. 2013. '"No Retreat No Surrender": Conflict for Survival Between Fulani Pastoralists and Farmers in Northern Nigeria.' *European Scientific Journal* 8(1): 331-346.

Abbink, J. 2011. 'Land to the Foreigners: Economic, Legal and Socio-Cultural Aspects of New Land Acquisition Schemes in Ethiopia.' *Journal of Contemporary African Studies* 29(4): 513–535.

Abdulai, R. T. and I. E. Ndekugri. 2007. 'Customary Landholding Institutions and Housing Development in Urban Centres of Ghana: Case Studies of Kumasi and Wa.' *Habitat International* 31(2): 257-267.

Abdullahi, A. 1997. *Colonial Policies and the Failure of Somali Secessionism in the Northern Frontier District of Kenya Colony, c. 1890–1968.* MA Thesis. History Department, Rhodes University.

Adisa, R. S. 2009. *Management of Farmer-herdsmen Conflicts in North-central State in Kano Region, 1900-2000.* Kano-Maradi Study of Long-Term Change: Drylands Research Working Paper 35. Crewkerne, UK Drylands Research.

Adjei, A. 1999. *Politics and Policies of Agriculture and Rural Development in Northern Ghana: The Case of the Upper East Region Agricultural Development Project (URADEP).* Bergen: Department of Administration and Organisation Science, University of Bergen.

Afgri. 2014. 'Entering a New Chapter as a Private Company: Information Sheet.' [online]. Available at: < http://www.afgri.co.za/downloads/ 2014/2014_AFGRI_ AgriGroupeQ&A_ENG.pdf> [Accessed 13 October 2014].

Agbosu, L., et al. 2007. 'Customary and Statutory Land Tenure and Land Policy in Ghana', ISSER Technical Paper, No. 70. Legon: Institute for Statistical, Social and Economic Research, University of Ghana.

Akram-Lodhi, A.H. and C. Kay, Eds. 2009. *Peasants and Globalization: Political Economy, Rural Transformation and the Agrarian Question.* London and New York: Routledge.

Alden Wily, L. 2012. 'Looking Back to See Forward: the Legal Niceties of Land Theft in Land Rushes.' *Journal of Peasant Studies* 39(3-4): 751-755.

Alden Wily, L. 2011a. '"The Law is to Blame": The Vulnerable Status of Common Property Rights in Sub-Saharan Africa.' *Development and Change* 42(3): 733–757.

Alden Wily, L. 2011b. *The Tragedy of Public Lands: The Fate of the Commons under Global Commercial Pressure.* Rome: International Land Coalition.

Alden Wily, L. 2008. 'Custom and Commonage in Africa: Rethinking the Ortho-doxies.' *Land Use Policy* 25(1): 43-52.

Al-Hassan, R. M. 2007. *Regional Disparities in Ghana: Policy Options and Public Investment Implications.* IFPRI Discussion Paper 00693. Washington DC: IFPRI, Development Strategy and Governance Division.

Allafrica 2012. Mozambique: Guebeza Visits Sugar Project in Massingir, 11 January. [online]. Available at: <http://allafrica.com/stories/201211120298. html> [Accessed October 27 2014]

Amanor, K.S. 2012. 'Land Governance in Africa: How Historical Context has Shaped Key Contemporary Issues Relating to Policy on Land'. *Framing the Debate Series* 1. Rome: International Land Coalition.

Amanor, K. S. 2005. 'Agricultural Markets in West Africa: Frontiers, Agribusiness and Social Differentiation.' *IDS Bulletin* 36(2): 58-62.

Amanor, K. S. 2001. *Land, Labour and the Family in Southern Ghana: A Critique of Land Policy under Neo-liberalisation.* Research Report 116. Upsalla: Nordiska Africainstitutet.

Amin, S. 1972. 'Underdevelopment and Dependence in Black Africa: Origins and Contemporary Forms.' *Journal of Modern African Studies* 10(4): 503–24.

ANRS. 2006. *Rural Land Administration and Use Proclamation 133/2006.* Bahir Dar: Amhara National Regional State, Ethiopia.

Anseeuw, W., M. Boche, T. Breu, M. Giger, J. Lay, P. Messerli and K. Nolte. 2012. *Transnational Land Deals for Agriculture in the Global South: Analytical Report Based on the Land Matrix Database.* Bern/Montpellier/Hamburg: CDE/CIRAD/GIGA.

Ansoms, A. and T. Hilhorst. 2014. 'Everyday Forms of Land Grabbing in the Great Lakes Region: Introduction.' In: A. Ansoms and T. Hilhorst, Eds. *Losing Your Land: Dispossession in the Great Lakes.* Woodbridge, UK: James Currey.

Antwi, A. Y. and J. Adams. 2003. 'Rent-seeking Behaviour and its Economic Cost in Urban Land Transactions in Accra, Ghana.' *Urban Studies* 40(10): 2083-2098.

Arezki, R, R. Deininger and H. Selod. 2011. *What Drives the Global Land Rush?* IMF Working Paper 11(251). Washington DC: International Monetary Fund.

Ariyo, J.A. and M. Mortimore. 2013. 'Youth Farming and Nigeria's Development Dilemma: the Shonga Experiment.' *IDS Bulletin* 43(6): 58-66.

Ariyo, J.A. and M. Mortimore. 2014. 'State, Land and Agricultural Commercialisation in Kwara State, Nigeria.' Working Paper. Brighton and Nairobi: Future Agricultures Consortium.

Aryeetey, E, J. Ayee, K. Ninsin, and D. Tsikata. 2005. *From the Crown Lands Bills to the Land Administration Project: The Politics of Land Tenure Reforms in Ghana.* Legon: Institute of Statistical, Social and Economic Research.

Aryeetey, E., J. Ayee, K. Ninsin, and D. Tsikata. 2007. *The Politics of Land Tenure Reform in Ghana: From the Crown Lands Bills to the Land Administration Project.* Technical Papers. Legon: Institute of Statistical, Social and Economic Research.

AU/AfDB/UNECA. 2009. *Framework and Guidelines on Land Policy in Africa.* Addis Ababa: African Union, African Development Bank, United Nations Economic Commission for Africa.

Awanyo, L. 2003. 'Land Tenure and Agricultural Development in Ghana: The Intersection of Class, Culture and Gender.' In: W. Tettey, K. Puplampu and B. Berman, Eds. *Critical Perspectives on Politics and Socio-Economic Development in Ghana.* Leiden: Brill.

Baglioni, E. and P. Gibbon. 2013. 'Land Grabbing, Large- and Small-scale Farming: what can evidence and policy from 20th century Africa contribute to the debate?' *Third World Quarterly* 34(9): 1558-1581.

Balaigwa, A. 2013. 'Low Sugarcane Price Frustrates Farmers.' *The Guardian*, 6 March. [online]. Available at: <http://www.ippmedia.com/frontend/index.php?l=51991>.

Bassett, T. and D. Crummey, Eds. 1993. *Land in African Agrarian Systems.* Madison WI: University of Wisconsin Press.

Bates, R. 1981. *Markets and States in Tropical Africa.* Berkeley and Los Angeles, CA: University of California Press.

Bauer, W. 2012. 'A Ride in the Congo.' *BikeSA Magazine.* September 2012: 50-58.

Baum, E. 1968. 'Land use in the Kilombero Valley: From Shifting Cultivation Towards Permanent Farming.' In: H. Ruthenberg, Ed. *Smallholder Farming and Smallholder Development in Tanzania: Ten Case Studies.* Munich: Weltforum Verlag.

Beekman, W. and G.J. Veldwisch. 2012. 'The Evolution of the Land Struggle for Smallholder Irrigated Rice Production in Nante, Mozambique.' *Physics and*

Chemistry of the Earth 50-52; 179-184.

Belay, K. and W. Manig. 2004. 'Access to Rural Land in Eastern Ethiopia: Mismatch between Policy and Reality.' *Journal of Agriculture and Rural Development in the Tropics and Subtropics* 105(2): 123-138.

Bernstein, H. 2010a. 'Introduction: Some Questions Concerning the Productive Forces.' *Journal of Agrarian Change* 10(3): 300–14.

Bernstein, H. 2010b. *Class Dynamics of Agrarian Change*. Halifax, NS: Fernwood Publishing and Sterling, VA: Kumarian Press.

Bernstein, H. 2004. 'Changing Before Our Very Eyes: Agrarian Questions and the Politics of Land in Capitalism Today.' *Journal of Agrarian Change* 4(1–2): 190–225.

Bernstein, H. 2002. 'Land Reform: Taking a Long(er) View.' *Journal of Agrarian Change* 2(4): 433–63.

Berry, S. 2009. 'Property, Authority and Citizenship: Land Claims, Politics and the Dynamics of Social Division in West Africa.' *Development and Change* 40(1): 23-45.

Berry, S. 2002. 'Debating the Land Question in Africa.' *Comparative Studies in Society and History* 44(04): 638-668.

Berry, S. 1997. 'Tomatoes, Land and Hearsay: Property and History in Asante in the Time of Structural Adjustment.' *World Development* 25(8): 1225-1241.

Berry, S. 1993. *No Condition is Permanent: The Social Dynamics of Agrarian Change in Sub-Saharan Africa*. Madison, WI: University of Wisconsin Press.

Berry, S., R.E. Downs and S.P. Reyna. 1988. 'Concentration Without Privatization? Some Consequences of Changing Patterns of Rural Land Control in Africa.' In: R.E. Downs and S.P. Reyna, Eds. *Land and Society in Contemporary Africa.* Hanover, NH: University of New Hampshire Press: 53-75.

Binswanger, H. P., K. Deininger and G. Feder. 1995. 'Power, Distortions, Revolt and Reform in Agricultural Land Relations.' *Handbook of Development Economics 3:* 2659-2772.

Boni, S. 2005. *Clearing the Ghanaian Forest: Theories and Practices of Acquisition, Transfer and Utilisation of Farming Titles in the Sefwi-Akan Area.* Legon: Institute of African Studies, University of Ghana.

Boone, C. 2014. *Property and Political Order in Africa: Land Rights and the Structure of Politics.* Cambridge: Cambridge University Press.

Borras Jr, S. M. and J.C. Franco. 2013. 'Global Land Grabbing and Political Reactions "From Below".' *Third World Quarterly* 34(9): 1723-1747.

Borras, S. and J.C. Franco. 2012. 'Global Land Grabbing and Trajectories of Agrarian Change: A preliminary analysis.' *Journal of Agrarian Change* 12(1): 34–59.

Borras Jr, S.M., R. Hall, I. Scoones, B. White and W. Wolford. 2011a. 'Towards a Better Understanding of Global Land Grabbing: an Editorial Introduction,' *Journal of Peasant Studies* 38:2: 209-216.

Borras Jr, S.M., D. Fig and S. Monsalve Suárez. 2011b. 'The Politics of Agrofuels and Mega-land and Water Deals: Insights from the ProCana Case, Mozambique.' *Review of African Political Economy* 38(128): 215-234.

Borras Jr, S.M., P. McMichael and I. Scoones. 2010. 'The Politics of Biofuels, Land and Agrarian Change: Editors' Introduction.' *Journal of Peasant Studies* 37(4): 575-592.

Borras Jr, S.M. and J. Franco. 2010. 'From Threat to Opportunity? Problems with the Idea of a" Code of Conduct" for Land-Grabbing.' *Yale Human Rights and Development Journal* 13(2): 508-523.

Breytenbach, W. 2003. 'Land Reform in Southern Africa.' In: D. Hansohm, W. Breytenbach and T. Hartenberg, Eds. *Monitoring Regional Integration in Southern Africa.* Windhoek: Gramsberg Macmillan.

Bryceson, D. F. 2004. 'Agrarian Vista or Vortex: African Rural Livelihood Policies.' *Review of African Political Economy* 31(102): 617-629.

Burke, W.J., T.S. Jayne and A. Chapoto. 2010. *Factors Contributing to Zambia's*

2010 Maize Bumper Harvest. Working Paper No. 48. Lusaka: Food Security Research Project.

Burgess, C. 2012. *Large Scale Biofuel Projects in Mozambique: A Solution to Poverty?* MSc Thesis. School of Social and Political Sciences, University of Melbourne.

Buur, L., C.M. Tembe and O. Baloi. 2011. 'The White Gold: The Role of Government and State in Rehabilitating the Sugar Industry in Mozambique.' *Journal of Development Studies* 48(3): 349-362.

Byres, T. 1991. 'The Agrarian Question and Differing Forms of Capitalist Agrarian Transition: An Essay with Reference to Asia.' In: J. Breman and S. Mundle, Eds. *Rural Transformation in Asia.* Oxford: Oxford University Press.

Byres, T. J. 1981. 'The New Technology, Class Formation, and Class Action in the Indian Countryside.' *Journal of Peasant Studies* 8(4): 405-54.

Catley, A., J. Lind and I. Scoones, Eds. 2013. *Pastoralism and Development in Africa: Dynamic Change at the Margins.* London: Routledge.

Channar, G. 1999. *Food security in Northern Ghana.* Accra: CIDA: Ghana Desk, Gulf of Guinea Division.

Chasukwa, M. 2013. 'An Investigation of the Political Economy of Land Grabs in Malawi: The Case of Kasinthula Cane Growers Limited.' LDPI Working Paper 30. [online] http://www.iss.nl/fileadmin/ASSETS/iss/Research_and_projects/Research_networks/LDPI/LDPI_WP_30.pdf [accessed 9 June 2015]

Chinsinga, B. 2012. 'Deconstructing the Success Myth: A Case of the Malawi Farm Input Subsidy Programme (FISP)'. Paper Presented at the 3rd International Conference of the Institute of Economic and Social Studies-Mozambique: Accumulation and Transformation in the Context of International Crisis, Maputo, 4-5 September 2012.

Chinsinga, B. 2011. 'The Politics of Land Reforms in Malawi: The Case of the Community Based Rural Land Development Programme (CBRLDP).' *Journal of International Development* 23: 380-393.

Chinsinga, B. 2007. *Democracy, Decentralization and Poverty Reduction in Malawi.* Cologne, Germany: Rudiger Koppe Verlag.

Chinsinga, B, M. Chasukwa, and S. Zuka. 2013. 'The Political Economy of Land Grabs in Malawi: Investigating the Contribution of Limphasa Sugar Corporation to Rural Development.' *Journal of Agricultural and Environmental Ethics* 26: 1064-1085.

Chinsinga, B. and M. Chasukwa. 2012a. 'Youth, Agriculture and Land Grabs.' *IDS Bulletin* 43(6): 67-77.

Chinsinga, B. and M. Chasukwa. 2012b. *The Green Belt Initiative and Land Grabs in Malawi*, FAC Policy Brief 55. Brighton: Future Agricultures Consortium.

Chirwa, E. 2008. *Land Tenure, Farm Investments and Food Production in Malawi.* IPPG Discussion Paper Series 18. Institute for Development Policy Management, University of Manchester.

Chirwa, E. W. 1998. 'Fostering Private Food Marketing and Food Policies after Liberalisation: The Case of Malawi.' In P. Seppala, Ed. *Liberalized and Neglected? Food Marketing Policies in Eastern Africa.* Helsinki: United Nations University/WIDER.

Chirwa, E., and D. Dorward. 2013. *Agricultural Input Subsidies: The Recent Malawi Experience.* Oxford: Oxford University Press.

Church, A.D., G.M. Groom, D.N. Thomson and V.R. Dlamini. 2008. 'Small-scale Cane Grower Development Models: Some Lessons from Sub-Saharan Africa.' *Proceedings of the South African Sugar Technologists Association*, 51: 116-127.

Clapp, J. 2014. 'Financialization, Distance and Global Food Politics.' *Journal of Peasant Studies* 41(5): 797-814.

Collier, P. and S. Dercon. 2014. 'African Agriculture in 50 Years: Smallholders in a Rapidly Changing World?' *World Development* 63: 92-101.

Concern Universal. 2012. *Household Income Survey Report for Sugar Capacity*

Building Project. Blantyre: Concern Universal.

Congo Agriculture. 2012. 'Congo Agriculture.' [online]. Available at: <http://www.agriallafrica.com/ congoagriculture.html> [Accessed 21 September 2012].

Congo Farmers' Union. 2014. 'Congo Farmers' Association (CFA) hou hulle Algemeene Jaarvergadering.' [online]. Available at:<http://www.congoagri.com/> [Accessed 13 October 2014].

Cooksey, B. 2013. *What Difference has CAADP Made to Tanzanian Agriculture?* Future Agricultures Working Paper 74. Brighton: Future Agricultures Consortium.

Corporate Citizenship. 2014. *Illovo Sugar: Mozambique Socio-economic Impact Assessment.* Internal Management Report. London: Corporate Citizenship. <http://www.illovosugar.co.za/UserContent/Documents/Illovo-Mozambique-Socio-economic-impact-12May14,pdf.

Cotula, L. 2013. *The Great African Land Grab?: Agricultural Investments and the Global Food System.* London: Zed Books.

Cotula, L. 2012. 'The International Political Economy of the Global Land Rush: A Critical Appraisal of Trends, Scale, Geography and Drivers.' *Journal of Peasant Studies* 39(3- 4): 649–680.

Cotula, L. and S. Vermeulen. 2010. 'Over the Heads of Local People: Consultation, Consent, and Recompense in Large-scale Land Deals for Biofuels Projects in Africa.' *Journal of Peasant Studies* 37(4): 899-916.

Cotula, L., C. Oya, E.A. Codjoe, A. Eid, M. Kakraba-Ampeh, J. Keeley, A.L. Kidewa, M. Makwarimba, W.M. Seide, W.O. Nasha, R.O. Asare and M. Rizzo. 2014. 'Testing Claims about Large Land Deals in Africa: Findings from a Multi-Country Study.' *Journal of Development Studies* 50(7): 903-925.

Cotula L., S. Vermeulen, R. Leonard and J. Keeley. 2009. *Land Grab or Development Opportunity: Agricultural Investment and International Land Deals in Africa.* London: IIED, and Rome: FAO and IFAD.

Cousins, B. 1997. 'How do Rights Become Real?: Formal and Informal Institutions in South Africa's Land Reform.' *IDS Bulletin* 28(4): 59-68.

Crewett, W and B. Korf. 2008. 'Ethiopia: Reforming Land Tenure.' *Review of African Political Economy* 116: 203–220.

Daramola, B. 2010. 'Public-Private Partnership in Commercial Agriculture in Nigeria: Issues, Constraints and Prospect.' Keynote paper presented at national seminar at ARMTI, Ilorin, 2 December 2010.

Davison, W. 2013. 'Ethiopia's Foreign Land Leases Fail to Deliver Food for Export.' [online]. Available at: <http://www.iol.co.za/business/international/ethiopias-foreign-land-leases-fail-to-deliver-food-for-export-1.1612220> [Accessed 26 November 2013].

De Schutter, O. 2011. 'How Not to Think of Land-grabbing: Three Critiques of Large-scale Investments in Farmland.' *Journal of Peasant Studies* 38(2): 249-279.

Deininger, K. W. 2003. *Land Policies for Growth and Poverty Reduction.* Washington DC: World Bank.

Deininger, K., T. Hilhorst and V. Songwe. 2014. 'Identifying and Addressing Land Governance Constraints to Support Intensification and Land Market Operation: Evidence from 10 African Countries.' *Food Policy* 48: 76-87.

Deininger, K. and D. Byerlee. 2012. 'The Rise of Large Farms in Land-abundant Countries: Do They Have a Future?' *World Development* 40: 701–714.

Deininger, K., D. Byerlee, J. Lindsay, A. Norton, H. Selod and M. Stickler. 2011. *Rising Global Interest in Farmland: Can It Yield Sustainable and Equitable Benefits?* Washington, DC: World Bank.

Devereux, S. 2002 'Can Social Safety Nets Reduce Chronic Poverty? *Development Policy Review* 20(5): 657-675.

Dorward, A. and E. Chirwa. 2011. 'The Malawi Agricultural Input Subsidy Programme: 2005-6 to 2008-9.' *International Journal of Agricultural Sustainability.* 9(1): 232-247.

Doss, C., G. Summerfield and D. Tsikata. 2014. 'Land, Gender, and Food Security.' *Feminist Economics* 20(1): 1-23.

Dubey, R. 2012. 'Indian Farmer's African Safari.' [online]. Available at: <http://www.businessworld.in/news/economy/indian-farmer%E2%80%99s-african-safari/415993/page-0.html> [Accessed 2 June 2013].

Dufey, A., S. Vermeulen, and B. Vorley. 2007. *Agrofuels: Strategic Choices for Commodity Dependent Developing Countries*. Amsterdam: Common Fund for Commodities.

Duvail, S., C. Medard, O. Hamerlynck and D.W. Nyingi. 2012. 'Land and Water Grabbing in an East African Coastal Wetland: The Case of the Tana Delta'. *Water Alternatives* 5(2):322-343.

Duvail, S. et al. 2010. 'Les Communautés Locales Face aux Grands Projets d'Aménagement desZones Humides Côtières en Afrique de l'Est.' *Politique Africaine* 117: 149-172.

Duvenage, I., R. Taplin, and L. Stringer. 'Bioenergy Project Appraisal in Sub-Saharan Africa: Sustainability Barriers and Opportunities in Zambia.' *Natural Resources Forum* 36(3): 167-180.

East African, The. 2008. 'Tana River Project not Economically Viable', 30 June 2008.

Edelman, M., C. Oya and S.M. Borras Jr. 2013. 'Global Land Grabs: Historical Processes, Theoretical and Methodological Implications and Current Trajectories.' *Third World Quarterly* 34(9): 1517-1531.

EEA/EEPRI. 2002. *A Research Report on Land Tenure and Agricultural Development in Ethiopia*. Addis Ababa: Ethiopian Economic Association (EEA)/Ethiopian Economic Policy Research Institute (EEPRI).

Englert, B. and E. Daley, Eds. 2008. *Women's Land Rights and Privatization in Eastern Africa*. Woodbridge, UK: Boydell & Brewer.

European Union. 2011. *Malawi-2011 Annual Action Programme for the Accompanying Measures for Sugar Protocol Countries,* Lilongwe: Delegation of European Commission to Malawi.

Fairbairn, M. 2014. '"Like gold with yield": Evolving intersections between farmland and finance.' *Journal of Peasant Studies* 41(5-6): 777-796.

Fairhead, J., M. Leach and I. Scoones, Eds. 2012. 'Green Grabbing: a New Appropriation of Nature?' Special Issue *Journal of Peasant Studies* 39(2).

FAO. 2013. *Trends and Impacts of Foreign Investment in Developing Country Agriculture: Evidence from Case Studies*. Rome: FAO.

FAO. 2012a. *Plan of Action for Malawi: 2012-2011*. Rome: FAO.

FAO. 2012b. *Voluntary Guidelines on the Responsible Governance of Tenure of Land, Fisheries and Forests in the Context of National Food Security*. Rome: FAO.

Favrot, M. 2012. *L'investissement de Fermiers Sud-africains dans l'Agriculture Congolaise: Accaparement Foncier ou Opportunité?* Mémoire de Master. Paris/Montpellier: AgroParisTech/CIRAD.

FDRE 2010. 'The Council of Ministers Directives regarding the administration of Agricultural Investment Land.' Unpublished document, March, Addis Ababa: Federal Democratic Republic of Ethiopia.

FDRE. 1997. *Rural Land Administration Proclamation 89/1997*. Addis Ababa: Federal Democratic Republic of Ethiopia.

FDRE. 1995. *The Constitution of the Federal Democratic Republic of Ethiopia*. Addis Ababa: Federal Democratic Republic of Ethiopia.

Forrest, T. 1993. *Politics and Economic Development in Nigeria*. Boulder, CO: Westview.

Galaty, J.G. 2012. '"Unused" Land and Unfulfilled Promises: Justifications for Displacing Communities in East Africa.' Paper presented at Global Land Grabbing II conference, Cornell University 12–19 October.

Government of Kenya. 2011. *National Food and Nutrition Security Policy*. Nairobi.

Ministry of Agriculture.

Government of Malawi. 2013. *The Third Integrated Household Survey (IHS).* Zomba: National Statistical Office.

Government of Malawi. 2012. *Integrated Household Survey.* Zomba: National Statistical Office.

Government of Malawi. 2010. *The Green Belt Initiative: Concept Paper.* Lilongwe: Ministry of Agriculture and Food Security.

Government of Malawi. 2009. *Nkhotakota Socio-Economic Profile.* Lilongwe: Ministry of Local Government and Rural Development.

Government of Malawi. 2002. *Malawi National Land Policy.* Lilongwe: Ministry of Lands, Housing and Surveys.

GRAIN. 2008. 'Seized! The 2008 Land Grab for Food and Financial Security.' Briefing Paper October. Barcelona: Genetic Resources Action International.

GRAIN 2011. *Pension Funds: Key Players in the Global Farmland Grab.* 20 June 2011.

Haggblade, S., P. Hazell and J. Brown. 1989. 'Farm-nonfarm Linkages in Rural Sub-Saharan Africa.' *World Development* 17(8): 1173-1201.

Hall, D. 2013. 'Primitive Accumulation, Accumulation by Dispossession and the Global Land Grab.' *Third World Quarterly* 34(9): 1582-1604.

Hall, D. 2012a. 'Rethinking Primitive Accumulation: Theoretical Tensions and Rural Southeast Asian Complexities.' *Antipode* 44(4): 1188-1208.

Hall, R. 2012b. 'The Next Great Trek? South African Commercial Farmers Move North.' *Journal of Peasant Studies* 39(3-4): 823-843.

Hall, R. 2011. 'Land Grabbing in Southern Africa: the Many Faces of the Investor Rush.' *Review of African Political Economy* 38(128): 193-214.

Hammar, A. 2010. 'Ambivalent Modalities: Zimbabwean Commercial Farmers in Mozambique.' *Journal of Southern African Studies* 36(2): 395-416.

Hanlon, J. 2011. 'Understanding Land Investment Deals in Africa. Country report: Mozambique'. Oakland CA: Oakland Institute.

Harriss, J. 1992. 'Does the "Depressor" Still Work? Agrarian structure and development in India: A review of evidence and argument.' *Journal of Peasant Studies* 19(2) 189-227.

Harvey, D. 2003. *The New Imperialism.* Oxford: Oxford University Press.

Herren, U. 1987. *The People of Mukogodo Division, Laikipia district: A Historical and Anthropological Baseline.* Nairobi: Institute of Geography, University of Nairobi.

Heyer, J., P. Roberts and G. Williams, Eds. 1981. *Rural Development in Tropical Africa.* New York: St Martin's Press.

High Court of Kenya. 2011. Mahamuka Farmers Co. Ltd (Plaintiff) Versus Soima Lekenge Ntaiyaiand Five Others. Before Honourable Justice J.K. Sergon. Civil Suit No. 152 of 2011.

HoAREC. 2013. 'Ecosystem Management and Conservation Programme: Protecting Valuable Natural Landscapes.' Horn of Africa Regional Environment Center [HoAREC]. [online]. Available at:<http://hoarec.org/index.php/2013-05-09-13-10-14/2013-05-23-14-04-04/2013-05-23-14-32-55> [Accessed 8 August 2013].

Hughes, L. 2006. *Moving the Maasai; A Colonial Misadventure.* St Antony's Series. Basingstoke, UK: Palgrave Macmillan.

Hughes, L. 2005. 'Malice in Maasai Land; The Historical Roots of Current Political Struggles.' *African Affairs* 104(415): 207-224.

ILC (International Land Coalition). 2011. *Land Rights and the Rush for Land: A report.* Rome: ILC.

Illovo Sugar. 2013. *Integrated Report for the Year Ending 31 March 2013.* [online]. Available at:<http://www.illovosugar.co.za/UserContent/Documents/Current-Year-Report-Overview/2013_Business-Overview.pdf> [Accessed 27 October 2014]

Illovo Sugar. 2014. 'More than Sugar: Integrated Annual Reports'. Available at http://www.o=illovosugar.co.za/investors/integrated-annual-reports.

Jayne, J.C. J. Chamberlin, D.D. Headey. 2014. 'Land Pressures, the Evolution of Farming Systems, and Development Strategies in Africa: A synthesis.' *Food Policy* 48: 1–17.

Kamuzora, A.K. 2011. 'Contractual Governance in Agro-Industry Institutions in Tanzania: A Case Study Analysis'. Unpublished Ph.D. thesis. University of Groningen. Available at: <http://dissertations.ub.rug.nl/faculties/jur/2011/a.k.n.kamuzora/.>

Kanyongolo, E. 2005. 'Land Occupations in Malawi: Challenging the Neoliberal Order.' In: S. Moyo and P. Yeros, Eds. *Reclaiming the Land: The Resurgence of Rural Movements in Africa, Asia and Latin America.* London and New York: Zed Books.

KBLP. 2005. 'Kilombero 2005'. Presentation as part of the Kilombero Business Linkages Project (KBLP). [online]. Available at <www.hedon.info/docs/p4a-Tanzania-Kilombero-TechnicalTour.pdf>.

Kenya Land Alliance. 2004a. *Righting Wrongs: Historical Injustices and Land Reforms in Kenya.* Policy Brief. Nakuru: Kenya Land Alliance.

Kenya Land Alliance. 2004b. 'The National Land Policy in Kenya: Addressing Historical Injustices.' *Kenya Land Alliance Issue Paper* 2(2004). Nakuru: Kenya Land Alliance.

Kiishweko, O. 2012. 'Tanzania: More Foreign Agricultural Investments Target Sugar Industry.' *Tanzania Daily News*, 6 December 2012. [online]. Available at <http://allafrica.com/stories/201212060232.html?viewall=1>.

Konadu-Agyemang, K. 2000. 'The Best of Times and the Worst of Times: Structural Adjustment Programs and Uneven Development in Africa: The Case of Ghana.' *Professional Geographer* 52:469-483.

KPHC. 2009. *Kenya Population and Housing Census (KPHC), 2009.* Nairobi: Central Bureau of Statistics.

Kyknet. 2014. 'Landbousake – Boere in die Kongo.' Dagbreek (Daybreak) Programme. 2 October 2014. [online]. Available at: <https://www.youtube.com/watch?v=Zivzt8T7b0s&feature=youtu.be&app=desktop> [Accessed 13 October 2014].

Land Matrix. 2014. 'South Africa.' [online]. Available at: <http://landmatrix.org/en/get-the-detail/by-investor-country/south-africa/1167/> [Accessed 13 October 2014].

Land Policy Initiative. 2014. *Guiding Principles on Large-Scale Land-Based Acquisition.* Addis Abba: African Union, African Development Bank and United Nations Economic Commission for Africa.

Lavers, T. 2012a. 'Patterns of Agrarian Transformation in Ethiopia: State Mediated Commercialisation and the "Land Grab".' *Journal of Peasant Studies* 39(3–4): 795–822.

Lavers, T. 2012b. '"Land Grab" as Development Strategy? The Political Economy of Agricultural Investment in Ethiopia.' *Journal of Peasant Studies* 39(1): 105–132.

Lawry, S., C. Samii, R. Hall, A. Leopold, D. Hornby and F. Mtero. 2014. *The Impact of Land Property Rights Interventions on Investment and Agricultural Productivity in Developing Countries: a Systematic Review.* Commissioned study for the UK Department for International Development. Brussels: The Campbell Collaboration.

Lebrun, D., O. Hamerlynk, S. Duvail and J. Nyunja. 2010. 'The Importance of Flexibility: An Analysis of Large-scale Tana Delta Irrigation Project in Kenya, Implemented Under an Estate System.' In: B. Calas and C.A. Mumma Martinon, Eds. *Shared Waters, Shared Opportunities.* Nairobi: Mkuki na Nyota.

Letai, J. 2011. 'Land Deals in Kenya: The Genesis of Land Deals in Kenya and its Implication on Pastoral Livlihoods: A Case Study of Laikipia District, 2011.' [online]. Available at: <http://landportal.info/sites/default/files/land_deals_in_

kenya-initial_report_for_laikipia_district2.pdf>

Letai, J. and J. Lind. 2012. 'Squeezed from all Sides: Changing Resource Tenure and Pastoral Innovations on the Laikipia Plateau, Kenya.' In: A. Catley, J. Lind and I. Scoones, Eds. 2013. *Pastoralism and Development in Africa: Dynamic Change at the Margins*. London: Routledge.

Li, T.M. 2011. 'Centering Labor in the Land Grab Debate.' *Journal of Peasant Studies* 38(2): 281–298.

Lindsay, W.K. 1987. 'Integrating Parks and Pastoralists: Some Lessons from Amboseli.' In: D. Anderson, R.H. Grove, Eds. *Conservation in Africa; People, Policies and Practice*. Cambridge: Cambridge University Press.

Lipton, M. 2009. *Land Reform in Developing Countries: Property Rights and Property Wrongs*. London: Routledge.

Little, P. D. and M. Watts, Eds. 1994. *Living Under Contract: Contract Farming and Agrarian Transformation in Sub-Saharan Africa*. Madison, WI: University of Wisconsin Press.

Locher, M. and E. Sulle. 2014. 'Challenges and Methodological Flaws in Reporting the Global Land Rush: Observations from Tanzania.' *Journal of Peasant Studies* 41(4): 569-592.

Locher, M. and E. Sulle. 2013. 'Foreign Land Deals in Tanzania: An Update and a Critical View on the Challenges of Data.' LDPI Working Paper 31. http://www.iss.nl/fileadmin/ASSETS/iss/Research_and_projects/Research_networks/LDPI/LDPI_WP_31_revised.pdf [accessed 9 June 2015]

Locke, A. and G. Henley. 2013. *The Possible Shape of a Land Transparency Initiative: Lessons from other Transparency Initiatives*. London: Overseas Development Institute. Available at: <www.odi.org/sites/odi.org.uk/files/odi-assets/publications-opinion-files/8599.pdf>.

Lund, C. 2008. *Local Politics and the Dynamics of Property in Africa*. Cambridge: Cambridge University Press.

Mabogunje, A.L. 2009. 'Land Reforms in Nigeria: Progress, Problems and Prospects'. Paper delivered at conference on Land Reform in Nigeria, Abuja, May 2009.

Makki, F. 2012. 'Power and Property: Commercialization, Enclosures, and the Transformation of Agrarian Relations in Ethiopia.' *Journal of Peasant Studies* 39(1): 81–104.

Makungu, C.M. 2011. 'Young People in Self-Care: Behaviours and Experiences in Farming Households in Kilombero Valley, Tanzania.' Unpublished Master's thesis. Durham University. [online]. Available at: <http://etheses.dur.ac.uk/3245>.

Manuel, L. and A. Salomão. 2009. 'Biofuels and Land Rights in Mozambique – the ProCana Case.' *Hamarata* 54: 17–19.

Margulis, M.E., N. McKeon and S.M. Borras Jr, Eds. 2013. 'Land Grabbing and Global Governance.' Special Issue. *Globalizations* 10(1).

Massimba, J., C. Malaki and B. Waized. 2013. *Consultancy Services for Collecting Policy Based Evidence for Enhancing Sugar Industry Regulatory Framework of Tanzania*. Morogoro: SUGECO.

Mathenge, G. 2000. 'Maasai Invade Ranches in Search of Pasture.' *Nation Media* 5 May.

Mbilinyi, M. and A.M. Semakafu. 1995. *Gender and Employment on Sugarcane Plantations in Tanzania*. Sectoral and Working Discussion Papers, Agriculture, SAP 2.44/WP.85. Geneva: ILO.

Mbonde, O. 2012. 'A Guide to the Environmental Impact Assessment Process.' *Swara* 35(2) 36-41.

McCarthy, J.F. 2010. 'Processes of Inclusion and Adverse Incorporation: Oil Palm and Agrarian Change in Sumatra, Indonesia.' *Journal of Peasant Studies* 37(1): 149–175.

McKeon, N. 2013. '"One Does Not Sell the Land Upon Which the People Walk": Land Grabbing, Transnational Rural Social Movements, and Global Governance.'

Globalizations 10(1): 105-122.

McMichael, P. 2012. 'The Land Grab and Corporate Food Regime Restructuring.' *Journal of Peasant Studies* 39(3-4): 681-701.

Mehta, L., G.J. Veldwisch and J. Franco, Eds. 2012. *Water Grabbing? Focus on the (Re)Appropriation of Finite Water Resources.* Special Issue *Water Alternatives.* [online]. Available at: < http://www.wateralternatives.org>.

Ministère de l'économie, du Plan, de l'aménagement du territoire et de l'intégration. 2011. *Convention d'établissement entre la République du Congo et la Société Congo Agriculture.* Brazzaville: République du Congo.

Ministry of Land Reform. 1975. *The Military Regime Land Proclamation No. 31/1975.* Addis Ababa: Ministry of Land Reform.

Mlingwa, G. 2009. 'Farming Systems for Ethanol – A Case of Block Farming'. Paper presented at the UDSM & PISCES workshop, Dar es Salaam, Tanzania, 24-25 September 2009.

MoARD. 2009. *Agricultural Investment Potential of Ethiopia.* Addis Ababa: Ministry of Agriculture and Rural Development.

MoFED. 2003. *Rural Development Policy and Strategy.* Addis Ababa: Ministry of Finance and Economic Development.

Moyo, S. 2008. *African Land Questions, Agrarian Transitions and the State: Contradictions of Neoliberal Land Reforms.* Dakar: CODESRIA.

Moyo, S., P. Jha and P. Yeros. 2013. 'The Classical Agrarian Question: Myth, Reality and Relevance Today.' *Agrarian South: Journal of Political Economy* 2(1): 93-119.

Moyo, S., P. Yeros and P. Jha. 2012. 'Imperialism and Primitive Accumulation: Notes on the New Scramble for Africa.' *Agrarian South: Journal of Political Economy* 1(2): 181-203.

Mustapha, A.R. 2010. 'Zimbabwean Farmers in Nigeria: Exceptional Farmers or Spectacular Support?' *African Affairs* 110(441): 536-561.

Mustapha, A.R. and K. Meagher. 2000. *Agrarian Production, Public Policy and the State in Kano Region, 1900-2000.* Drylands Research Working Paper 35. CrewKerne, UK Drylands Research.

Nalepa, R.A. 2013. 'Land for Agricultural Development in the Era of "Land Grabbing": A Spatial Exploration of the "Marginal Lands" Narrative in Contemporary Ethiopia.' LDPI Working Paper 40: 29. [online]. Available at: <http://www.iss.nl/fileadmin/ASSETS/iss/Research_and_projects/Research_networks/LDPI/LDPI_WP_40.pdf> [Accessed 15 July 2013].

Nalepa, R. A. and D.M. Bauer. 2012. 'Marginal Lands: the Role of Remote Sensing in Constructing Landscapes for Agrofuel Development.' *Journal of Peasant Studies* 39(2): 403-422.

National Centre for Statistics and Economic Studies. 2010. *General Census of Population and Housing 2007: Analysis of the Final Results.* (Vol IV). Brazzaville: National Centre for Statistics and Economic Studies.

Negelkerken, I., S.J.M. Blaber, S. Bouillon, P. Green, M. Haywood, L.G. Kirton, J.O. Meynecke, J. Pawlik, H.M. Penrose, A. Sasekumar, and P.J. Somerfield. 2007. 'The Habitat Function of Mangroves for Terrestrial and Marine Fauna: A Review.' *Aquatic Botany* 89(1): 155-185.

Nhantumbo, I. and A. Salomão. 2010. *Biofuels, Land Access and Rural Livelihoods in Mozambique.* London: International Institute for Environment and Development.

Nombo, C. 2010. 'Sweet Cane, Bitter Realities: the Complex Realities of AIDS in Mkamba, Kilombero District, Tanzania.' In: A. Niehof, G. Rugalema and S. Gillespie, Eds. *AIDS and Rural Livelihoods.* London: Earthscan.

Nshala, R., A. Locke and J. Duncan. 2013. *A Proposed Land for Equity Scheme in Tanzania: Issues and Assistance.* ODI Discussion Paper. London: Overseas Development Institute.

Obeng-Odoom, F. 2012. 'Neoliberalism and the Urban Economy in Ghana: Urban Employment, Inequality, and Poverty.' *Growth and Change* 109: 43–85.

ODI and CEPA. 2005. *Economic Growth in Northern Ghana. Revised Report for DfID.* London: Overseas Development Institute (ODI) and Accra: Center for Policy Analysis (CEPA).

OI. 2011. *Understanding Land Investment in Africa: Ethiopia Country Report.* Oakland, CA: Oakland Institute.

Okoth-Ogendo, H.W.O. 2008. 'The Nature of Land Rights under Indigenous Law.' In: A. Claassens and B. Cousins, Eds. *Land, Power and Custom: Controversies Generated by South Africa's Communal Land Rights Act.* Cape Town: University of Cape Town Press: 95-108.

Olanya, D.R. 2012. 'From Global Land Grabbing for Biofuels to Acquisitions of African Water for Commercial Agriculture.' *Current African Issues* 50, Uppsala, Sweden: Nordisk Africa Institute.

ONRS. 2007 *Rural land Administration and* Utilization *Proclamation No.130/2007.* Finfine: Oromia National Regional State, Ethiopia.

Osei, R. 2007. 'Integrated Tamale Fruit Company: Organic Mangoes improving livelihoods for the poor. Growing inclusive markets'. New York: United Nations Development Programme

Oxfam. 2011. *Land and Power: The Growing Scandal Surrounding the New Wave of Investments in Land.* Oxfam International Briefing Paper 51.

Oya, C. 2013a. 'Contract Farming in Sub-Saharan Africa: A Survey of Approaches, Debates and Issues.' *Journal of Agrarian Change* 12(1): 1–33.

Oya, C. 2013b. 'Methodological Reflections on "Land Grab" Databases and the "Land Grab" Literature "Rush".' *Journal of Peasant Studies* 40(3): 503-520.

Oya, C. 2013c. 'The Land Rush and Classic Agrarian Questions of Capital and Labour: a systematic scoping review of the socioeconomic impact of land grabs in Africa.' *Third World Quarterly* 34(9): 1532-1557.

Pearce, F. 2013. 'Splash and Grab: the Global Scramble for Water.' *New Scientist* 2906 (March 4). [online]. Available at: http://www.newscientist.com/article/mg21729066.400-splash-and-grab-the-global-scramble-for-water.html [accessed 7 June 2013].

Pearce, F. 2012. *The Land Grabbers: The New Fight Over Who Owns the Earth.* Redruth: Eden Project Books.

Peluso, N.L. and C. Lund. 2011. 'New Frontiers of Land Control: Introduction.' *Journal of Peasant Studies* 38(4): 667-681.

Peters, P. E. 2013. 'Land Appropriation, Surplus People and a Battle over Visions of Agrarian Futures in Africa.' *Journal of Peasant Studies* 40(3): 537-562.

Peters, P.E. 2009. 'Challenges in Land Tenure and Land Reform in Africa: Anthropological Contributions.' *World Development* 37(8): 1317-1325.

Peters, P.E. 2004. 'Inequality and Social Conflict Over Land in Africa.' *Journal of Agrarian Change.* 4(3): 269-314.

Peters, P., and D. Kambewa. 2007. 'Whose Security? Deepening Social Conflict over Customary Land in the Shadow of Land Tenure Reform in Malawi.' *Journal of Modern African Studies* 45(3): 447-472.

Phillips, D. 2009. 'Global Sugar and Fairtrade: Insights from Malawi.' *Food Ethics Magazine* (2): 24-25.

Pongui, B.S. 2012. *Study on the Situation of Reference of the Intervention Area South African Farmers in the Valley of Niari: Socioeconomic Data.* Brazzaville: Marien Ngouabi University.

Poulton, C. 2014. 'Democratisation and the Political Incentives for Agricultural Policy in Africa.' *Development Policy Review* 32(2): 101-122.

Puplampu, K.P. 1999. 'The State of Agricultural Policies and Food Security in Ghana (1983-1994).' *Canadian Journal of Development Studies* 2: 337-359.

Rabobank. 2013. 'Tanzania Sugar.' Rabobank Industry Note 386. [online]. Available at: <www.nmbtz.com/index.php?option=com_joomdoc&task=doc_details&gid=55>.

Rahmato, D. 2011. *Land to Investors: Large-scale Land Transfer in Ethiopia.* Addis

Ababa, Ethiopia: Forum for Social Studies.

Rahmato, D. 2009. *The Peasant and the State: Studies in Agrarian Change in Ethiopia 1950s–2000s.* Addis Ababa: Addis Ababa University Press.

Rakner, L., L. Mukubiru, N. Ngwira, S. Kimberley and A. Schneider. 2004. *The Budget as Theatre: The Formal and Informal Institutional Makings of the Budget Process in Malawi.* Lilongwe: Department for International Development.

RAPDA (Réseau Africain pour le droit à l'alimentation / African Network on the Right to Food). 2010. *Etat Des Lieux sur le Droit à L'Alimentation (The State of the Right to Food). Report by the Focal Point.* Brazzaville: RAPDA. [online]. Available at: <http://www.rtfn-watch.org/uploads/media/Etat_des_lieux_Congo_Brazzaville.pdf>. [Accessed 12 October 2012].

Reporter, The. 2014. 'Foreclosure notice forces Karuturi to pay off 25 percent debt.' 7 June 2014. http://www.thereporterethiopia.com/index.php/news-headlines/item/2105-foreclosure-notice-forces-karuturi-to-pay-off-25-percent-debt> [Accessed on 04 November 2014].

Reporter, The. 2015. 'Karuturi under the spotlight.' 17 January 2015. http://www.thereporterethiopia.com/index.php/news-headlines/item/3045-karuturi-under-the-spotlight> [Accessed on 01 March 2015].

Richardson, B. 2010. 'Big Sugar in Southern Africa: Rural Development and the Perverted Potential of Sugar/Ethanol Exports.' *Journal of Peasant Studies* 37(4): 917–38.

Rimmer, D. 1992. *Staying Poor: Ghana's Political Economy 1950-1990.* Oxford: Pergamon Press.

RoK. 2010. 'Releasing Our Full Potential', Unpublished Draft Sessional Paper on National Policy for the Sustainable Development of Northern Kenya and other Arid Lands, Nairobi: Office of the Prime Minister, Ministry of State for the Development of Northern Kenya and other Arid Lands, Kenya.

Rothchild, D. 1991. 'Ghana and Structural Adjustment: An Overview.' In: D. Rothchild, Ed. *The Political Economy of Recovery.* Boulder and London: Lynne Rienner Publishers: 3-20.

RSA (Republic of South Africa). 2010. *2010/11-2012/13 Industrial Production Action Plan.* Pretoria: Economic Sectors and Employment Cluster, Republic of South Africa, February 2010.

Rutten, M. 1992. *Selling Wealth to Buy Poverty: The Process of Individualization of Land Ownership among the Maasai Pastoralists of Kajiado District, Kenya, 1890-1990.* Saarbrucken, Germany: Verlag Breitenbach Publishers.

SAGCOT. 2012. 'SAGCOT Investment Partnership Program: Opportunities for Investors in the Sugar Sector'. [online]. Available at <www.sagcot.com>.

SAGCOT. 2011. 'Southern Agricultural Growth Corridor of Tanzania: Investment Blueprint.' [online]. Available at <http://www.sagcot.com/uploads/media/Invest-Blueprint-SAGCOT_High_res.pdf>.

Sassen, S. 2013. 'Land Grabs Today: Feeding the Disassembling of National Territory.' *Globalizations* 10(1): 25-46.

Sassen, S. 2010. 'A Savage Sorting of Winners and Losers: Contemporary Versions of Primitive Accumulation.' *Globalizations* 7(1-2): 23-50.

Schoneveld, G.C. and M. Shete. 2014. 'Modernising the Periphery: Citizenship and Ethiopia's New Agricultural Investment Policies.' In: A. Zoomers and M. Kaag, Eds. *Beyond the Hype: Land Grabbing in Africa.* London: Zed Books.

Scoones, I., R. Smalley, R. Hall and D. Tsikata. 2014. *Narratives of Scarcity: Understanding the 'Global Resource Grab'.* FAC Working Paper 076. Brighton: Future Agricultures Consortium.

Scoones, I., R. Hall, S.M. Borras Jr, B. White and W. Wolford. 2013. 'The Politics of Evidence: Methodologies for Understanding the Global Land Rush.' *Journal of Peasant Studies* 40(3): 469-483.

Seufert, P. 2013. 'The FAO Voluntary Guidelines on the Responsible Governance of Tenure of Land, Fisheries and Forests.' *Globalizations* 10(1): 181-186.

Sharife, K. 2010. 'The South Africa-Congo Concession: Exploitation or Salvation?' *Pambazuka News* 7 January 2010. [online]. Available from International Land Coalition at: <http://www.landcoalition.org/cpl-blog/?p.4172.1>. [Accessed 19 November 2010].

Sherry, S. 2013. 'Farmers in Bid to Block R2.5bn Afgri Sale.' *Business Day* 13 November 2013. [online]. Available at: <http://www.bdlive.co.za/business/agriculture/2013/11/13/farmers-in-bid-to-block-r2.5bn-afgri-sale>.

Shete, M. 2011. 'Implications of Land Deals for Livelihood Security and Natural Resource Management in Benshanguel Gumuz Regional State, Ethiopia.' Paper presented at the Global Land Grabbing conference, University of Sussex, Brighton, 6-8 April 2011.

Siyao, P.O. 2012. 'Barriers in Accessing Agricultural Information in Tanzania with a Gender Perspective: the Case Study of Small-Scale Sugar Cane Growers in Kilombero District.' *Electronic Journal of Information Systems in Developing Countries* 51(6): 1–19.

Smalley, R. 2013. *Plantations, Contract Farming and Commercial Farming Areas in Africa: A Comparative Review.* FAC *Working Paper* 55. Brighton: Future Agricultures Consortium.

Smalley, R. and E. Corbera. 2012. 'Large-scale Land Deals from the Inside Out: Findings from the Kenya's Tana Delta.' *Journal of Peasant Studies* 39(3-4): 1039-1075.

Smart, T. and J. Hanlon. 2014. *Chickens and Beer. A Recipe for growth in Mozambique.* [online]. Available at: <http://bit.ly/chickens-beer>.

Smith, N. 2014. 'Convoy to the Congo.' *Farmer's Weekly* 30 September 2014. [online]. Available at: <http://www.farmersweekly.co.za/news.aspx?id=63321&h=Convoy-to-the-Congo>. [Accessed 13 October 2014].

SNNP. 2007. *Rural Land Administration and Utilization Proclamation No. 110/2007.* Awasa: Southern Nations Nationalities and Peoples Regional State (SNNP), Ethiopia.

Songsore, J. and A. Denkabe. 1995. *Challenging Rural Poverty in Northern Ghana: The Case of the Upper West Region.* Trondheim: Centre for Environment and Development, University of Trondheim.

Sprenger, E.L.M. 1989. *Sugarcane Outgrowers and Kilombero Sugar Company in Tanzania.* Nijmegen: Third World Centre.

Standard, The. 2009. 'Qatar Land Deal not Unique to Kenya.' 6 January 2009.

Storck, H., B. Adenew, A. Emana, S. Birowiecki and W. Hawariate. 1991. *Farming System and Farm Management Practices of Smallholders in the Hararghe Highlands: A Baseline Survey* (Farming Systems & Resource Economics in the Tropics). Wissenschaftsverlag Vauk Kiel KG.

Sulle, E. 2010. 'A Hybrid Business Model: the Case of Sugarcane Producers in Tanzania.' In: L. Cotula and R. Leonard, Eds. *Alternatives to Land Acquisitions: Agricultural Investment and Collaborative Business Models.* London: IIED.

Sulle, E. and R. Hall. 2015. 'Agrofuels and Land Rights in Africa.' In: K. Dietz, A. Brunnengräber, B. Engels and O. Pye, Eds. *The Political Ecology of Agrofuels.* London: Routledge.

Sumberg, J, N. Akua Anyidoho, M. Chasukwa, B. Chinsinga, J. Leavy, G. Tadele, S. Whitfield and J. Yaro. 2014. *Young People, Agriculture, and Employment in Rural Africa.* WIDER Working Paper 2014/080. Helsinki: WIDER.

Temper, L. (Undated). 'Let Them Eat Sugar: Life and Livelihood in Kenya's Tana Delta'. [online]. Available at: <http://www.ceecec.net/case-studies/let-them-eat-sugar-life-and-livelihood-in-kenyas-tana-delta/>

TGE (1991). *Ethiopia's Economic Policy during the Transitional Period.* Addis Ababa: Transitional Government of Ethiopia.

TNRS. 2006. *Rural Land Administration and Use Proclamation* No.97/2006. Mekelle: Tigray National Regional State, Ethiopia.

Tsikata, D. and J. A. Yaro. 2014. 'When a Good Business Model is Not Enough: Land

Transactions and Gendered Livelihood Prospects in Rural Ghana.' *Feminist Economics* 20(1): 1-25.

Tsikata, D. and J.A. Yaro. 2011. 'Land Market Liberalization and Trans-National Commercial Land Deals in Ghana since the 1990s.' Paper presented at International Conference on Global Land Grabbing. Future Agricultures Consortium, Institute of Development Studies, University of Sussex, 6-8 April 2011.

TSPA (Tanzania Association of Sugar Producers). 2013. Presentation to the Parliamentary Committee on Development, Dar es Salaam.

UNDP. 2007. *Ghana Human Development Report 2007: Towards a More Inclusive Society.* Accra: UNDP, Ghana Office.

URT (United Republic of Tanzania). 2013. *Tanzania Development, Vision 2025, Big Results Now: National Key Result Area: Agriculture Lab.* Dar es Salaam: URT.

Van der Ploeg, J.D. 2009. *The New Peasantries: Struggles for Autonomy and Sustainability in an Era of Empire and Globalization.* London: Routledge.

Van Schalkwyk, H., J. Groenewald and A. Jooste. 2003. 'Agricultural Marketing in South Africa.' In: L. Niewoudt and J. Groenewald, Eds. *The Challenge of Change: Agriculture, Land and the South African Economy.* Scottsville: University of Natal Press.

Van Zyl, J, N. Vink, J. Kirsten and D. Poonyth. 2001. 'South African Agriculture in Transition: the 1990s.' *Journal of International Development* 13(6): 725–739.

Vaughan, S. and M. Gebremichael. 2011. *Rethinking Business and Politics in Ethiopia: The Role of EFFORT, the Endowment Fund for the Rehabilitation of Tigray.* Research Report 02. London: Overseas Development Institute.

Verma, R. 2014. 'Land Grabs, Power and Gender in East and Southern Africa: So What's New?' *Feminist Economics* 20(1): 52-75.

Vermeulen, S. and L. Cotula. 2010a. *Making the Most of Agricultural Investment: A Survey of Business Models that Provide Opportunities for Smallholders.* London: IIED.

Vermeulen, S and L. Cotula. 2010b. 'Over the Heads of Local People: Consultation, Consent, and Recompense in Large-scale Land Deals for Biofuels Projects in Africa.' *Journal of Peasant Studies* 37(4): 899-916.

Von Braun, J. and R. Meinzen-Dick. 2009 *'Land Grabbing' by Foreign Investors in Developing Countries: Risks and Opportunities.* IFPRI Policy Brief 13. Washington DC: IFPRI.

White, B., S.M. Borras Jr., R. Hall, I. Scoones and W. Wolford. 2012. 'The New Enclosures: Critical Perspectives on Corporate Land Deals.' Editors' introduction to special issue, *Journal of Peasant Studies* 39(3-4): 619-647.

Wolford, W., S.M. Borras Jr, R. Hall, I. Scoones and B. White, Eds. 2013. 'Governing Global Land Deals: The Role of the State in the Rush for Land.' Special Issue, *Development and Change* 44(2). [online]. Available at: <http://onlinelibrary. wiley.com/doi/10.1111/dech.2013.44.issue-2/issuetoc>.

Woodhouse, P. 2012. 'New Investment, Old Challenges: Land Deals and the Water Constraint in African Agriculture.' *Journal of Peasant Studies* 39(3–4): 777–794.

World Bank. 2013. *Growing Africa: Unlocking the Potential of Agribusiness.* Washington D.C.: World Bank.

World Bank. 2011. *Rising Global Interest in Farmlands: Can it Yield Sustainable and Equitable Benefits?* Washington, DC: The World Bank.

World Bank. 2009. *Awakening Africa's Sleeping Giant: Prospects for Commercial Agriculture in the Guinea Savannah Zone and Beyond.* Washington, DC: World Bank.

World Bank. 2008. *World Development Report 2008, Agriculture for Development.* Washington, DC: World Bank.

World Bank 1984. *Ghana: Policies and Program for Adjustment.* Washington, DC: World Bank.

World Bank. 1981. *Accelerated Development in Africa. An Agenda for Action.* Washington, DC: The World Bank.

World Bank and Government of Malawi. 2011. *Malawi: Poverty Reduction Support Credit: Fertilizer Procurement Review of the 2010/11 Farm Input Subsidy Programme (FISP), December 2010-February 2011.* Washington, DC: World Bank and Lilongwe: Government of Malawi.

Yaro, J.A. 2012. 'Re-inventing Traditional Land Tenure in the Era of Land Commoditization: Some Consequences in Peri-urban Northern Ghana.' Geografiska Annaler: Series B. *Human Geography* 94(4): 351–368.

Zewde, B. 2008. 'Environment and Capital: Notes for a History of the Wonji-Shoa Sugar Estate (1951–1974).' In: B. Zewde, Ed. *Society, State and History: Selected Essays.* Addis Ababa: Addis Ababa University Press.

Zoomers, A. and M. Kaag, Eds., 2014. *Beyond the Hype: Land Grabbing in Africa.* London: Zed Books.

Zoomers, A. 2010. 'Globalisation and the Foreignisation of Space: Seven Processes Driving the Current Global Land Grab.' *Journal of Peasant Studies* 37(2): 429-447.

INDEX